Shakespeare and Youth Culture

Shakespeare and Youth Culture

Jennifer Hulbert, Kevin J. Wetmore, Jr.,
and
Robert L. York

palgrave
macmillan
OCM 68786822

SHAKESPEARE AND YOUTH CULTURE

First published in 2006 by
PALGRAVE MACMILLAN™
175 Fifth Avenue, New York, N.Y. 10010 and
Houndmills, Basingstoke, Hampshire, England RG21 6XS
Companies and representatives throughout the world.

PALGRAVE MACMILLAN is the global academic imprint of the Palgrave Macmillan division of St. Martin's Press, LLC and of Palgrave Macmillan Ltd. Macmillan® is a registered trademark in the United States, United Kingdom and other countries. Palgrave is a registered trademark in the European Union and other countries.

ISBN-13: 978–1–4039–7284–2
ISBN-10: 1–4039–7284–2

Library of Congress Cataloging-in-Publication Data is available from the Library of Congress.

A catalogue record for this book is available from the British Library.

Design by Newgen Imaging Systems (P) Ltd., Chennai, India.

First edition: June 2006

10 9 8 7 6 5 4 3 2 1

Printed in the United States of America.

Transferred to digital printing in 2007.

This book is dedicated to
Jason Hulbert
Eleanor Maher Wetmore
and
Sherry Bevins Darrell, for her ongoing encouragement,
and Lisa, for her undying love and support

Contents

Acknowledgments

The authors would like to thank the editorial staff at Palgrave. We also thank the anonymous readers for the excellent suggestions on how to shape and strengthen the volume.

Jennifer Hulbert would like to thank Rob Gander in the Denison University Theatre Department for his guidance and sarcasm. She also extends her thanks to Kevin for pretty much the same thing. Thanks to Judy Hulbert and Jay Hulbert for putting up with her now and in her "Ophelia" years. Denison University also provided financial and academic support for this research, for which she is also grateful.

Kevin Wetmore would like to thank Matt Walker and the Troubadour Theatre Company of Santa Monica, the faculty and staff of the Department of Theatre and the College of Arts, Media and Communication at California State University, Northridge for their support (in all its forms), Hy Bender, and David Pellegrini. Thanks also to Susan Kattwinkel and Matthew Philips and the participants and board members of the 2003 Southwestern Theatre Conference Theatre Symposium for their insights and feedback on chapter 3. Similarly, thanks are due to the participants in the 2002 American Society for Theatre Research seminar on theatre and expropriation for their feedback on an earlier version of chapter 4: Sarah Bay-Cheng, Mark Cosdan, David A. Crespy, Mark Gordon, Norman Hart, Victor Holtcamp, Chris Olson, and Doug Rossom. Thanks as well to Denison University and Loyola Marymount University. Last but not the least, he would like to thank his wife, Maura Chwastyk for her patience, insights, and support.

Robert York would like to thank Ivy Tech Community College of Indiana, Southern Indiana Campus and his students.

About the Authors

Jennifer Hulbert completed her degree in acting at Denison University, where she was also the recipient of a Provost's Young Scholar Grant to carry out her research on contemporary feminist adaptations and appropriations of Shakespeare. She currently lives and works in Los Angeles.

Kevin J. Wetmore, Jr. lives and works in Los Angeles, teaching in the Department of Theatre and Dance at Loyola Marymount University. He is the author of *The Athenian Sun in an African Sky*, *Black Dionysus: Greek Tragedy and African-American Theatre*, and *The Empire Triumphant: Race, Religion and Rebellion in the Star Wars Films*. He is the Founding Artistic Director of the Pittsburgh-based Unseam'd Shakespeare Company and has directed or acted in over half the Shakespearean canon.

Robert L. York is an Assistant Professor of English at Ivy Tech Community College of Indiana in Sellersburg, where he teaches composition and literature courses. Also a poet and songwriter, York has released an independent compact disc of ten songs, *Neverever*, in 2002.

"Dude, Where's My Bard?"

Reducing, Translating, and Referencing Shakespeare for Youth: An Introduction

He was indeed the glass
wherein the noble youth did dress themselves.

—Henry IV, Part II 2.3.21–22

This work takes as its starting point the strange intertextual space Shakespeare has come to occupy in contemporary America: His works are read in schools, used as raw material for film, television, and stage adaptations, re-created as graphic novels, referenced in commercials and advertisements, and used as a framework to understand adolescent girls, contemporary cultural and social conflicts, and business practices. We no longer have "Shakespeare," but rather "Shakespeares." As Frederic Jameson argues in *Postmodernism, or the Cultural Logic of Late Capitalism*, the border has broken down between high art and mass culture: commercial culture is incorporated directly into postmodern art and high culture has become a commodity. What might at first glance be dismissed as immature, trendy, silly, or insignificant is actually indicative of both Shakespeare's place in contemporary culture as well as indicative of the dominance of youth culture, even in the face of the "universality" and classical status of Shakespeare.

Our second concern is the points of intersection between Shakespeare, who represents and embodies education, high culture, and "the old," and youth culture, itself both created by and for youth and also the product of corporate marketing. The usual first encounter with Shakespeare by youth is in secondary education, in which the classroom becomes a site of resistance—to Shakespeare, that is. There are two key youth objections to Shakespeare: boredom and inaccessibility, and although the two are related, they are not synonymous. The enemy of youth-culture Shakespeare is "boring Shakespeare," the word most often linked with Shakespeare by nonacademics and the highest compliment apparently one can pay to film and theatrical productions: "It wasn't boring at all." "Boring" is apparently an essential attribute of Shakespeare that is the first aspect of his work who any that would expropriate or appropriate or produce it must overcome: Shakespeare does not interest youth.

Inaccessibility ("I don't get it") is the other charge leveled against the bard. Even if one finds the plays interesting, the language, culture, and concepts that make up the canon are difficult and strange. Inaccessibility usually leads to boredom. Therefore, many of the youth culture mediations of Shakespeare that we examine in this volume both make Shakespeare accessible and make him "interesting."

Often the role of the educator, told to teach Shakespeare, is to find a way to make Shakespeare both interesting and accessible to the students. Many of the books about teaching Shakespeare in the class-room deal with the anxiety of relevance: How do "we" make Shakespeare interesting to "them?" How do we convince the students that Shakespeare is relevant to their lives and worth reading and know-ing? An entire industry has sprung up for the purpose of marketing Shakespeare to youth and to market products to market Shakespeare to educators and scholars. Books, videos, graphic novels, software, CD-ROMs, "translations" of the plays, and other activity-based products are available to teach Shakespeare's texts to youth at all levels of education from primary through university.

Use of youth-culture Shakespeare is another means to impress relevance upon students. Want to understand "O"? You need to read *Othello* (or at least see the version with Laurence Fishburne). *Romeo and Juliet* is relevant to young people's lives—just look at the film version with Leonardo DiCaprio. In his essay in *The Shakespeare Myth*, Derek Longhurst argues that "How do we make it relevant?" is the question that haunts both classrooms and theatres.[1] The two strategies employed, observes Longhurst, are to make it relevant by other means (visual overlay of another time period on the text, such as Ian McKellen's fascist *Richard III*), or to argue for the texts' "time-lessness" or universality.[2]

We would argue that a third method to deal with the anxiety of relevance is translation, via a variety of means, into youth culture. As opposed to actual translation of Shakespeare's language, which will be explored in detail below, and which is a strategy for dealing with inaccessibility, the use of a "translation" of the play into the youth milieu, using the common elements of youth culture (e.g., teen film, comic book, popular music or pop psychology), ensures relevancy. This third method uses elements of the first while contradictorily claiming and refuting the second. While using "O" to prove that Shakespeare's *Othello* is timeless and universal, an instructor is relying upon a translation of the play into the media of film that keeps almost none of the original lines, renames the characters and maintains the plot only loosely. If anything, the film proves the timelessness of Giraldi Cinthio's plot from *Hecatommithi*, Shakespeare's source. And yet "O" then becomes synonymous with *Othello* in the mind and experience of the student.

We should note that Shakespeare's texts are now Shakespeares' texts. One can read any one of a variety of editions of the "original" play, not taking into account editorial emendations, variations between folio and quarto texts, and other variables that destabilize the Shakespearean original. Next comes the performance text: the play in active performance in a theatre. Lastly, one might encounter a video text—either a filmed stage production or a cinematic or television adaptation of a play.

Often in educational sites we encounter not one but several texts of the same play. The student will read (or skim) the original text, and (most likely or) read a commercial publication such as *Cliff's, Spark,* or *Monarch Notes* that summarizes and analyzes the text. The student then views the film or video version (perhaps more than one in cases such as *Hamlet* or *Romeo and Juliet*) or follow the BBC Shakespeare version of the play, and most likely engages in text-related activities (such as those found in Folger Shakespeare Library's Shakespeare Set Free series, in which teachers are encouraged to use creative exercises to encourage the students to experience and understand the text on several levels). In addition, the original text might be read out loud or performed by the students, and, lastly, the student will write a paper involving research and critical and analytical writing. To the student, all of this becomes *Romeo and Juliet*, for example, and "Shakespeare."

Three key strategies emerge for combating both the boredom and the inaccessibility of the original texts. The three strategies for making Shakespeare accessible to contemporary youth audiences (even in educational settings) in both textual and performance forms are translation, reduction, and reference. Although much fuller, complex definitions will be given below, we might consider these to mean a changing of language (translation), a cutting down of the play(s) to its (their) constituent elements (reduction), and referring to quotation, character, plot, or even the man (Shakespeare) either directly or indirectly and with or without explanations (reference). These three strategies are not mutually exclusive and often overlap.

Youth-culture Shakespeare involves both strategies for making Shakespeare "unboring" and accessible and the creation of an easily marketed product / commodity. Furthermore, "It's Shakespeare" can elevate the trivial as well as sell more merchandise. The transaction between Shakespeare and youth culture allows youth culture to gain cultural credibility, linking youth culture to the synecdoche for the height of western culture, and allows Shakespeare to be made more "accessible" and therefore more cool and ultimately more marketable.

Furthermore, we might note that youth-culture Shakespeare is a contested site with multiple constituencies engaged in multiple dynamics. Many critics have observed the use of Shakespeare within youth culture to form a counter-narrative to that of previous generations. John Story argues that youth (sub)cultures engage in a symbolic and literal resistance to dominant (read: their parents') cultures.[3] Youth culture is not simply a representative product of the culture industry under late capitalism and the corporations that manufacture it. It can also be a bottom-up movement, even within the classroom. It is also a discerning movement—one that places different values based on individual taste and levels of artistry. There is no unified youth culture and distinctions, critical evaluations and divides exist. Both REM and Britney Spears are examples of popular music, but REM is much more highly respected by both critics and young audiences. However, if one is a fan of the latter, none of that matters.

As many have argued, the young viewer/reader/listener is not other or object or the passive member of a one-way transaction, but has agency to engage, reimagine and re-create the plays on his or her own terms. Barbara Hodgson, taking *William Shakespeare's Romeo + Juliet* as her subject, correctly observes that young people "made *Romeo + Juliet* their cultural property and took into their hands knowledge-making and its attendant power."[4] Or, as Donald Hedrick and Bryan Reynolds argue in the introduction to *Shakespeare without Class*, Shakespeare is both "socially and historically determined playground" and "an ambiguous space that makes possible and in fact encourages alternative opportunities for thought, expression and development."[5] In other words, when youth engage Shakespeare, whether in the classroom or on their own, it is always a contested site, but one in which they have agency and power.

In order to understand this dynamic, we will first define "youth culture" and then consider the relationship between youth culture and Shakespeare. We will then take a brief "side trip" into Shakespeare and the education industry, school being a place where youth are obligated to engage Shakespeare on terms other than youth culture, then examine the individual (yet often used in combination) strategies used both to appropriate Shakespeare and to help youth understand the original text, including a consideration of how referencing Shakespeare in film, television, and other popular cultures both includes and excludes youth.

Pop Goes the Theatre: Popular Culture, Mass Media, and Youth or Enterprises of Great Pith and Moment Lose the Name of Transaction

We move from a multiplicity of Shakespeares to the contradictory and complex nature of youth culture. Comparatively speaking, Youth Culture is a fairly recent development. Michael Barson and Steven Heller argue that the teenager emerged as a cultural icon during the Second World War: *Seventeen* magazine premiered in September 1944.[6] Until this point in Western history, youth culture was not separate from mainstream culture. After the war, however, a transformation occurred as a result of the sociocultural and economic changes in the face of the Holocaust and Hiroshima. Jon Lewis argues, correctly, that in the postwar generation there arose "a distinct, moneyed, seemingly homogenous subculture with its own set of rituals and practices."[7] This generation had economic power—they went to the movies, they purchased books, magazines, record albums, and they defined themselves by these choices. Being an Elvis fan distinguished one from those who were fans of other types of music, and these preferences shaped (and continue to shape) identity.

The 1950s developed an entire culture around youth and the material culture and cultural practices associated with it: rock-and-roll music, hot rod cars and drag racing, juvenile delinquency, and malt shops. As Herbert J. Gans observes, youth culture came into its own in the 1960s. The new youth culture was not mere delinquency, however. Gans argues that youth culture became a counterculture, defined by

[I]nformality of dress and manners, the rejection of traditional forms of art and other high culture . . . the use of drugs, the borrowing from black and folk cultures and the radical values which can be traced back to earlier, avant-garde high culture.[8]

The rejection of tradition and parental authority by the youth was accompanied by the experimentation with narcotics and a growing sense of political empowerment. Two things should be noted, however: first, the fundamental cultural appropriativeness of youth culture. Mainstream youth culture, then as now, borrows everything from other cultures, be it the African American influences on popular music (from rock to hip-hop) or the Japanese influences on contemporary animation and action cinema. Second, beginning in the 1960s, youth culture was also defined by products and material culture.

Furthermore, youth is a "fundamentally mediated culture."[9] Individual and collective identity are established by and associated with the products that one buys and uses, everything from deodorant and hair care products to the music, film, and Web sites one likes. Even the specific types of media that one uses are culturally coded: MP3, CD, DVD, and iPod are all youth-driven forms. The culture itself is created and disseminated through mediated forms: radio, television, cinema, the Internet, etc., and is driven by the notion of brand.

Branding, as James Twitchell writes, is the new means by which many audiences know great works of art. We know the original through commercials "quoting" it.[10] We recognize neither the original nor its context, but by the popular culture reference, be it an Absolut advertisement or popular film. This quoting of canonical works from all the arts, insists Twitchell, "has become so insistent and redundant that it has drained certain objects d'art of their value."[11] Beethoven's Fifth and Ninth Symphonies, the "William Tell Overture," the paintings *Mona Lisa, American Gothic* and *The Scream*, and Michelangelo's *David* have been transformed into clichés. Shakespeare's most popular works, especially *Hamlet* and *Romeo and Juliet*, have lines that have become drained of meaning and value. "Romeo, Romeo, wherefore art thou Romeo?" and "To be or not to be" are as known out of context as they are in context. It is the corporate and pop cultural use of these phrases that have made them familiar even to those who have never picked up a play. They are also marketing slogans for the branding of Shakespeare. "Shakespeare" is not only an industry and a trade, but it is also a brand. And, like all brands, it can convey a sense of identity and of community.

Youth culture is a consumptive one: it consumes. Herbert J. Gans refers to contemporary youths as "omnivores," people who, because of wealth and position, consume all cultures.[12] Teens, as Wheeler Winston Dixon, observes, "dominate the global theatrical box office."[13] Following Joe Roth, Wheeler further notes that teens are ready consumers because they don't work, have no responsibilities, but do have money, time, and interests.[14]

The fundamental problem, however, with Dixon and Roth's supposition of youth culture ignores differences in social class. It is primarily the affluent youth found typically in the middle-class (mostly white) suburbs that they describe. Affluent youth are a leisure class; poor youth are marginalized and disaffected, and yet even their culture, whether ghetto slang, hip-hop music, or "gangsta" stylings, are appropriated and consumed by the affluent, which is evidence of Gans's theory of cultural omnivourism among youth culture. So powerful is this market that Gans argues that "youth culture" is an archaic term, "in part because so much of American popular culture now caters to youth.[15] Even after the teenage years, the younger members of society wield considerable economic power: 18 to 34 is the key demographic for almost every media.

In youth-culture Shakespeare two important markets converge: youth culture and what Michael D. Bristol, after Terence Hawkes, terms "Bardbiz"—that is, the "Shakespeare industry," a multimillion pound and dollar business incorporating many other businesses and industries, from theatre and film to the makers of souvenirs emblazoned with Shakespeare's visage for towns named Stratford.[16] As most popular culture caters to youth, as per Gans's argument, and consumers of Bardbiz also represent a significant market, added to the fact that the education industry, in the form of producers of textbooks, learning aids, and other educational tools, also commands a fairly large market all indicate that youth-culture Shakespeare is a sizeable and growing market. This book, therefore, examines the transformations undergone by Shakespeare (the man, the canon, the culture, etc.) in order to appeal to a youth audience.

We might also note that almost all youth-culture theatre is, therefore, part of a cultural (and therefore economic) exchange. As Graham Holderness notes, speaking of Shakespeare on film: "The repute of cinema art and of the film industry can be enhanced by their capacity to incorporate Shakespeare; the institution of Shakespeare itself benefits from the transaction by a confirmation of its persistent universality."[17] Holderness is right to use the word "transaction" here, for every youth-culture Shakespeare follows on the exchange Holderness describes: youth culture, such as rock or hip-hop music, graphic novels or teen films, gives Shakespeare "street cred," whereas Shakespeare gives youth "cultural cred," so to speak. In each chapter of this book we consider the transactions and exchanges involved in youth-culture Shakespeare: what does each element bring to the transaction and what does each element take or get from it.

This exchange allows Shakespeare to overcome the divide Lawrence Levine presents in *Highbrow / Lowbrow*, thereby making Shakespeare's plays once more an element of popular culture, rather than the high cultural ground they often occupy in the United States. Yet a tension remains in the different form now, as there is not Shakespeare but Shakespeares. The marketing of Shakespeare via youth culture also creates a hierarchy among these Shakespeares that are also ranked vertically: "our" Shakespeare is the cool one. Baz Luhrmann's film is cooler than Franco Zeffirelli's. Ethan Hawke is cooler than Mel Gibson, now better known as Christ's cinematic biographer than for his performance as Hamlet. *10 Things I Hate about You* is way better than the Burton/Taylor film version of *Taming of the Shrew* and infinitely better than the written text. Shakespeare represents a certain kind of cultural authority, but popular culture represents another, perhaps more powerful, cultural authority. Youth culture ranks the Shakespeares and gives some, but not all of them, a commercial credibility. Shakespeare thus also becomes a brand name. Shakespeare is "branded" in Alissa Quart's sense of the word, and as one determines which soft drink or video game best represents one's identity as a youth, so, too must one determine which Shakespeare is yours.[18]

Youth-culture Shakespeare, like all youth culture, is about identity and cliques. In theatrical terms, the use of Shakespeare in youth culture serves to define and create in groups and out groups. Youth identity determines which Shakespeare one "likes," and conversely the Shakespeare with which one identifies determines one's identity as well. The audience for *Tromeo and Juliet* is not necessarily the audience for Baz Luhrmann's *Romeo + Juliet* or "*O.*" The target audiences are also different, depending on the mediating culture: one who enjoys graphic novels such as *The Sandman* may not enjoy a teen romance such as *10 Things I Hate about You* or *Clueless*. Or he or she might. Heath Ledger and Neil Gaiman may appeal to different audiences, but there is also overlap there.

"Youth" in this case is also not a single audience but audiences. The Shakespearean scholar seeking youth Shakespeare must understand the difference between audience identity and individual identity. To which youth is this Shakespeare being marketed: urban, lower class?

Suburban, upper-middle class? College students? High school students? Teens, young adults or "tweens"? An "R" rating, for example, on an ostensible "teen" film, creates inordinate problems in reaching a target audience.

Given these different audience bases, how youth-culture Shakespeare "means" to these different audiences is also determined by one's knowledge of Shakespeare and one's knowledge of other cultures. Only if one knows the original songs does one "get" the musical jokes of The Troubadours in their theatrical pastiches. Familiarity with the "DC Universe" in graphic novels published by that corporation will frame the use of Shakespeare and his characters in DC's *Sandman*. One practically needs advanced degrees in popular and classical culture in order to comprehend all of the references in *The Simpsons*. Thus, a multiplicity of Shakespeares is met by a multiplicity of audiences with a multiplicity of contexts and frames for understanding.

Shakespeare can also become part of youth identity. As a means of rebelling against conformity, some students embrace Shakespeare, fetishizing his works, using them as a marker of intelligence, maturity, sophistication, and nonconformity. In response to the groans elicited from students by the introduction of the bard in class, other youth will wholeheartedly make Shakespeare a part of their identity and be branded (again in all senses of that word) by that publicly acknowledged identification.

The late twentieth century witnessed an explosion of popular culture and youth-culture Shakespeare. In 1968, the movement was heralded by Franco Zeffirelli's *Romeo and Juliet*, arguably the first youth-market Shakespeare film. It also went on to become a staple in American classrooms, serving to explicate, and in some cases replace, the text. Another precursor to the movement was Paul Mazurski's *The Tempest* (1982), which features the 1980s teen movie goddess Molly Ringwald as Miranda. Yet the film that began the last decade's pop culture Shakespeare spate was Kenneth Branagh's *Henry V* (1989), with its younger-than-usual king and playful sense of humor. Many Shakespeare films that had at least some youth appeal followed: Zeffirelli's *Hamlet* with Mel "Mad Max" Gibson (1990), Ian McKellen's *Richard III* (1995, which, cast member and perennial bad boy Robert Downey, Jr., remarked to the press, "might be the first film that bridges the gap between entertainment and Shakespeare"[19]), and Baz Luhrmann's obvious teen film *William Shakespeare's Romeo + Juliet* (1996). 1996 proved to be a good year for Shakespeare, as Luhrmann's film was followed by Branagh's *Hamlet*, Al Pacino's *Looking for Richard*, an exploration of *Richard III* featuring actors better known for Hollywood action and drama than Shakespearean history, Trevor Nunn's *Twelfth Night*, and a made for television *The Tempest* with Peter Fonda as Prospero and Katherine Heigel (yet another teen television actress) as Miranda, set during the American Civil War with Ariel and Caliban as black slaves.

These films were followed by the multiple award-winning *Shakespeare in Love* and Almereyda's *Hamlet*, featuring heartthrob Ethan Hawke and Julia Stiles (both 1998), Julie Taymor's *Titus* and Gil Junger's *10 Things I Hate about You* (a teen *Taming of the Shrew* explored in greater detail in the first chapter) (both 1999). The year 2000 saw "*O*" (a teen *Othello* in which high school basketball takes the place of war with the Turk), *A Midsummer Night's Dream* (again featuring performers better known for their film and television roles than their stage work, including a then-popular Calista Flockheart—television's *Ally McBeal*, which was used as a selling point in the marketing campaign) and yet another adaptation by Branagh, *Love's Labour's Lost*.

As noted in this list, often when Hollywood turns to Shakespeare, the performers called on to play the major roles (and sometimes minor ones, too—witness Robin Williams and Billy Crystal as the gravediggers in Branagh's *Hamlet*) are better known for their television and cinema work, and often have an appeal to the key youth demographic. As a result, however, when celebrities perform Shakespeare on stage or on screen, they bring with them their pop cultural personas. When Kenneth Branagh casts Keanu Reeves as Don John in *Much Ado about Nothing*, or when Gus van Sant uses him as a Prince Hal figure in *My Own Private Idaho*, or when he plays *Hamlet* at Ashland, Oregon, all of these Shakespearean characters become invested with "Bill" from *Bill and Ted's Excellent Adventure*, his "cool cop" characters in *Speed* and *Point Break*, and, retroactively, Neo from the *Matrix* trilogy. Shakespeare is received and understood in terms of the popular context.

Marvin Carlson refers to this phenomenon as "ghosting": the process of using the memory of previous encounters to understand and interpret encounters with new and somewhat different but apparently similar phenomena," which "plays a major role in the theatre, as it does in all the arts."[20] In the case of youth-culture Shakespeare, however, Carlson's timeline is interrupted. Whereas Carlson argues that in the theatre the current performance is haunted by the past, the use of electronic media means that one does not necessarily encounter the works of a performer (or writer) in the order in which they were created. A student in the classroom is much more likely to have seen *The Matrix* or *Constantine* before than *Much Ado about Nothing*, so his or her respective viewing is haunted by Keanu Reeves in those roles, even though they came after his Shakespearean turn. When one applies Carlson's theory to film, one can be haunted not only by past performances, but those performances can be "haunted" by ones that followed. Kenneth Branagh's *Henry V* (the film for which he was known for years after its release) is now haunted by his appearance as the Defense against the Dark Arts teacher in *Harry Potter and the Chamber of Secrets*. *Romeo + Juliet* is haunted by *Titanic*. Even the Shakespearean films of Julia Stiles, the subject of chapter 2, are haunted by *Save the Last Dance*. Any other role in which the performer has appeared can and will be linked to the Shakespearean character.

Similarly, Kenneth M. Chanko observes of the 1995 film version of *Othello* featuring Laurence Fishburne in the title role that not only did Fishburn not read the Shakespearean original, but also that people connected his character to his Oscar-nominated performance as Ike Turner in *What's Love Got to Do with It?*[21] In other words, Othello becomes conflated with Tina Turner's abusive husband. Just as Ike beat Tina, Othello beats Desdemona. The two become one in the audience's minds. Shakespeare thereby becomes just another reference point within the popular culture.

We might also consider youth-culture Shakespeare within the history of Shakespearean adaptation. "New" versions of Shakespeare's plays are old hat; they have existed since the very beginning. Shakespeare has been adapted since he was still alive: quarto text versus folio, London production at the Globe or Blackfriars versus scaled-down touring productions, significant textual and production transformations from the Restoration on. Different names have been applied to this phenomenon: Jonathan Bate (1989) and Jonathan Miller both refer to this as a play's "afterlife," Ruby Cohn (1976) calls them "offshoots," Michael Scott (1989) refers to them as "feedoffs," Charles Marowitz (1988) prefers to term his experiments as "transmutations," whereas Martha Rozett (1994) calls them "transformations." Alan Sinfield (1988) offers "reconstitutions," and Michael D. Bristol refers to "vernacular Shakespeare" and "crossover Shakespeare," the latter specifically referring to the movement from high culture, where Bristol posits Shakespeare, to low or popular culture.[22] Other authors and critics have used the terms adaptation, spin-off, parody, appropriation, variation, and so forth. The specific term used establishes the relationship between the original text and the new work based upon it.

Yet we must also consider Shakespearean reference. Not an adaptation of the original play, per se, but rather linking the new work to Shakespeare's. This connection can be achieved by referencing the man himself or his works, directly or indirectly. Sometimes the reference acknowledges the source; other times only those who recognize the reference understand that Shakespeare is being invoked. This use of reference will be explored in much greater detail later, but the question is raised, is it merely a game of "identify the quote," or more significant than that? Furthermore, the question is begged why would a dead white male from England 400-years-gone matter in the least to a hip, American crowd for whom over-30 is already too old?

Lastly, it is important to note that while cultural and political conservatives decry youth Shakespeare as a corruption, a vulgarity, and "not Shakespeare" while at the same time voicing concern that Shakespeare is vanishing from university campuses, replaced by rap music, Toni Morrison, and multicultural literature, the irony is that much of youth- culture Shakespeare is culturally conservative. Henry A. Giroux observes that films such as *Stand and Deliver* and *Dead Poets Society* (to which we might add *Renaissance Man* and *10 Things I Hate About You*) "appropriate elements of a progressive pedagogy" by showing a nontraditionalist instructor using Shakespeare to help disenfranchised or alienated young people learn and achieve through Shakespeare. Yet these films also affirm the canonical knowledge (read: Eurocentric, "classical" culture) as important and superior. Authority is not resisted through Shakespeare in these films, argues Giroux, but rather finds its position affirmed as the height of culture, which even misguided youth can value and use. Thus, these films are inherently conservative, reaffirming the value of Shakespeare in education and for its own sake as well.[23] In *10 Things I Hate About You* the young African American English teacher remarks, "I know Shakespeare's a dead white guy, but he knows his shit, so we can overlook that." Apparently Shakespeare transcends race, gender, nationality, time, and even death, and can be appreciated and valued by all cultures and peoples. Youth-culture Shakespeare affirms Shakespeare's canonicity, value, and appropriate place at the top of the curriculum and the culture. Youth-culture Shakespeare as often as not reaffirms the same lessons taught at school.

Shakespeare in the Schools: Another Brick in the Wall

Thou hast most traitorously corrupted the youth of the realm in erecting a grammar school; and whereas, before, our forefathers had no other books but the score and the tally, thou hast caused printing to be used; and, contrary to the king, his crown, and dignity, thou hast built a paper mill.

—Henry VI, Part II *4.7.32–37*

We don't need no education... all in all you're just another brick in the wall.

—Pink Floyd, Another Brick in the Wall, Part 2

All of the issues discussed thus far come into play when attempting to teach Shakespeare in the secondary or university classroom. As noted, an entire industry exists to teach teachers how to market Shakespeare in the classroom, how to overcome the challenges of inaccessibility and irrelevance, and means by which the students can be encouraged to engage the plays on their own level, ostensibly in the hope that doing so will lead them to other levels. Ghosting is seen as a useful way to interest students in Shakespeare videos. Jo MucMurtry, for example, in *Shakespeare Films in the Classroom* evaluates each film in terms of "pluses" and "minuses" as well as "textual cuts," "settings," "costumes," and "interpretation." Under pluses for *Much Ado about Nothing*, she cites the fact that students will "recognize many members of the cast" and identifies those members with more familiar roles they've played: "Denzel Washington (*Malcolm X*) and Michael Keaton (*Batman*).[24] While the recognizability of the cast may be a selling point to students, how does it benefit Shakespeare (or the student) to link Don Pedro with Malcolm X and Dogberry with Batman?

Numerous publications offer suggestions to engage the students with Shakespeare through a variety of means. Fred Sedgwick, for example, advocates creative writing as a means of engagement.[25] Milla Cozart Riggio has edited an anthology that advocates teaching Shakespeare through performance, from reading out loud in the classroom to fully mounted productions.[26] Other anthologies propose a variety of approaches and techniques, many with variations on the title *Teaching Shakespeare*.[27] But what Shakespeare is being taught, how, and to what end? And how and why is youth culture that has appropriated Shakespeare being appropriated by the education industry as a teaching tool of the original Shakespeare? In some senses,

Shakespeare in school becomes a series of mirrors, in which one reads reflected texts, watches reflected movies and then engage the experience through discussion, writing, performance, and activities.

In his aptly titled "Give an Account of Shakespeare and Education, Showing Why You Think They Are Effective and What You Have Appreciated about Them; Support Your Comments with Precise References," Alan Sinfield argues that the educational system serves primarily as a means to continue capitalism and patriarchy, and that Shakespeare is not only a tool of that process, but also primarily "has been made to speak for the right."[28] Sinfield seeks to change this situation, acknowledging that standardized tests on Shakespeare serve as a means of controlling and defining his work.[29] Yet we must acknowledge that Sinfield, too, is guilty of attempting to control and define Shakespeare's work, and of empowering the right by attempting to define Shakespeare against it. In the words of Pink Floyd, Sinfield is also "just another brick in the wall."

As we have argued, there are multiple Shakespeares that are negotiated during the educational process, not all of which are controlled and defined by the instructor. Even the assertion Sinfield made twenty years ago, that British O-levels and American AP exams privilege texts is made further difficult by the substitution of all these other Shakespeares for the text. Sinfield quotes an O-level exam: "Questions refer to the books you have read, NOT to any radio, television, musical or film version of them."[30] And yet these are precisely the materials that teachers are encouraged to use in order to make the texts "come to life." The past two decades have done much to transform the understanding of Shakespeare in the classroom and the understanding of Shakespeare by youth.

What Jon Lewis argues for teen films might apply to all of teen culture: it focuses on "the breakdown of traditional forms of authority," and yet in all these films (as in all of Shakespeare's plays), the traditional authority that has broken down is restored by narrative's end.[31] In the lives of teens, as seen in popular culture and in reality, the two key institutions that break down are the family and the school. Both are sources of authority and both move to contain unruly youth and transform them into productive members of society. As school is also where textual Shakespeare is most often first encountered, the name and the plays are linked inextricably to school and education. Yet, as we have acknowledged, there are already Shakespeares in the student's lives.

The linkage of Shakespeare, youth, and education is made manifest in the number of films that appropriate Shakespeare's narratives, characters, plots, and themes to high school settings: "*O*," *10 Things I Hate about You*, and *The Glass House* to name but three are all films that set Shakespeare's narratives among high school students, setting the events of *Othello, Taming of the Shrew* and *Hamlet*, respectively, in the 14 to 18 age set.

Numerous other films aimed at the youth audience feature classroom scenes during which Shakespeare is discussed: the above-mentioned *Dead Poets Society* and *Stand and Deliver* both feature scenes of students reading (and performing) Shakespeare in exclusive prep schools and inner city public schools. *Porky's II: The Next Day* features a production of Shakespeare. This phenomenon extends to television, in which students are frequently shown studying Shakespeare and rehearsing and performing the plays, usually for comic effect, in such sitcoms as *3rd Rock from the Sun, Malcolm in the Middle*, and *Arrested Development*. The one thing that unites all teens in these films and television programs, regardless of genre and narrative is that they all study Shakespeare in the classroom. The films arguably reflect the reality: as Samuel Crowl argues, Shakespeare is "the one constant fixture in American high school classrooms."[32]

By linking Shakespeare so firmly to education, we firmly ensconce him within the world of youth culture, but in a dualistic role, at once both adversarial to youth and wholly recognizable to them. Shakespeare is part of the youth world, and yet the plays are an imposition on that world from outside, under the authority of education. And yet the Shakespeare received in the classroom is always a mediated one, as noted above. Teachers at both the high school and college level employ mediated Shakespeare to teach the texts—videos, activities, such as those in the *Shakespeare Set Free* books, attendance of theatrical performances can often be a part of the curriculum. More recently, textbooks are being replaced with DVDs, videos, CD-ROMs and the Internet. In school, one is as likely to watch or download Shakespeare as read him.

Tied to the number of media through which Shakespeare is now available is the phenomenon of repeated viewing. Youth culture encourages repeated experiences: see/read/do it again and again and again, often with minor variations. *William Shakespeare's Romeo + Juliet* was seen by many in the theatre, who could then rent or buy the videotape or DVD, which was then re-released in a special edition and finally in a box set with additional features. One not only sees the film, one watches it again with the commentary tracks, watches the deleted scenes and alternate endings, interviews with the cast, and "making of" featurettes. Just as Shakespeare culture encourages repeated viewings of different versions of the same texts (every time scholars get together they inevitably compare the number and type of productions they have seen—did you see the Ralph Fiennes *Hamlet*? How about Mark Rylance in the role? Richard Thomas?), so, too, does youth culture encourage repeated experiences with variation: cinema, DVD, special edition DVD, and director's cut DVD.

Yet we might also note that concern over Shakespeare disappearing from the classroom has been a rather constant feature in the culture wars of the past few decades. In *The Culture of Fear*, Barry Glassner observes that the concerns of cultural conservatives, "the image [that] appeared widely in the press of PC thugs in ivory towers forcibly evicting the Bard," that Toni Morrison is replacing Shakespeare in secondary schools and universities, are unfounded.[33] Rather, figures such as Allan Bloom, William Bennett, and E.D. Hirsh rely upon anecdote and intuition, rather than numbers.

Rather than being concerned about the canon of classroom literature growing more inclusive, one wonders why such figures are not more concerned about the aforementioned growing mediation of Shakespeare when he is present in the classroom. The reason is quite simple. Even if text is replaced with DVD, CD-Rom, and Internet searches, Shakespeare is still given primacy in education. Shakespeare is still "number one." Even a mediated Shakespeare is preferable to no Shakespeare or nontraditional authors. Yet Shakespeare is alive and well and part of the larger education schema, despite these concerns.

As Shirley R. Steinberg and Joe L. Kincheloe write in *Kinderculture: The Corporate Construction of Childhood*, students are also taught by "cultural pedagogy . . . education takes place in a variety of social sites including, but not limited to schooling."[34] Libraries, churches, youth groups, even via movies and education television from *Sesame Street* to the Discovery Channel are sites where students might learn. Thus, even as the youth culture industry looks to Shakespeare for source material, the education industry looks to the youth-culture industry for pedagogical tools. The use of technologically mediated youth-culture Shakespeare in the classroom has shaped the current generation's students' perceptions of Shakespeare. As Martha Tuck Rozett observes, "Assign a paper on *Hamlet* and the Hamlet that will come back to you might look remarkably like Mel Gibson in Zeffirelli's film . . ."[35] More recently, Hamlet will look remarkably like Ethan Hawke, even as Romeo and Juliet look like Leonardo DiCaprio and Claire Danes.

We do not necessarily suggest that this linkage is a negative aspect of the popularization of Shakespeare, but educators need to recognize the nature of such tactics in teaching Shakespeare. Richard Keller Simon has been a strong advocate of using "popular culture as a potentially powerful teaching tool," for linking a classic work of literature with a work of popular culture in another media and by juxtaposition understand both better.[36] In *Trash Culture: Popular Culture and the Great Tradition*, he argues that television soap operas "are very similar to some of the great Jacobean revenge tragedies of the English Renaissance."[37] By juxtaposing the classic with the contemporary, one can perceive the classic as an example of the popular culture of its own day and "see the complexity in the popular form that you were unable to see before."[38] The danger, of course, is that one simply exchanges the classical Other for a contemporary Self, and difference and cultural context are erased.

In a subsequent article, Simon advocates teaching Shakespeare via popular television situation comedies. His examples of choice are *Much Ado about Nothing* and the show *Friends*. Both are about "a small group of unmarried young men and women [who] flirt with each other, play a series of tricks on each other, and fall in and out of love."[39] While true on one level, Simon's analysis is also hopelessly reductivist, as both Shakespeare's play and the NBC situation comedy are much more than these mere plot elements. To see *Much Ado* as an Elizabethan *Friends*, with Ross and Rachel as Claudio and Hero, Chandler and Monica as Benedick and Beatrice, and Joey and Phoebe as "clowns," as Simon suggests, is to reduce both down to component elements and ignore the complexities of each.

We shall go into greater detail below on the role of reduction in linking Shakespeare to youth, but a pattern can be seen emerging here. Both popular culture and the educational system, in seizing upon Shakespeare as a means to connect to youth, must deal with the issues of boredom and inaccessibility, and therefore use the strategies of translation, reduction, and reference.

Translating Shakespeare into English

Bless thee, Bottom, bless thee. Thou art translated.

—Peter Quince to Nick Bottom,
A Midsummer Night's Dream *3.1.119*

There's a matter in these sighs, these profound heaves.
You must translate: 'tis fit we understand them.

—Claudius to Rosencrantz and Guildenstern,
Hamlet 4.1.1–2

The latter quotation above appears on the title page of every edition of No Fear Shakespeare, which purports to "translate" Shakespeare into "plain English." Each text is "a translation anyone can understand," and the cover of each play boasts that the reader who encounters *this* version of the text will encounter the play "in all its brilliance and actually understand what it means."[40] Yet it is the former quotation that may be more accurate in describing the translation of Shakespeare for young and/or American readers.

In the quotation from *Hamlet*, Claudius is speaking to two of Hamlet's college friends, instructing them to translate his behavior into terms that he and Gertrude, Hamlet's stepfather and mother, respectively, can understand. Claudius argues that it is "fit," that is, that it is proper, appropriate, and perhaps even necessary that Hamlet's parents understand his actions and attitudes. Others who know him better must translate his actions for his parents so that they become comprehensible on Claudius and Gertrude's terms. It would seem that the editors of No Fear Shakespeare, in employing the quote epigrammatically, posit that it is fit to translate Shakespeare's plays into language comprehensible to modern American students (the clearly designated market for these books) so that the plays become comprehensible to the students on their own terms as well.

Quince, on the other hand, is speaking to a Bottom who has been given the head of an ass as a jest by Puck. While here the term translated refers to transformation, we might use Quince's words in their actual meaning: what was once human and artistic has now been translated into something vulgar and frightening. Jan Kott named one of his critical treatises *The Bottom Translation*, by which he argues that translation is not only metamorphosis, but also "in Shakespeare, 'translation' is the sudden discovery of desire." It is also a "carnival ritual" in the Bakhtinian sense and "the wisdom of folly and the delight of the fool."[41] In other words, Shakespeare's theatre engages desire, transformation, and social inversion in a mad, celebratory manner. One might consider these translations of Shakespeare into contemporary vernacular prose as a sort of "Bottom translation." What was once "high culture" is now transformed into the common and everyday.

If one considers the varied meanings of the word translation—to render from one language to another, to change into another media, and to explicate or explain—it seems obvious that youth-culture Shakespeare engages in all of these activities. Yet there is also another, more archaic, Catholic meaning to the word. In church terminology, to translate is to move the relics of a saint from place of interment to another. We might also view this as a larger metaphor for the youth-Shakespeare movement. It is a movement from one generation to the next, as well as moving the "relics" of Shakespeare from the province of purists, traditionalists, and academics to the mall cinemas, DVDs, CDs, MP3s, and other digital and technological churches of the youth, always with the announcement that such activity is blessed by Shakespeare: "Its what he would have done were he alive today." At the close of the introduction to the texts of Shakespeare's *Romeo and Juliet* and the shooting screenplay of Baz Luhrmann's *William Shakespeare's Romeo + Juliet*, Lurhmann and cowriter Craig Pearce note, "We're trying to make this movie rambunctious, sexy, violent, and entertaining the way Shakespeare might have if he had been a filmmaker."[42] Or, as Lloyd Kaufman, president of Troma Entertainment and producer, director and cowriter of *Tromeo and Juliet*, the exploitive parody of Luhrmann's film, notes of his version, "We've given Shakespeare the car crashes, the kinky sex, the dismemberment, all of the wonderful ingredients that Shakespeare always wanted but never had." One can (and many do) justify any number of translations from the tropes of one media to another by arguing it is what Shakespeare himself would have done. And who are we to argue with Shakespeare about his own plays?

> Life is a story told by an idiot, full of noise and
> emotional disturbance but devoid of meaning.
> "Translation" of *Macbeth* 5.5.26–28,
> *No Fear Shakespeare: Macbeth*

Another recent trend has been the literal translation of Shakespeare's plays into modern English, usually aimed at the student market. For example, the "No Fear Shakespeare" series references both Shakespeare and the "No Fear" clothing and product line. The cover of each book proclaims that the series was created by Harvard students "for students everywhere." Shakespeare's original text is on the left side of the text, on the right is an "accessible, plain English translation" of that text. Neither critical introduction, nor scholarly apparatus is included. Instead the reader is given a list of characters with a brief summary of their identity and relationship to each other and the occasional side note in the text indicating cultural, historical, or contextual information. Whereas students of a generation ago would read the *Cliffs Notes* or *Monarch Notes*, which summarized the play, now students can simply read a translation. The "student aid" text is now incorporated into the original text.[43]

No Fear, we might note, also creates an intertext with the "No Fear" clothing line—a trendy set of jackets, hats, t-shirts, other garments and gear linked to so-called extreme sports: motocross, BMX bike racing, surfing, snowboarding, skateboarding, etc. By calling the series No Fear, the editors are linking their product with a name that suggests youth, coolness, hipness, and "extreme" activities. No Fear Shakespeare is clearly designed to seem like "Extreme Shakespeare" for the current generation of youth.

This idea is not original to the Harvard students who created this series. A previous version, all edited by Alan Durband was published in the 1980s and titled "Shakespeare Made Easy." The series was published by Barrons, who also published "Simply Shakespeare," yet another translations series and best known for standardized test preparation guides that seek to prepare students to do well on standardized tests such as the PSAT, SAT, GRE, LSAT, and MCAT, to name but a few. Such guides serve the purpose of studying to the test—the goal is not learning or education, but to pass with a high score. These Shakespeare translations might be seen in the same light. So long as one can answer questions about the narrative, the original language, subtlety, ambiguity, and cultural references are not important.

As an example, consider the following translations from *Hamlet*, act 3, scene 1, line 55 in the original:

> To be or not to be, that is the question.
> No Fear Shakespeare translation:
> The question is: is it better to be alive or dead?[44]

> Shakespeare Made Easy translation:
> [To himself] To live or not to live. That is the issue.[45]

The challenge of these translations is that, unlike standard texts of Shakespeare that footnote difficult words, phrases and concepts, these translations must present the entire text in translation. The translation of such famous lines as "To be or not to be . . ." is almost always reductivist and falls into self-parody. Consider act 3, scene 1, lines 120–121:

> Original:
>   Get thee to a nunnery. Why wouldst thou be a breeder of sinners?
> No Fear Shakespeare:
>   Get yourself to a convent at once. Why would you want to give birth
> to more sinners?[46]
> Shakespeare Made Easy:
>   Become a nun! What, do you want to give birth to sinners?[47]

Something is lost in translation, literally.

Sometimes the translations, when juxtaposed against other translations of the same line, almost contradict each other.

> Act 3, scene 2, lines 1–2:
>   Speak the speech, I pray you, as I pronounced it to you,
> trippingly on the tongue.
> No Fear Shakespeare:
>   Perform the speech just as I taught you, musically and smoothly.[48]
> Shakespeare Made Easy:
>   Please speak the speech as I recited it to you, in a natural way.[49]

If one considers "musically" to mean with the structure and flow of music (an artificial construct and an artificial manner of speaking), then one cannot speak the speech "in a natural way." In this case, not only is something lost in translation, the meaning of the line as rendered in translation may not be entirely accurate.

The larger question, as noted above is—given that much of the play is comprehensible to a contemporary reader—why is translation of every line necessary? Consider the opening scene of *Macbeth* (1.1.1–7), which ordinarily requires only three or four footnotes to explain the culturally specific references.

Original:

> *First Witch:*   When shall we three meet again
>   In thunder, lightening, or in rain?
> *Second Witch:*   When the hurly-burly's done,
>   When the battle's lost and won.
> *Third Witch:*   That will be ere the set of sun.
> *First Witch:*   Where the place?
> *Second Witch:*   Upon the heath.
> *Third Witch:*   There to meet with Macbeth.

This scene is translated in No Fear Shakespeare thus:

> *First Witch:*   When should the three of us meet again? Will it be in thunder, lightning, or rain?
> *Second Witch:*   We'll meet when the noise of the battle is over, when one side has won and the other side has lost.
> *Third Witch:*   That will happen before sunset.
> *First Witch:*   Where should we meet?
> *Second Witch:*   Let's do it in the open field.
> *Third Witch:*   We'll meet Macbeth there.[50]

This text is less translation than paraphrase—the "translator" has in some cases slightly rephrased the text and in some cases the same exact phrasing is used. What is the clarification for students achieved by changing "There to meet with Macbeth" to "We'll meet Macbeth there"?

In some cases, the translation is useful, especially at countering popular misreadings of the text. Both translations of *Romeo and Juliet* kill the old bugbear of "Wherefore art thou, Romeo?," long translated by both popular and youth culture to mean "Where are you, Romeo?," rendering it as "Why do you have to be 'Romeo'?"[51]

The purpose of these translations, however, is to make the text accessible. Translate the play from an unfamiliar language (renaissance English) to a familiar one (modern English). The result is that the reader, rather than going to Shakespeare and the original language, insists that Shakespeare come to him or her. Rather than encountering the original text and engage the original context, the translation modernizes and moves the text (yet another translation!) into the shrine of the familiar.

A similar, but different approach is in texts that seek to serve as keys or guides for translation. Books such as Nick Groom and Piero's *Introducing Shakespeare*, Brandon Toporov and Van Howell's *Shakespeare for Beginners*, Norrie Epstein's *The Friendly Shakespeare*, and John Doyle and Ray Lischner's *Shakespeare for Dummies*, all of which employ a variety of techniques and tools to translate Shakespeare into a comprehensible form. Cartoons, icons, scorecards, flow charts, paraphrases, sidebars, and photographs and film stills, among other devices, are used to inform the reader of character, narrative, and context. While useful in aiding understanding, often these books are substitutes for reading (or seeing) the plays themselves. One can read them and know the plot, the major characters, significant lines, and important productions of each of the major plays. In the case of these volumes, the plays have been translated even out of a dramatic format and are simply summarized. In short, these works link translation with reduction, another strategy for bringing Shakespeare to youth culture, removing boredom and making the plays accessible.

We might note that No Fear Shakespeare renders the Bottom translation thus: "God bless you, Bottom, God bless you. You've been changed. Reborn."[52] Shakespearean translation is also Shakespeare changed and reborn. As Puck later states in the same translation: "Lord, what fools these mortals are!"[53]

Reducing Shakespeare

> We found a way to satisfy your cravin'
> When you're bored of the Bard of Stratford-upon-Avon:
> We think old Bill's too stuffy, he needs to loosen
> so we take his boring plays and we reduce 'em.
> We cut the poetry, the subplots, the imagery that's illin'
> And we get right to the sex and to the killin'.
>
> —"OTT Rap," The Reduced Shakespeare
> Company Radio Show[54]

"OTT" stands for "Over the Top," which is how the Reduced Shakespeare Company describes many of their own productions. As the rap suggests, the attitude of the company is one of mockery, expressing familiarity with Shakespeare by calling him Bill and that he is "too stuffy" and his plays are "boring." The solution to this problem, posits the Other RSC, as they call themselves, is to reduce Shakespeare. As their name suggests, the company specializes in doing so.

The Reduced Shakespeare Company began in 1981 in Northern California with a thirty-minute *Hamlet* inspired by Tom Stoppard's *Fifteen-Minute Hamlet*. A two-man, truncated *Romeo and Juliet* followed. In 1987, planning to attend the Edinburgh Fringe Festival, the company created *The Complete Works of William Shakespeare (Abridged)*, which, as its title suggests, is a condensation of all of Shakespeare's plays into a single two-hour performance. As the company name (and the rap above) suggests, the strategy for creating such a work is to "reduce" the plays to their component elements (and sometimes even less than that!). As Daniel Singer, cocreator of the Other RSC and cowriter of *The Complete Works of William Shakespeare (Abridged)* writes, "[A]udiences of the last quarter of the twentieth century apparently possessed an urgent need to see Shakespeare performed as if it were a Tex Avery cartoon . . ."[55]

The play displays a loving, knowledgeable disrespect for the original plays. These guys know their Shakespeare, they simply do not adore him, worship him, or acknowledge him as the source of all that is good in world culture as Harold Bloom or Allen Bloom do. Instead, they engage the plays in the personae of young, slightly confused actors. In doing so, they can arrange a clever parody, such as presenting *Titus Andronicus* as a cooking show. On the other hand, some of the scenes are sophomoric and rely upon no actual knowledge of the play being "reduced." For example, they refuse to perform *Coriolanus* as one of the performers does not "like the 'anus' part. I think it's offensive," prompting the other two members to agree that "we skip the anus play."[56]

After several successful world tours, including performances in London, New York, and Los Angeles, the company began to expand their own contributions to bardbiz. The text of their "complete works" was published in 1994, and the company also had a radio series on the BBC. It is on the radio show that one might see the principle at work behind their versions of Shakespeare. In the first radio show, a thirty-minute adaptation of *Romeo and Juliet*, the announcer proclaims that "The RSC is proud to prevent *Romeo and Juliet*." There is something accurate there, not just the pun involving between the similar sounds of "present" and "prevent," but in the idea that this performance prevents Shakespeare's version from being performed. They reduce the play to a series of narrative moments taken from the original, along with the main characters, and then replace Shakespeare's language with common vernacular and contemporary reference.

The meeting of Romeo and Juliet occurs at a costume party at the Capulets, in which Romeo and Benvolio have dressed together as a horse. Romeo is the back half, allowing for bad joke about him being a "horse's ass." Then, as Romeo recites actual lines from Shakespeare's play,

> Romeo: Oh, she doth teach the torches to burn bright!
>   It seems she hangs upon the cheek of night
>   Like a rich jewel in an Ethiope's ear,
>   Beauty too rich for use, for earth too dear.
>
> (1.5.44–47)

Benvolio then interrupts to ask Romeo if he's on drugs—"What was all that stuff about an Ethiope's ear? Are you stoned?" Romeo responds, "That was poetry, man. Back off!" and the rest of the scene is dropped, so that Romeo and Juliet may meet sooner.

This exchange demonstrates the modus operandi of the Reduced Shakespeare Company—familiar narrative and textual landmarks surrounded by jokes and contemporary references, with most of the original text removed. As noted in the epigram above, they remove all subplots, imagery, poetry, and extended dialog and get to not only the violence and the sex, but to the familiar, the recognizable.

As with translation, reduction is a word of several meanings. The definitions of reduce include to make smaller and/or simpler, to break down to essential elements, to lessen or make less, to remove essential parts. To reduce Shakespeare, in the Other RSC sense, is to do all of these. The plays are made simple, preserving only the most essential elements and in the end barely resemble the original. More accurately, to reduce is to turn original into reference.

We might also note that in *The Complete Works of William Shakespeare*, as well as many teen cinematic adaptations of Shakespeare, multiple references to California abound. Many of the teen Shakespeare films are set in California. Partly this fact can be attributed to the fact that Hollywood and Southern California are the center of the international entertainment industry, and many films are shot there, but also we might note that California is center of youth culture (and especially Shakespearean Youth culture). From Jan and Dean's "Little Old Lady from Pasadena" and the complete catalogue of the Beach Boys to such films as *Clueless* and *Bill and Ted's Excellent Adventure*, youth culture is sited in California, or at least holds the greater Los Angeles area as a model.

The Reduced Shakespeare Company are not the only reducers—we might employ the term of reduction as a larger metaphor for what others do. For example, *Shakespeare for Dummies* by John Doyle and Ray Lischner and *The Complete Idiot's Guide to Shakespeare* by Laurie Rozakis, both mentioned above, are also part translation, part reduction.[57]

In his own survey of what he calls "Kiddie Shakespeare," Richard Burt (1998) calls youth-culture Shakespeare "inane or just plain stupid" and "precisely a dumbed down Shakespeare," citing contemporary youth culture as regressive, childish and infantile.[58] Popular culture and youth culture have embraced the dumb, the stupid and the reductivist. The icons of the last decade of the twentieth century were Beavis and Butthead, *Dumb and Dumber* and *Jackass*—all celebrations of stupidity. Films of this period such as the one this introduction references by its title, *Dude, Where's My Car?* celebrate the successful attempt of chronically stupid young people to live their lives oblivious to the world around them, pursuing infantile goals. The Shakespeare that is given to this generation, or the one created by and for it, perhaps, is a reduced one. Dude, where's my Bard?

"Nobody Outcrazies Ophelia": *The Simpsons* References the Bard

Christy Desmet states in the introduction to *Shakespeare and Appropriation* that many cultural products will engage in "individual acts of 're-vision' . . . for the sheer fun of playing 'identify that quotation.' "[59] Partly this game involves the pleasure of recognition, and partly the pleasure of exclusion. If one gets the reference and others do not, then one is a member of an elite group of insiders. Reference can also generate another level of meaning, as well as elevate what might commonly be considered base to a higher level of culture. On the other hand, reference can also be used to mock or deride: "Recitation," observes Desmet, "can turn citation into parody."[60]

In *A Theory of Parody*, Linda Hutcheon argues that often Shakespeare's texts can be a means of parody, rather than the target itself: "It is not Shakespeare who is being mocked," but rather a political, social, or cultural target. Shakespeare is merely "the vehicle for their satire."[61] In either case, whether Shakespeare is the target of parody or the means by which another target may be parodied, reference to his works is common in popular culture.

The Simpsons, a half-hour animated show on Fox television, currently in its fourteenth season, is popular youth culture par excellence. Two thirds of the viewers are under the age of 34, and the show is the best-rated regularly scheduled network show among teens and also among males 18 to 34.[62] The show's disrespect for all traditional authority figures and its lack of trust also makes it appeal to younger viewers, who can laugh at Homer (the father) as fool, but still find empathy for Bart, the young rebel, and Lisa, the daughter whose intelligence isolates her from both her family and her peers.

The show has often employed references to Shakespeare on several levels and for different reasons and in different manners. We will here use *The Simpsons* as a model for understanding the different ways that youth culture references Shakespeare. *The Simpsons* is by no means the only animated show to tackle Shakespeare, only the most recent in a long line of animated Shakespeareana, including 1916s *The Barnyard Hamlet*, which re-created the tragedy with farm animals,

Bugs Bunny performing Romeo, *Shakespeare: The Animated Tales*, and even the *Hamlet*—inspired Disney's *The Lion King.*[63]

The first type of reference is an out-of-context quotation, usually unidentified in context:

> Lisa: A rose by any other name would smell as sweet.
> Bart: Not if you call them stenchblossoms.

The reference is never acknowledged, though Lisa is quoting directly from *Romeo and Juliet*. Bart's response is to devalue the famous quotation from Shakespeare. This type of reference is one of the most common, and serves to parody both Shakespeare and the idea of quoting his plays as a means of practical advice or wisdom. Similarly, when Principal Skinner dates Marge's sister Patty, Shakespeare is referenced when they break up. Patty says, "Good night, Sweet Principal," a direct reference to the last scene of *Hamlet*, but no other acknowledgement is made of the reference. In such situations, we may be witnessing nothing more than Desmet's game of identify the quotation, or we might then link the scene with the death of Hamlet, which has nothing to do with the moment on the television screen.[64]

The second type of reference is to reference the man directly. Shakespeare has come to represent intellect and a certain stuffiness in the popular mind. To call someone a Shakespeare is not always complimentary, as it implies bookishness and a privileging of the intellectual over the physical, and in certain cultures this quality is not valued. In popular and youth-culture depictions, Shakespeare is inevitably shown in Elizabethan period costume, speaking in a very classical British accent in a heightened, highly artificial style. On one of the Halloween episodes of *The Simpsons*, titled "Treehouse of Horror," this is the version of Shakespeare presented. Homer uses a shotgun to dispose of zombies who have come to life when Bart accidentally casts a spell raising the dead. He identifies each famous zombie before shooting it, saying, "Take that, Washington! Eat lead, Einstein! Show's over, Shakespeare!" One might wonder why Shakespeare's corpse is even buried in Springfield, but it allows Shakespeare to speak, the only zombie to do so. "Is this the end of Zombie Shakespeare?" he proclaims in an overdramatic, cultured British accent after being shot by Homer and falling dramatically to the ground. Again, Shakespeare the man is the target and the means for parody in this example. What is being mocked is the high culture that surrounds the idea of Shakespeare the man as well as linking

Shakespeare to Edward G. Robinson's Rico, an absurd connection that requires a third level of reference for the viewer.

Similarly, in another "Treehouse of Horror," this time number XIII, a parody of *The Island of Dr. Moreau* is enacted in which Dr. Julius Hibbert, in the Moreau role, attempts to justify the positive benefits of his human/animal experiments: "Think of what Shakespeare could have accomplished if he had the eyes of an eagle, or could spray stink on his critics like a skunk." The man is being referenced here, although no longer is high culture the object of parody. Instead, Shakespeare is the means for an absurdist parody of Wells's novel and the various film versions of it.

The third type of reference is to acknowledge the plots, characters, and titles of specific plays. Bart's friend Milhouse, describes his ill-fated romance with Lisa: "We started out like Romeo and Juliet, but it ended in tragedy." The object of parody here is not Shakespeare. Rather, the reference requires the audience's knowledge that Shakespeare's play is a tragedy that ends very badly for Romeo and Juliet. What is being mocked is Milhouse's misunderstanding of *Romeo and Juliet*, and perhaps even the public's conception of Romeo and Juliet as idealized lovers, despite a less than ideal relationship. Given the number of poplar songs that reference Romeo and Juliet, as analyzed in chapter 2, it might be that this reference also mocks a public that sees in their tragedy the model of teenage love.

The fourth type of reference is to show Shakespeare in performance. Bart, auditioning for a film about a superhero named "Radioactive Man," impresses his peers with his performance. Announcing that "it's all in the delivery," Bart draws his cape around him and intones, "Now is the winter of our discontent . . ." prompting Ralph Wiggum to cry out, "Oh no! Run!" While the reference is never cited (thus also making this an example of the first type of reference), it is clear that Bart is performing and parodying the idea of performing Shakespeare—that one must be over dramatic and not at all realistic.

In another episode, Krusty the Clown plays Lear at a local dinner theatre. The servant informs him of his daughter's death:

Krusty: Hey, lighten up, it's a comedy!
Servant (whispering):   No, it's not.

This exchange relies upon the audience's knowledge of *King Lear* and how inappropriate it is to have Krusty, who is, as his name suggests, a clown with his own children's show, play the role of the king. One might even view this reference as a parody of celebrity Shakespeare, as discussed above, in which Keanu Reeves, Michelle Pfeiffer, Michael Keaton, Billy Crystal, Calista Flockheart, and other Hollywood actors are cast in roles simply on the strength of their celebrity rather than appropriateness of the role, acting experience, or even ability to play it.

Krusty, the host of a children's show and a clown, is clearly not ready or right to play Lear:

> *Servant:* "Your daughters are here: Regan, Goneril, and Cordelia."
> *Krusty:* "Hey, what is this, *Petticoat Junction?*

While the other characters continue to perform, one of the other actors shows Krusty the actual script. Krusty decides to change Shakespeare to suit his talents:

> *Krusty:* (Looking at the script) Whoa! This material stinks! I'm going to have to punch it up on the fly. Oh, got one. How do you make the King Lear? Put the queen in a bikini!"

The crowd begins to boo, causing Krusty to remark to a fellow actor, "Tough crowd, they're booing Shakespeare." Krusty conflates his performance with Shakespeare's text. The celebrity actor who is inappropriate for the role is parodied, as well as the idea of how Shakespeare should be played. In the following scene, in the background the newspaper headline the next day can clearly be seen: "Krusty: Worst Lear in 400 Years."

Fifth is the full-on adaptation of a specific play utilizing the characters as themselves in specific roles. Thus, in one particular episode, "Tales from the Public Domain," *Hamlet* is dramatized, along with the life of Joan of Arc, and *The Odyssey*. Homer's discovery of an unreturned library book results in his reading stories from it to his children. Shakespeare's play is the final tale to be told. In it, Hamlet is conflated with Bart, the Ghost with Homer, Gertrude with Marge, and Lisa with Ophelia. Other characters from the series play the other characters, and meaning is derived from the overlap of the two sets of characters. References are made both to the Shakespearean original as well as to the world of the Simpsons.

Bart objects to the choice of material: "Dad, these old stories can't compare with our modern superwriters. Steven Bochco could kick Shakespeare's ass," he claims, referencing the creator of *NYPD Blue* and other contemporary television dramas, and raising the traditional objections of youth to Shakespeare: it is boring and inaccessible

Lisa counters that Shakespeare is more interesting than Bart thinks, and that the play begins with a murder. Bart asks if Hamlet gets to marry his mom, to which Homer responds, "I don't know, but that would be hot," referring to Ernest Jones's theory that Hamlet suffered from an Oedipal complex. In their radio show for the BBC the Reduced Shakespeare Company also uses the popular conception of Jones's analysis of Hamlet as Hamlet puts on a dress and chases Claudius with a chainsaw, crying out "You killed my father and married my mother. I WAS SUPPOSED TO DO THAT!" Again, Shakespeare is the means of parody, not just the target.

When the play within the show begins, Bart, as Hamlet, sleeps in a bedroom with a poster that says "Danes Do It Melancholy" and a pennant that reads "Feudalism." Homer, as the Ghost, enters in a manner more suggestive of *Casper the Friendly Ghost* than any Shakespeare play. He cries "Avenge me!" and explains the plot, to which Bart responds, "Yeah, that was quite a weekend." This line serves to deride the unreality of the events of *Hamlet* and use them to serve as the set up for a joke. Shakespeare's play is neither being taken seriously, nor on its own terms. What is necessary to understand the humor, however, is the original text and context.

The adaptation leaps from the last scene of the first act all the way to act 3, scene 2, the play-within-the-play scene. Marge is Gertrude. Moe the bartender is Claudius. Lisa plays Ophelia while Ralph Wiggum plays Laertes and his father, Chief Wiggum is Polonius. The players are represented by Krusty the Clown, Sideshow Mel, and Mr. Teeny (Krusty's monkey), who all regularly appear on Krusty's children's show that Bart watches.

As the show begins, Krusty tells the audience, "Now we'd like to warn you, our performances tend to make audience members blurt out hidden secrets," a line that is only humorous if one knows the Shakespearean original, because it is parodying the events that occur when "The Mousetrap" is played before Claudius. Upon hearing this, Hamlet/Bart says, "The play's the thing, wherein I'll catch the conscience of the king." In a mockery of the convention of the aside, Moe/Claudius looks up in confusion and says, "Catch my conscience? What?" Bart/Hamlet responds, "You're not supposed to hear me. That's a solilo-quy." Moe/Claudius snaps back, "Well, I'll do a soliloquy, too! Note to self: kill that kid." The entire scene is parody of the convention of the soliloquy, a device for which *Hamlet* and Hamlet are arguably known.

Instead of The Mousetrap, Krusty announces that they will "open it up with a little improv," which translates the play into more modern terms, even as it reduces the complexity of the play-within-the-play to a simple theatre game. Krusty, as leader of the improvisation asks the audience for suggestions and Bart/Hamlet shouts the answers from Shakespeare's play:

Krusty: Give me a Location.
Bart: This castle.
Krusty: Occupation
Bart: Usurper of the throne.
Krusty: And an object
Bart: Ear poison.

"The Murther of Gonzago" is reduced to an improvisational exercise that will be performed before the court. Moe/Claudius looks increasingly guilty as the play is set up. A dumb show is then acted out with Krusty as the Player King, Sideshow Mel as Lucianus, and Mr. Teeny as the Player Queen. Lucianus begins pouring the poison into the Player King's ear and Moe/Claudius yells, "Wait a minute! I didn't use that much poison!" The play-within-a-play scene of *Hamlet* is thus broadly parodied in contemporary terms. There is no other target than Shakespeare.

Bart/Hamlet runs to a portrait of Homer and says, "Daddy, it's true! Uncle Claudius murdered you!" Lisa, as Ophelia, sees this and sighs, "Oh, great, now Hamlet's acting crazy. Well *nobody* outcrazies Ophelia!" and, singing "Hey nonny nonny, hey / with a wooo and a haw . . ." jumps up on a table, kicks over some flowers, and throws herself out a window into the moat, and everyone's attention goes back to Bart/Hamlet. Here the idea of Ophelia is parodied. No oppressed daughter or shrinking violet, Lisa/Ophelia is strong and confrontational, as Lisa Simpson is. Ophelia goes mad and kills herself in the original, but here the competition between the Simpson children is played out. Ophelia goes mad with grief not because Hamlet abuses her and her father dies. Lisa/Ophelia goes mad and dies out of a sense of competition: "Nobody outcrazies Ophelia." Her death is still indirectly caused by Hamlet, but now it is not his cruelty and rejection but the fact that he is acting mad when that is her "thing" that drives her to kill herself in order to prove that she is the more insane. The figure of Ophelia is parodied, but the parody is achieved by placing Lisa in the role, and Lisa is being parodied as much as Ophelia.

The rest of the cartoon continues to deconstruct the play, offering new and comic explanations as to why the characters of *Hamlet* act the way they do. Bart /Hamlet runs to Marge/Gertrude's chamber and stabs Wiggum/Polonius, who was hiding behind the arras because he "has a fear of getting stabbed." Ralph Wiggum, as Laertes, is present, observing, "Daddy's stomach is crying," a remark consistent with Ralph's character, but not Laertes's. Polonius tells him, "Laertes, you gotta do a special, big boy job for Daddy: I need you to revenge my death," not only infantilizing Shakespeare's original text, it reduces a pivotal plot point to a joke. Revenge, taken very seriously in the English Renaissance context, is reduced to a child's responsibility, along with cleaning one's room or feeding a pet.

The show immediately jumps to the climactic scene in which Moe/Claudius poisons everything in the castle right before the duel, "just in case": food, drapes, Laertes's sword. He even poisons "Rosencarl" and "Guildenlenny" (Carl and Lenny, two of Homer's friends who are regulars on the show) so that, should Hamlet touch them, he will die. They "high-five" to celebrate their part in the plot and kill each other.

The two arrive for the duel, and Moe/Claudius announces: "Laertes here gets one practice stab," after which Ralph/Laertes stabs himself and dies. Again, not very Laertes but very Ralph Wiggum. Bart takes the sword out of Ralph (parodying the switching of the swords in the original) and kills Moe/Claudius without hesitation, but then slips on the bloody floor and is impaled himself. Marge/Gertrude looks at all the blood and says, "No way I'm cleaning up this mess," and kills herself by striking herself in the head with a spiked mace. We emerge from the story-within-the-cartoon to Lisa informing the family, "And that's the greatest thing ever written!" Clearly the audience is meant to interpret this line ironically. Bart rejects her interpretation, stating, "Are you crazy? I can't believe a play where every character was murdered could be boring!" As the voice of parental wisdom, Homer informs Bart, "Son, it's not only a great play, it also became a great movie . . . called *Ghostbusters*!" The episode ends with the entire family dancing to Ray Parker, Jr.'s "Theme from Ghostbusters."

The episode, by presenting a parody of *Hamlet* by overlaying the world of *The Simpsons* on Shakespeare's greatly reduced play, engages many, if not all, of the issues associated with youth-culture Shakespeare. Bart's objection is that even after hearing only the sex and violent parts, the play is still boring. Homer's counterargument tries to prove that Shakespeare is not boring by pointing out its greatness not as a play, but a film. In other words, even if Shakespeare is boring, others have found ways to make him interesting to a modern audience, and we can value those films and products. Don't like *Taming of the Shrew*? *10 Things I Hate about You* is both fun and accessible. Don't like *Much Ado about Nothing*? How about if it has Denzel Washington and Michael Keaton in it?

Homer's real difficulty, however, lies in his own lack of ability to recognize the reference and the referent. He believes that *Ghostbusters* was based on *Hamlet*, and so the latter must be brilliant because the former is so enjoyable. This reference can be read as both simply an absurdist statement and also as a parody of pseudo-intellectuals who express appreciation for something because of its perceived intellectual value. Homer still doesn't understand *Hamlet*, but he likes dancing to the theme from *Ghostbusters*, and that makes him someone who "enjoys all the meats of our cultural stew."

The sixth, and final point of reference occurs outside of the actual show of *The Simpsons*. The works of Shakespeare and the man can serve as a comparative point of reference when discussing *The Simpsons*, as witnessed in a recent newspaper article about the success of the program. Bob Baker writes in the *Los Angeles Times* that Homer is "a classic Shakespearean clown in the model of Falstaff in *Henry IV, Part 2*."[65] For Baker, Shakespeare is a reference point to observe the intelligence behind the artistry of *The Simpsons*. The only problem is that Falstaff is not a "classic Shakespearean clown" himself, a title perhaps better left to Touchstone, Launcelot Gobbo, Feste, or Dogberry. Baker also observes that the literary references in the show are "evidence that America's intellectual traditions are safe."[66] We can understand Shakespeare in terms of *The Simpsons* and *The Simpsons* in terms of Shakespeare, as Richard Keller Simon has suggested above, hopefully avoiding the pitfalls of reductivism and the erasure of difference in doing so.

Similarly, a writer/performer has been touring the world recently with *MacHomer*, a one-man version of *Macbeth* performed as if by the characters of *The Simpsons*. Homer is Macbeth, Marge is Lady Macbeth, Flanders (the next door neighbor) is Banquo, and so forth. As with "Tales from the Public Domain," the characters of Shakespeare's play are conflated with the characters of *The Simpsons* and exhibit the tendencies of both. Mr. Burns is Duncan, reducing "This castle hath a pleasant seat," to a purred "Excellent." Malcolm is "played" by Waylon Smithers. The witches are the sea captain, Moe Szyslak the bartender, and Principal Seymour Skinner. But all of these characters are played by Rick Miller, who also wrote the piece.[67]

As Miller presents each character's voice performing the lines of *Macbeth* filtered through Simpson's sensibilities, a picture of the character (some in kilts, some not) is projected upon a screen behind him. In other cases, Miller's own live image is projected on the screen from a camera on the set, so that he is simultaneously performing in front of the audience and represented in two dimensions in the world of *The Simpsons*. It is a literal blending of worlds.

As with the Reduced Shakespeare Company's *The Complete Works of William Shakespeare (Abridged)*, *MacHomer* has proven very popular, especially with young audiences. Yet it also shares with that work reductivist tendencies. Boredom and inaccessibility are replaced with easily understood referents and references, but the text of Shakespeare has been translated and reduced and is no longer present, it is now only referenced.

Youth culture's language is inherently self-referential—it is a language that feeds on and off of youth culture. In the postmodern sphere, Shakespeare is conflated with all other youth cultures. Mel Gibson is Hamlet, but Hamlet is now also Mel Gibson, and therefore Mad Max, William Wallace, and *The Man without a Face*. In translating and reducing Shakespeare, youth culture uses the language of youth culture to make the works accessible to a modern young audience by contextualizing that work within the youth world.

This volume is not intended to be a comprehensive survey of the intersections between Shakespeare and youth culture. Nor is it meant to be geographically or canonically encompassing. We specifically focus on twentieth-century American youth culture with each author considering one particular aspect of youth culture and Shakespeare, considering how that aspect intersects with Shakespeare and how the two worlds are translated into each other. Each chapter considers the material adapted (which plays and why), the manner of adaptation/ expropriation (translation/reduction/reference), the purpose of adaptation, and how the adaptation/expropriation means within the larger contexts of Bardbiz, youth culture, and Shakespeareana.

This volume has been written by three different authors with three different perspectives on Shakespeare (and, for that matter, on youth culture). We are a professor of English (who is also a musician), a theatre professor (who is also an actor and professional director), and an actress. Our backgrounds are textual and performative, rooted in language, image, and sound. All three are American. We are from various points along the "ages of man," to quote Jacques. Although our different voices come through in the different chapters, we have attempted to create a unified work that offers different perspectives on the points of confluence between Shakespeare and youth culture.

Beginning with a consideration of the "William Shakespeare Action Figure," which places him in the same category as Darth Vader, Captain Kirk, and Doctor Zaius, the fifth chapter surveys two performing object theatres that utilize toys to bring Shakespeare to the stage. From the Toy Theatre of the nineteenth century, in which children could stage versions of Shakespeare's most popular plays with paper puppets to the Tiny Ninja Theatre, which has staged Shakespeare's plays in the twenty-first century using "Tiny Ninja" action figures, the use of toys in the staging of Shakespeare in public and private is comparatively analyzed by Kevin Wetmore.

Chapter 2, "Smells Like Teen Shakespirit: The Shakespearean Films of Julia Stiles" is Robert York's evaluation of youth-oriented cinematic adaptations of Shakespeare's plays, specifically those featuring popular actress Julia Stiles such as *10 Things I Hate about You* (a teen *Taming of the Shrew* set at "Verona High School"), "*O*" (a teen *Othello* in which high school basketball replaces the wars of Venice and the Turks), and *Hamlet* (set in present-day corporate America with Stiles as Ophelia). York explores how the films translate and reduce the plays through the language and elements of cinema with some final consideration of two other teen films: *Get Over It* and *The Glass House*.

The next two chapters consider popular music and Shakespeare. In chapter 3, Wetmore considers the various ways rock-and-roll music have intersected with the works of Shakespeare, both in terms of lyrical content of popular rock songs and in terms of using rock music in stage and filmed productions of Shakespeare as a cultural shorthand to generate new meanings. In the fourth chapter, Wetmore evaluates rap music in a similar fashion. In both chapters, the role of these music forms in contemporary theatrical productions of Shakespeare is considered, especially the productions of Joe Papp in the 1960s and Los Angeles's Troubadour Theatre Company, which specializes in rock-and-roll Shakespeare with titles like *Fleetwood Macbeth*, *Romeo Hall and Juliet Oates*, *Comedy of Aerosmith* and *Hamlet, The Artist Formerly Known as Prince of Denmark* in the former chapter and *The Bomb-itty of Errors* in the latter. Translation, reduction, and reference all play a role in pop musical Shakespeare and Shakespeare in popular music.

In the fifth chapter, Wetmore examines comic book and graphic novel adaptations of Shakespeare, another kind of translation from one medium involving text and image (the theatre) into another. Wetmore considers both comic adaptations of Shakespeare's plays and the reference of Shakespeare in traditional comic books and graphic novels, especially the groundbreaking work in the Neil Gaiman-authored *Sandman* series. In several issues of that title, Morpheus, the Lord of Dreams, interacts with William Shakespeare, and the award-winning *A Midsummer Night's Dream* issue offers an explanation of how that play came to be written. Later in the series, a deconstruction of *The Tempest* is offered. Interestingly, in his book *Big-Time Shakespeare*, Michael D. Bristol cites "Morpheus, Lord of Dreams" as if he were an actual author commenting on Shakespeare, and although actual author Neil Gaiman does not appear in the index, "Morpheus, Lord of Dreams" does.[68]

In the final chapter, Jennifer Hulbert explores the "Ophelia-ization" of teenage girls in such books as *Reviving Ophelia*, *Ophelia's Mom* and *Ophelia Speaks*. All of these books represent a form of reference—couching the problems of contemporary teenage girls in terms of Shakespeare's character from *Hamlet*. The difficulty, argues Hulbert, is that Shakespeare's Ophelia bears little resemblance to the model girl proposed in these books. The converse problem is that these books construct teenage girls as "Ophelias," not exactly a positive construction, nor entirely accurate in this sense either. She then offers alternative models for pop psychology to engage Shakespeare.

This volume is a collaborative project between three authors whose points of interest in Shakespeare have coincided in the role in which Shakespeare plays in the creation of youth culture and the role youth culture plays in the construction and understanding of Shakespeare as he and his works are received today. We are also "fans" of the forms that we are engaging, which gives us a unique perspective on the subject. As Jeffery H. Mills writes of *Star Trek*, we write of these aspects of Shakespearean offshoots:

> It is a strange thing to critique that which you love. Strange because it doesn't feel good, but you know you must do it anyway . . . There's a certain sense of heightened responsibility that comes with being a fan of something: because the fan knows the object of his love so very well, he is able to identify standards of quality that the casual observer may not see.[69]

In our specific topic, we believe we benefit not only by being scholars of Shakespeare, we are also fans of the specific forms of adaptation about which we write. One of the challenges we have found in other writings about, for example, graphic novels, is that the average Shakespearean has not read the entire run of *Sandman*, and thus only comments on two issues that directly relate to Shakespeare, without understanding the greater context those issues must be placed in. Also then missed are all of the other, smaller references and uses of Shakespearean characters and lines. The Shakespearean reads *Sandman* for Shakespeare. The fan reads *Sandman* for *Sandman*.

In another sense, scholars are fans of their specific subject matter. Their behavior is certainly fan-like: they meet in conventions, they spend a good deal of time and money becoming acquainted with the minutiae of their chosen object of devotion, be it Shakespeare or *Star Trek*, they argue over topics that the unwashed and uninitiated have no knowledge (or even interest), and they form a rough hierarchy amongst themselves. As Mills notes, the Shakespeareans "love" Shakespeare, feel heightened responsibility, and are able to identify standards of quality in the plays and productions that the casual observer would not see. We believe our membership in the multiple fan constituencies allow us both the responsibility and the unique position to explore youth-culture Shakespeare.

Part of the difficulty in tracking youth culture is its rapid transitory nature. By the time trends are reported, they are over. As such, this volume is neither comprehensive nor necessarily up to date. Instead, we offer it as a beginning and not an end. If the perception of Shakespeare has changed with each generation, as Gary Taylor suggests in *Reinventing Shakespeare*, then the current generation has a very young, hip, and extreme Shakespeare. If Shakespeare is always our contemporary, as Jan Kott suggests, then he uses a cell phone, goes to the cinema but sees it again on DVD for the extended scenes and special features, and is outraged by the price of gasoline but won't give up his SUV. It is this figure that we seek to understand.

One final note: although the individual authors have worked separately, we have all used *The Riverside Shakespeare* as our canonical text for citation and quotation. We have also presented a unified list of works cited, divided into a bibliography, and a filmography, and a discography.

> Youth's a stuff will not endure.
> *Twelfth Night*, 2.3.52

> Hope I die before I get old.
> The Who,
> "My Generation"

Notes

1. Derek Longhurst, " 'You base football-player': Shakespeare in Contemporary Popular Culture," in *The Shakespeare Myth*, edited by Graham Holderness (Manchester: Manchester University Press, 1988), p. 61.
2. Ibid.
3. John Storey, *An Introductory Guide to Cultural Theory and Popular Culture* (Athens: University of Georgia, 1993), p. 109.
4. Barbara Hodgson, "*William Shakespeare's Romeo + Juliet*: Everything's Nice in America?" *Shakespeare Survey* 52 (1999), p. 91.
5. Donald Hedrick and Bryan Reynolds, "Shakespeare and Transversal Power," in *Shakespeare without Class: Misappropriations of Cultural Capital*, edited by Donald Hedrick and Bryan Reynolds (New York: Palgrave, 2000), p. 9.
6. Michael Barson and Steven Heller, *Teenage Confidential: An Illustrated History of the American Teen* (San Francisco: Chronicle Books, 1998), p. 22.
7. Jon Lewis, *The Road to Romance and Ruin: Teen Films and Youth Culture* (New York: Routledge, 1992), p. 3.
8. Herbert J. Gans, *Popular Culture and High Culture* (New York: Basic Books, 1999), p. 120.
9. Lewis, *The Road to Romance*, p. 4.
10. James B. Twitchell, *Branded Nation* (New York: Simon and Schuster, 2004), p. 203.
11. Ibid., p. 210.
12. Gans, *Popular Culture*, p. 12.
13. Wheeler Winston Dixon, "Fighting and Violence and Everything That's Always Cool: Teen Films in the 1990s," in *Film Genre* 2000, edited by Wheeler Winston Dixon (Albany: State University Press of New York, 2000), p. 126.
14. Ibid., p. 127.
15. Gans, *Popular Culture*, p. 155.
16. Michael D. Bristol, *Big-Time Shakespeare* (London: Routledge, 1996).
17. Graham Holderness, "Radical Potentiality and Institutional Closure: Shakespeare in Film and Television," in *Political Shakespeare: New Essays in Cultural Materialism*, edited by Jonathan Dollimore and Alan Sinfield (Ithaca and London: Cornell University Press, 1985), 182.
18. Alissa Quart, *Branded: The Buying and Selling of Teenagers* (New York: Basic Books, 2004).
19. Quoted in Wendy Jenson, "Faces and Places," *US Magazine*, January 1996, p. 13.
20. Marvin Carlson, *The Haunted Stage: The Theatre as Memory Machine* (Ann Arbor: University of Michigan Press, 2001), p. 7.
21. Kenneth M. Chanko, "Dangerous Fun: Fishburne as Othello," *Boston Globe*, December 24, 1995, pp. 31, 33.
22. Bristol, *Big-Time Shakespeare*, pp. 88–89.
23. Henry A. Giroux, *Living Dangerously* (New York: Peter Lang, 1996), p. 51.
24. Jo McMurtry, *Shakespeare Films in the Classroom: A Descriptive Guide* (Hamden: Archon Books, 1994), p. 157.

25. Fred Sedgwick, *Shakespeare and the Young Writer* (London: Routledge, 1999).
26. Milla Cozart Riggio, ed. *Teaching Shakespeare through Performance* (New York: Modern Language Association of America, 1999).
27. See, for example, Richard Adams, ed. *Teaching Shakespeare: Essays on Approaches to Shakespeare in Schools and Colleges* (London: Robert Royce, 1985) and Walter Edens, Christopher Durer, Walter Eggers, Duncan Harris, and Keith Hall, eds. *Teaching Shakespeare* (Princeton: Princeton University Press, 1977).
28. Alan Sinfield, "Give an Account of Shakespeare and Education, Showing Why You Think They Are Effective and What You Have Appreciated about Them; Support Your Comments with Precise References," in *Political Shakespeare: New Essays in Cultural Materialism*, edited by Jonathan Dollimore and Alan Sinfield (Manchester: Manchester University Press, 1985), pp. 134–135.
29. Ibid., p. 135.
30. Ibid., p. 151.
31. Lewis, *The Road to Romance*, p. 3.
32. Samuel Crowl, "Introduction: Where the Wild Things Are: Shakespeare in the American Landscape," in *Teaching Shakespeare Today: Practical Approaches and Productive Strategies*, edited by James E. Davis and Ronald E. Salomome, (Urbana: National Council of Teachers of English, 1993), p. xiv.
33. Barry Glassner, *The Culture of Fear* (New York: Basic Books, 1999), p. 16.
34. Shirley R. Steinberg and Joe L. Kincheloe, "Introduction: No More Secrets— Kinderculture, Information Saturation and the Postmodern Childhood," in *Kinderculture: The Corporate Construction of Childhood*, edited by Shirley R. Steinberg and Joe L. Kincheloe (Boulder: Westview, 1998), p. 3.
35. Martha Tuck Rozett, *Talking Back to Shakespeare* (Newark: University of Delaware Press, 1994), p. 176.
36. Richard Keller Simon, "Much Ado about 'Friends': What Pop Culture Offers Literature," *The Chronicle of Higher Education* 46, no. 41 (June 16, 2001), p. B4.
37. Richard Keller Simon, *Trash Culture: Popular Culture and the Great Tradition* (Berkeley: University of California Press, 1999), p. 3.
38. Ibid., p. 8.
39. Simon, "Much Ado," p. B4.
40. All quotations in this sentence are taken verbatim from the front and back cover of every edition of *No Fear Shakespeare*.
41. Jan Kott, *The Bottom Translation* (Evanston: Northwestern University Press, 1987), pp. 30, 52, 58.
42. Baz Luhrmann and Craig Pearce, "Introduction," *William Shakespeare's Romeo + Juliet: The Contemporary Film, The Classic Play* (New York: Bantam, 1996), p. v. What is especially interesting about this text is that the authors are listed on the cover as "Craig Pearce, Baz Luhrmann, and William Shakespeare" and all three are listed under "About the Authors," with biographies of all three, as if Shakespeare were just one of the collaborators on this project, but also conversely elevating Pearce and Luhrmann to the level of Shakespeare.

43. The No Fear series is obviously aimed at the high school and college market. Not only are these the largest consumers of Shakespeare's plays as well as the largest consumers and target market for textual aids such as *Cliffs Notes*, the very plays chosen as part of the series are those most likely to be encountered in the high school or college classroom: *Hamlet, Macbeth, Romeo and Juliet, Julius Caesar, The Tempest, King Lear, The Merchant of Venice, A Midsummer Night's Dream, Othello, Twelfth Night, Much Ado about Nothing* and *The Taming of the Shrew*. It seems unlikely (and perhaps unnecessary) that an "English translation" by No Fear Shakespeare for *Timon of Athens* or *Henry VI, Part III* will be seen anytime soon.

44. John Crowther, ed. *No Fear Shakespeare: Hamlet* (New York: Spark Publishing, 2003), p. 139.

45. Alan Durband, *Shakespeare Made Easy: Hamlet* (Hauppauge: Barron's, 1986), p. 143.

46. Crowther, *No Fear Shakespeare: Hamlet*, p. 143.

47. Durband, *Shakespeare Made Easy: Hamlet*, 148.

48. Crowther, *No Fear Shakespeare: Hamlet*, p. 151.

49. Durband, *Shakespeare Made Easy: Hamlet*, p. 153.

50. John Crowther, *No Fear Shakespeare: Macbeth* (New York: Spark Publishing, 2003), p. 3.

51. This famous line is arguably the most corrupted and misunderstood line in the Shakespearean canon, largely because of the pop cultural translation of "wherefore" to mean "where." From Bugs Bunny as Romeo, responding "Here I am" to the question in a Looney Tunes cartoon to Lucille Ball, appearing with Orson Welles (playing himself) on the television program *I Love Lucy* in a nightclub act featuring magic tricks and Welles reciting Shakespeare, in which Lucy is left floating in the air at the end of a magic trick, crying out to Welles, "Wherefore art thou, Romeo?" the line has become a cornerstone of Shakespeare parody, especially in youth culture. See Michael Anderegg, *Orson Welles, Shakespeare and Popular Culture* (New York: Columbia University Press, 1999), pp. 3–5.

52. John Crowther, *No Fear Shakespeare: A Midsummer Night's Dream* (New York: Spark Publishing, 2003), p. 77.

53. John Crowther, *No Fear Shakespeare: A Midsummer Night's Dream*, p. 93.

54. Reduced Shakespeare Company, *Reduced Shakespeare Company Radio Show* (London, 1994), 1897774915.

55. Daniel Singer, "Author's Note," in *The Complete Works of William Shakespeare (Abridged)*, edited by Jess Borgeson, Adam Long, and Daniel Singer (New York: Applause, 1994), p. xxiii.

56. Reduced Shakespeare Company, *Complete Works*, p. 57.

57. John Doyle and Ray Lischner, *Shakespeare for Dummies* (New York: Wiley Publishing, 1999) and Laurie Rozakis, *The Complete Idiot's Guide to Shakespeare* (Indianapolis: Alpha Group, 1999).

58. Richard Burt, *Unspeakable Shaxxxspeares: Queer Theory and American Kiddie Culture* (New York: St. Martins, 1998), pp. xiii, 4.

59. Christy Desmet, "Introduction," in *Shakespeare and Appropriation*, edited by Christy Desmet and Robert Sawyer (London: Routledge, 1999), p. 2.

60. Desmet, "Introduction," p. 9.
61. Linda Hutcheon, *A Theory of Parody* (New York: Urbana, 1985), p. 58.
62. Bob Baker, "The Real First Family," *Los Angeles Times*, February 16, 2003, p. E34.
63. For more on animated Shakespeare, see Eddie Sammons, *Shakespeare: A Hundred Years on Film* (Lanham, MD: Scarecrow Press, 2004); Richard Finkelstein, "Disney cites Shakespeare: The limits of appropriation," in *Shakespeare and Appropriation*, edited by Christy Desmet and Robert Sawyer (London: Routledge, 1999); and Laurie Osborne, "Mixing Media and Animating Shakespeare's Tales," in *Shakespeare the Movie II*, edited by Richard Burt and Lynda E. Boose (New York: Routledge, 2003).
64. This use of quotation is not out of the ordinary in popular culture, although one wonders why a title or line might reference Shakespeare when no other purpose is to be served. For example, in *Harry Potter and the Prisoner of Azkaban*, the Hogwarts School Choir sings a song whose lyrics consist entirely of "Double double, toil and trouble," and then concludes with "Something wicked this way comes," which connects the concerns of Harry with those of Macbeth (4.1.10 and 4.1.45). The same line is used for the title of a 1993 video by Mary-Kate and Ashley Olson ("Double, Double, Toil and Trouble"), which begs the question what hath Mary-Kate and Ashley to do with Macbeth or he with them? Short answer: nothing. It is a recognizable quotation along the lines of Twitchell's assertion that the certain canonical works of art have been drained of intrinsic meaning because of overuse in other contexts. Still, why one might wish to connect the misadventures of a pair of wacky twins with Shakespeare's supernatural tragedy of ambition gone wrong must raise a few eyebrows.
65. Baker, "The Real First Family," p. E34.
66. Ibid. The irony, of course, is that despite Baker's almost self-congratulatory pronouncement, suggesting that if one recognizes the literary reference, then one has engaged in "intellectual tradition," his argument is vastly undercut in the very next paragraph by his stating that *MacHomer* is based upon *Hamlet*, even quoting from *Macbeth* ("Is this a dagger I see before me?") in the article and calling it a line from *Hamlet*. America's intellectual traditions seem none too safe if one can only misidentify references at best. As Bart Simpson himself would (mis)state, "The ironing is delicious."
67. For more information, visit Miller's Web site <www.machomer.com>
68. Bristol, *Big-Time Shakespeare*, pp. 121–124, 126, 138, 231.
69. Jeffrey H. Mills, "*Star Trek IV*: The Good, The Bad, The Unquenched Thirst," in *The Best of Trek 15*, edited by Walter Irwin and G.B. Love (New York: Roc, 1990), p. 126.

1

"Great Reckonings in Little Rooms," or Children's Playtime: Shakespeare and Performing Object Theatre of Toys

Kevin J. Wetmore, Jr.

When that I was and a little tiny boy
With hey ho the wind and the rain;
A foolish thing was but a toy,
For the rain it raineth every day.

—Twelfth Night 5.1.389–392

Shakespeare the Action Figure

For a generation raised on action figures, from *Star Wars* and *Star Trek* to *G.I. Joe* and *Transformers*, a principle means of play is to use figures from pop culture narratives to create new, original, self-generated narratives. Beyond reenacting the original narrative, action figures mean one can create one's own fun with characters one knows well from other media, oftentimes blending two completely separate narratives into one. In such child's play, Luke Skywalker fights Captain Kirk while Princess Leia makes out with Spock. While such play is emblematic of what Richard Burt calls "American kiddie culture," especially with its asexual sexuality, such play is also inherently inter-textual.[1] It involves the referencing of many texts beyond the original narrative that inspired the figures.

It also represents a form of agency, as the child playing with the toys often does not re-create the narrative of the film or television show exactly, but rather can change it in any manner he or she wishes.

Endings can be changed, new relationships created, situations transformed and new elements introduced. In this author's own experience, unable to afford both the X-Wing and TIE Fighter ships for the *Star Wars* action figures at the tender age of eight, Luke Skywalker was forced to learn to fly a new ship that was even better than the X-Wing and engineered out of an old shoebox. It had all the powers of an X-Wing, but with a transporter from *Star Trek* and a bed. Play with the action figures allows one to participate in the narrative, control the narrative, control the characters, and ultimately move the narrative beyond the confines of the original into a limitless intertextual space.

The child is encouraged to use his or her imagination, but also is learning the lessons of capitalism and marketing. One is encouraged to purchase "them all" in order to have a complete set. One links the film to the toys it generates and the toys to the film. In order to participate fully, one must purchase fully. Ownership of the narrative comes at a cost. Even though I deeply loved my shoebox, I would have gladly traded dozens of them for a "real" X-Wing. Of course, the manufacturers of action figures assert authenticity through the action figures. When one purchases Han Solo (Hoth Gear)™ in his cardboard and blister pack packaging, one knows that one is purchasing something "Official," as it says so right on the packaging. Authenticity and totality become the hobgoblin of play or even collecting action figures. One must own a "complete" set of "official" action figures in order to fully participate. This is Jean Baudrillard's theory of simulacra taken to its extreme and logical conclusion. One purchases the likeness of the actors in the persona of the characters, replicas of sets, props, and vehicles in order to simulate and expand the world of the film or television program. One then controls the simulation and can alter it in any manner one pleases. All of this is done in the name of profit for the filmmakers and the toy makers.

The popularity (and profitability) of action figures has moved well past film and television since my days of collecting back in the 1970s. In 2003, a company called Accoutrements, the self-styled "Outfitters of Popular Culture" released the Shakespeare action figure.[2] Other "Action Figures" in the series include Casanova, Oscar Wilde, Mozart, Alexander the Great, Bigfoot, Sherlock Holmes, Edgar Allen Poe, Annie Oakley, Beethoven, Ben Franklin, Cleopatra, Moses, Einstein, Jesus, and Freud. The official and authentic action figures that allow one to play and use imagination and control the narrative are now literary figures, historical figures, literary characters, and religious figures.

As with previous action figure series, often the back of the box is used to advertise other action figures in the series. Whereas when one purchases a "Tusken Raider" action figure and learns one can (and should) also purchase a "Jawa" or "Darth Vader" from *Star Wars*, the newer line creates an intertext between Poe, an author, Moses, the Biblical figure, and Bigfoot, a cryptozoological creature, making them part of the same curious continuum. Lost is the need to collect them all; one may pick and choose according to one's preference. The interconnection between the figures has been made, however.

Shakespeare as action figure translates, reduces, and references Shakespeare all at once. Shakespeare is literally reduced, both in size and nature, to a toy. He is reduced to the same status as a character from a genre film or television program. It is also possible to "own" Shakespeare. His "Bottom translation" has made him into an object that can literally be contained, owned, manipulated, circumscribed, and forced to make out with Princess Leia as well.

Like the Droeshout engraving or the bust in Holy Trinity Church, the Shakespeare action figure is a physical icon upon which one may project the notions of authorship and high culture. If, as Douglas Lanier asserts, portrayals of Shakespeare the man in popular culture "inevitably serve ideological ends," then the action figure version of the author meets many ideological needs at once, all of them culturally conservative, reinforcing notions of authorship, individual achievement, and ownership.[3]

The packaging is a parody of action figure packaging; Shakespeare as Han Solo, Captain Kirk or Cobra Commander, relying upon familiar catchphrases, information about the "character," and special accessories included with the toy. Written on the front of the box, above the figure of Shakespeare, is "All the world's a stage, and all the men and women merely players" (*As You Like It*, 2.7.239–240), one of the most recognizable metatheatrical phrases taken out of context from the canon. Next to the figure a sticker loudly proclaims, "With Removable Quill Pen and Book!" The viewer is simultaneously reminded of Shakespeare's theatrical greatness and his affiliation with the high-culture world of the theatre and reminded that this figure is indeed an action figure, and may be posed with the tools of his trade. The text asserts Shakespeare's primacy as a man of the theatre while offering the opportunity to create narratives of him as author (or even reader). The sticker, however, is meant to be read ironically by a generation that grew up "With Real-Action™ Fire Gun!" "With removable lightsaber!" or "With Dino-Buddy" next to the character.

Shakespeare can hold the quill and book, to simulate writing the plays and poems, or he can stand iconically without them. But the primacy of the author Shakespeare is asserted by their inclusion.

Lanier further argues that, in opposition to the theoretical constructions of Barthes and Foucault in which the author disappears, "popular culture remains invested in authorship and particularly in Shakespeare the author" and "locate the meaning of Shakespeare's works firmly with the man himself."[4] The action figure most certainly follows this formulation. The back cover contains biographical information: Birth and death dates, occupation ("English poet, dramatist, and actor"), accomplishments ("Published 37 plays, 154 Sonnets and several narrative poems"), weapon of choice ("Quill pen (Mightier than the sword)"), and an interesting fact ("An outbreak of the plague, which closed public theatres for a time, led Shakespeare to try writing poetry as a creative outlet"). A brief essay follows that notes the authorship controversy, the nature of his dramaturgy, and praise for his plays. The reader is then cautioned that the action figure is "Not suitable for children under 36 months" and that it is "Made in China." Again, the narrative of the packaging conflates Shakespeare the author with the idea of Action Figure. Shakespeare's writings are his "accomplishments," his pen is a "weapon," and he was driven to create, even when the theatres were closed. The actual meaning and significance of his plays is ignored. In fact, not a single play title is named anywhere on the box, nor are any of the poems. Instead, one is given statistics ("37 plays, 154 Sonnets," etc.), again following the action figure model. What Shakespeare wrote is not as significant as the fact that he wrote, that he was a writer and that he was "the greatest literary mind of all time." In other words, Shakespeare's actual writings don't matter. The man does. One does not need to read the plays to know his greatness; one merely needs to know that he was great.

Lanier argues that "Shakespeare the man often serves within pop culture as a focus for fantasy and iconoclasm, a way to bring elements of Shakespeare's cultural significance to bear on pop's own productions."[5] Shakespeare as action figure asserts the primacy of creation, imagination, and play. The quotation from the front of the box reminds us that all the men and women are players, not merely performers but people who play. The packaging ironically suggests that the very grown-up pursuit of acting Shakespeare is intrinsically similar to playing with action figures. Characters re-create a narrative over and over and over. In the case of the theatre, because of its liveness, that repetitive narrative also comes with variations. Although one follows the script, the unexpected can and does happen. Playing is a form of playing, contained by narrative, but free within it to circumvent or subvert the text in unfamiliar and remarkably personal ways.

Lanier concludes that it is "a truism that portrayals of Shakespeare reveal less about Shakespeare the man or author than they do about the biographer."[6] If this is true, then Shakespeare the action figure represents quite a bit about the current generation that would purchase and (not) play with such a toy. I say not play as the action figure is intended ironically. No one plays with it, nor are they intended to. It is the reduction of Shakespeare (whom may of those who purchase the figure encounter not at the age of action figure play but in high school and college) to the familiar figure of a toy. It can be and often is not a toy but décor.[7] One does not play with the figure, but place him on a shelf in an office or dorm room as the ultimate form of containment, control, and ownership.

In this sense, we might see the Shakespeare action figure as the embodiment of the conflict over the ownership of Shakespeare. Numerous constituencies fight over to whom Shakespeare belongs: artists, scholars, teachers, youth, Hollywood, England, the world, etc. Each constituency claims a special relationship that grants them primacy over the others: the scholars know more about Shakespeare than the others; theatre artists believe that Shakespeare wrote for the theatre and belongs to them, even as English professors assert the poetry and the text belongs to them. And, of course, nearly every commentary track on a Shakespeare DVD sees a Hollywood figure asserting that if Shakespeare were alive today he'd be working in Hollywood, and that he is a man of the people, not of the cultural elite. The action figure literally allows anyone and everyone to own Shakespeare.

For a generation raised on action figures, Shakespeare the action figure is nostalgia, ironic distancing and assertion of authorial hegemony simultaneously. The packaging is meant to evoke childhood toys even as it subverts, parodies, and satirizes the form. The end result is to create an ironic distance from both the toy itself and what it represents: Shakespeare. Yet even as it mocks both Action Figure and Shakespeare, the figure is firmly invested in Shakespeare as greatest author of all time. The figure reduces Shakespeare and links him and his work to the narratives of popular culture—Shakespeare as Spock, Captain Picard, or The Six Million Dollar Man. In doing so, it also controls and circumscribes Shakespeare.

Shakespeare as toy, however, is not the first interaction between Shakespeare and toy. While the gift stores at Shakespeare theatres and in Stratford find ways to create Shakespeare-related, age-appropriate souvenirs for young people, there have historically been periods of toys as theatre. Although Shakespeare the action figure is not intended to be played with, theatre using toys based on his plays much less ironically connects the canon with youth culture and with the idea of "play."

Toy Theatre—The Original Action Figure

As stated in the introduction, youth-culture Shakespeare is a fairly recent phenomenon. In Shakespeare's day there were youth in the audience alongside the adults in the form of apprentices stealing away from work to see a play. There were youth on stage as well: boys played the female roles. Youth were a part of Shakespeare, never separated out from adults until the Victorian era, with its separation of high and low culture and its transforming attitude toward children. Although during this period children did not normally attend the theatre, those in their early teens who could afford it would go fairly regularly.[8] Instead, what one might term the original "home theatre" or the original set of action figures was invented for children: the Toy Theatre. The same era that saw the development of Charles and Mary Lamb and the bowdlerization of Shakespeare also saw the development of a toy designed to simulate the theatre-going experience of children. A staple of Victorian England and, to a lesser extent the United States, the Toy Theatre is an example of performing object theatre that was simulacrum of the theatre of its day, children's toy, family entertainment, and means to introduce children to Shakespeare's works, among others.

The term "Performing object theatre" was coined by Frank Proschan, who defines the term as, "material images of humans, animals or spirits that are created, displayed or manipulated in narrative or dramatic performance."[9] Performing object theatre includes such various examples as Japanese *bunraku*, *Sesame Street Live*, *Tiny Ninja Theatre*, Javanese Shadow Puppetry, Julie Taymor's stage version of *The Lion King*, and *Avenue Q*. It embraces puppetry, masks, and the use of other objects to represent living beings live on stage.

One of the strengths of performing object theatre is that it blends the fantastic more seamlessly than live performers can. Another strength is that, like action figures, the toy theatre variant of performing object theatre can simulate famous, professional narratives in the home. It is democratic, imagination-encouraging, and allows the agency of the "performer" to either faithfully reproduce the narrative, or go "off script" and allow for new variants, endings, relationships and scripts, just as with contemporary action figures, although, as will be argued later, the toy is also, contradictorily, a means of controlling the behavior of both young performer and young audience member, encouraging them not to go off script, but to perform as expected.

One should note that the English Toy Theatre is different from the other forms of Shakespearean appropriation in this volume in that it is not a part of the postwar milieu that defines youth culture. It is instead a phenomenon of the eighteenth and nineteenth centuries. It does, however, represent one of the first attempts to adapt Shakespeare (among others) to a form specifically designed for children. George Speaight refers to it as "a rough and ready toy for children" and "an entertaining occupation for 'juveniles.' "[10] In some senses, the Toy Theatre was the original action figure playset: the juvenile would purchase the theatre and then could purchase various "plays": sets of characters printed on sheets, scenery, and the script, the cost of which was memorialized in Robert Louis Stevenson's tribute to the form, "A Penny Plain and Two Pence Coloured."[11] Like action figures, Toy Theatre was "primarily the domain of teenage boys."[12]

The playset consists of a cardboard theatre with sheets of characters that the owner would assemble, paste onto cardboard, cut out, and re-create plays. The sheets often featured important characters in every costume, rather than just a single figure.[13] This aspect makes the toy theatre very similar to contemporary action figures, where there will be several different versions of key figures in popular series. For example, there are dozens of different "Luke Skywalkers," "Han Solos" and "Obi-Wan Kenobis" in the *Star Wars* action figure series, and even characters glimpsed only for a second in the background get their own action figure. The reason for both the toy theatre and the contemporary action figure to include so many variants is the same: completeness of the collection in order to reproduce every aspect of the original, as well as the profit motive. More sheets and more figures mean more disposable income spent to maintain a "complete set."

Candles or small oil footlights would simulate the theatre-going experience. The theatre was intended to be placed on a table top and create a miniature proscenium theatre when chairs were placed in front of it. In other words, it was a simulation of a real theatre, utilizing many of the same elements of scenery, lighting, and changes of costume in order to simulate the theatre-going experience for children (and adults, it should be noted). The plays would be performed by cardboard actors simulating live counterparts but in front of a live audience. The live actors were replaced by performing objects.

Toy Theatre had its own canon in original plays such as *Black Eyed Susan* and *The Miller and His Men*, as well as plays that were based on literary classics and showed distant lands and cultures, such as *Aladdin* and *Ali Baba and the Forty Thieves*.[14] But more often than not, the plays were based on literary and dramatic works. Over the lifetime of the form there were more plays from Shakespeare (14) than from the next most popular writer (Sir Walter Scott, with ten).[15] During the Victorian period *Hamlet* was especially popular. But the form also re-created dozens of different plays, often several versions by different publishers. Not every play was printed by every publisher, but there was a good deal of crossover. *Richard III* was published at different times by nine different publishers. *Hamlet* and *Julius Caesar* were published by three different publishers. William West was the only one to publish *Coriolanus*, *The Merry Wives of Windsor*, and *Richard II*. Orlando Hodgeson was the only one to publish a version of *Two Gentlemen of Verona*.

The plays published were also mostly inspired by the offerings on London's stages. A successful run of a play would often inspire a Toy Theatre adaptation; for example, Kean as Richard III was made into a Toy Theatre play.[16] The *Macbeth* that was published in July, 1811 was based on the Covent Garden production earlier that year.[17] The toy theatre itself was often a cardboard reproduction of a famous London theatre: Theatre Royal, Covent Gardens, Drury Lane, The Lyceum, or Sadler Wells.[18] Even those who had not seen the production, however, were invited to purchase the sheets of characters and imagine their version, which echoes contemporary marketing of *Star Wars: Episode III: Revenge of the Sith* action figures. The film was rated PG-13, thus eliminating many in the age group that buys action figures from seeing the film. Brian Goldner, who oversees the U.S. market for the makers of the *Star Wars* action figures, advocated the toys as a means to participate in the world of the film, even if one was not old enough to see it: "Even if they can't go to the movie, they can be a part of it."[19] In this sense, like action figures, the toy theatre was also purely commercial as well.[20] The sets were marketed following popular productions, and although some sheets of characters were quite well done, just as often they were also hack work, done quickly and cheaply to cash in on the popularity of a show. The manufacturers of the sheets, scripts and theatres did not do so out of love for the form or to bring great plays to children. They were in business to make money, and they made quite a bit of it before the form eventually lost popularity and other forms of play replaced it.

The Toy Theatre declined primarily because of the rise of realism and the subsequent rise of cinema. The forms that would give rise to contemporary action figures killed the original action figures. The toy theatre, however, represented, the first major attempt to modify, reduce, and translate Shakespeare's plays (and the theatregoing experience) for young people. The toy theatre was not only a performing object theatre, representing live actors through cardboard objects and representing famous productions through play; it was also an attempt to mediate Shakespeare for young people. The scripts of Shakespeare, complete with stage directions were published alongside sheets of characters. The child at play would re-create Shakespeare in miniature for a home theatre.

The form introduced young people to the theatregoing experience and, presumably for Victorian era families, it was educational not only in terms of introducing text and performance but also the expectations of audience behavior, as younger siblings presumably were encouraged to sit straight and attentive in their chairs, to stop squirming, to pay attention, and to appreciate Shakespeare. It was thus contradictorily not only a form of agency for the child creating the play, it was also a form of social control, teaching young people how to behave in a public audience. One might also argue that the agency of the child might even be stifled by adults who presumably would encourage them not to innovate or be creative, but to follow the script and "do it right." Like much of youth-culture Shakespeare, this early form both set young people free to play with Shakespeare, but it also circumscribes and contains that play, limiting it.

Toy Theatre Now—Action Figures as Figures of Action

All is but toys . . .

—Macbeth 2.3.94

Contemporary performing object Shakespeare echoes its Victorian predecessor in that it is influenced by previous productions of the plays, and in that it uses children's toys, but is not children's theatre, nor even necessarily aimed at children, although the same age groups that appreciate the irony of the Shakespeare action figure would also appreciate contemporary Toy Theatre. The form began in the early 1990s by such groups as Tiny Ninja Theatre and Great Small Works. Although the use of toys makes the form function best in small spaces with small audiences, John Bell calls it a "small scale medium of extraordinary power."[21] It has its roots in the Victorian Toy Theatre, but it is not the province of amateurs and children any more. Contemporary Shakespeare in the Toy Theatre is performed by professionals in major venues.

Tiny Ninja Theatre is the creation of Dov Weinstein. As per its name, it uses Tiny Ninja action figures as performers in it productions. The ninjas could be found in vending machines throughout New York City in the early 1990s. Weinstein serves as director, designer, playwright and performer, adapts the play and performs it using Tiny Ninjas.[22] *Tiny Ninja Macbeth*, his first Shakespearean adaptation, received its world premiere on the Lower East Side in the 2000 New York International Fringe Festival.

Weinstein attributes the origins of the form to an observation of the absence of Shakespearean toy theatre: "I had noticed that there were these tiny plastic ninjas in vending machines all across the city, but no one was using them to perform classical theater. Something had to be done."[23] He also attributes the need to perform to the toys themselves: "I created *Macbeth* because tiny plastic ninjas had a lack of opportunity to perform classical theater," he states, "It was my dream to fill that void!"[24] Although the comment is wry and amusing, it does note that part of what is going on with Tiny Ninja Theatre is the substitution of tiny ninja action figures for real performers and the notion that pop theatre using action figures was a void that needed to be (or at least could be) filled. The ninja are performing objects, and much of the show consists of watching Weinstein create worlds with the toys.

What prevents *Tiny Ninja Macbeth* from being a young man playing with action figures in public or a continuation of Victorian Toy Theatre is the context. Tiny Ninja Theatre is a professional theatre that plays in professional (and serious) venues. In addition to the Fringe Festival, the Tiny Ninja Shakespeare plays (among others) have played at a variety of theatres and festivals, including *Tiny Ninja Hamlet* in fall 2004 at P.S. 122 in New York. Tickets are fairly costly. The plays are aimed at those who are already knowledgeable in Shakespeare and conventions of Shakespeare productions in New York. Youth culture in the form of toys is the mediating factor, but the plays are not aimed at youth, they are aimed at those who seek out alternative New York theatre.

The form has also grown and developed since its origins, allowing it to be performed in front of much larger crowds than its nineteenth-century predecessor. On average, only 15 people at a time can see the show, but projection screens have allowed the audience size to increase substantially. A pen-like camera magnifies the action "on stage," Weinstein sitting at a table upon which sits the set. He manually manipulates the figures or moves them with magnets. The magnified image is projected upon a screen behind him. While this use of technology allows for more audience as well as stunning visual effects, it does make the form more professional in all senses of the word. Whereas Trudi Cohen argues that "affordability and accessibility . . . make this do-it-yourself medium democratic by nature," although anyone could conceivably afford two dozen Tiny Ninja sold in vending machines, only a few can afford the camera and other technologies for which the critics single out the show.[25] As Tiny Ninja Theatre grows in popularity, it grows in complexity, and thus becomes less accessible, both to audiences as ticket prices go up and to practitioners, as the cost of the technical equipment to do anything more than the equivalent of Victorian Toy Theatre is prohibitive, or at least less democratic than Cohen asserts.

Shakespeare in Tiny Ninja form is greatly reduced (in every sense of the word), is translated (in the Bottom sense), and references not only "Shakespeare" but other productions of Shakespeare. One of the first plays to be developed was *Olivier's Hamlet*, a twenty-minute adaptation using Shakespeare's play, Laurence Olivier's autobiography, and images from the film. In the case of the three straightforward adaptations of Shakespeare: *Macbeth*, *Romeo and Juliet*, and *Hamlet*, Shakespeare is reduced not only in terms of the size and scope (they are, after all, *Tiny* Ninjas, standing an inch or two tall), but in terms of text, which is heavily cut. Most performances last less than an hour, and include spectacular scenes and special effects, as well as large casts.

It is the cast size and the assigning of roles in the program that indicates that Tiny Ninja Theatre is a parody of contemporary theatre practice, with toys. It is a simulacrum of the theatre-going experience. The program for *Tiny Ninja Macbeth* lists the "cast" as including "Duncan, King of Scotland, played by: Ninja," "Malcolm, son to Duncan, played by: Ninja," "Macbeth, a general in the King's army, played by: Mr. Smile," "Banquo, a general in the King's army, played by: Ninja," and "Lady Macbeth, played by: Mrs. Smile." Even minor characters, such as Caithness, were "played by: Ninja," and the cast list ended with "introducing Ninja as Young Siward." As the Shakespeare action figure is a parody of action figures, on some levels the Tiny Ninja version of *Macbeth* is a parody of the theatre-going experience. It is difficult to distinguish between the different characters, as they are all played by similarly dressed and posed toy ninjas. Macbeth and Lady Macbeth are distinguished by being played by "Mr. Smile" and "Mrs. Smile," action figures whose heads consist of the "Have a Nice Day" smiling face. It is a version of the focus on the stars, while the other characters are played by lesser-known or unknown actors who blend together.

The form allows for stage performances that could not have occurred with real actors. As Dan Bacalzo notes in his review of *Tiny Ninja Macbeth*, "The show's format allows its creator to stage some elaborate effects that would be difficult to pull off in a more traditional production."[26] In *Hamlet*, for example, the Ghost is placed in Weinstein's mouth, creating a startling image that is evocative of a medieval hellmouth. One wonders if a *Tiny Ninja Doctor Faustus* might ever be a possibility. In *Macbeth*, as Bacalzo reports

> During the final battle scene, he dumps a bagful of tiny ninjas onto the stage; then, to the accompaniment of an appropriately dramatic sound effect, he has the figure of Macbeth crash down onto this pile of bodies. The sheer power of this moment had audience members clapping in appreciation.[27]

Their appreciation, however, was not based on a man dumping a bag of toys on stage. The image is powerful only in contrast to other versions of *Macbeth* that one has seen. Unlike the Victorian Toy Theatre, which sought to re-create famous productions of London's stages, *Tiny Ninja Macbeth* builds off of every production of the play one has ever seen, especially productions that feature armies of two or three supernumeraries marching off to Dunsinane, or actors running in to fight and be killed as they fall off stage, only to run in on the other side as another character. Weinstein actually has entire armies on the set. Even as it parodies professional theatre, Tiny Ninja Theatre seeks to outdo it on its own terms, better representing reality through the highly artificial nature of toys on a tiny stage.

While clearly playful, the Shakespearean canon of the Tiny Ninja Theatre is played seriously, not for laughs. It is reductive, and in being so, it can achieve greater heights than a production featuring human actors. Melinda Barlow, profiling the theatre for *American Theatre* observes, "The contrast between the grandiosity of Shakespeare's tragedy and the mundanity of its brightly colored, inch-high, vending machine actors makes Tiny Ninja Theatre's productions surprisingly profound."[28]

What was once a theatre by and for children has now become a theatre using children's toys to create a new matrix of interpretation of

Shakespeare's plays. It is simulation along the same lines as the Shakespeare action figure. We make take it seriously, despite its level of irony, but the Toy Theatre is not child's play. The action figures are now figures with the true name of action. Child's play (and children's toys) has been appropriated by professional theatre, but the resulting parody is a theatre that is spectacular, profound and playful, even as it reduces, translates, and references Shakespeare.

Notes

1. Richard Burt, *Unspeakable Shaxxxspeares: Queer Theory and American Kiddie Culture* (New York: St. Martin's, 1998).
2. See the manufacturer's web page for more information <www.accoutrements. com.>
3. Douglas Lanier, *Shakespeare and Modern Popular Culture* (Oxford: Oxford University Press, 2002), p. 113.
4. Ibid., p. 114.
5. Ibid., p. 112.
6. Ibid., p. 141.
7. The author must confess that most of the individuals I know who own the Shakespeare action figure are professors of English or Theatre who were given the figure at least partly as a joke and who use the figure as office décor. This group includes the author.
8. George Speaight, *Juvenile Drama: The History of the English Toy Theatre* (London: MacDonald and Company, 1946), p. 116.
9. Frank Proschan, "The Semiotic Study of Puppets, Masks, and Performing Objects," *Semiotica* 47, no. 1–4 (1983), p. 4.
10. Speaight, *Juvenile Drama*, p. 21.
11. Robert Louis Stevenson, "A Penny Plain and Twopence Coloured," *Memories and Portraits* (New York: Charles Scribner's Sons, 1900), pp. 213–227.
12. Melinda Barlow, "Size Matters," *American Theatre* 22, no. 2 (February 2005), p. 61.
13. Speaight, *Juvenile Drama*, p. 20.
14. Ibid., p. 69.
15. The plays are *Coriolanus, Hamlet, Henry IV, Julius Caesar, Macbeth, The Merry Wives of Windsor, A Midsummer Night's Dream, Othello, Richard II, Richard III, Romeo and Juliet, The Tempest, The Two Gentlemen of Verona, and The Winter's Tale.* See the appendices in Speaight, *Juvenile Drama*, p. 236.
16. Speaight, *Juvenile Drama*, p. 69.
17. A.E. Wilson, *Penny Plain Two Pence Coloured* (London: George G. Harrap and Company, 1932), p. 111.
18. Speaight, *Juvenile Drama*, p. 54.
19. Quoted in Geoff Boucher, "Gone to the Dark Side," *Los Angeles Times*, May 10, 2005, E10.
20. See Wilson, *Penny Plain*, p. 27.

21. Quoted in Barlow, "Size Matters," p. 63.
22. See Eric Grode, "Bard or Bust: A Fanatics Vow," *American Theatre* 19, no. 7 (September 2002).
23. Quoted in Brook Pierce, "Reviews: Tiny Ninja Macbeth, Finally, Little Green Man," *TheatreMania.com* (August 18, 2000) <http://www.theatermania.com/content/news.cfm/story/970> Accessed August 1, 2005.
24. Quoted in "Off-off Color: Toy Story," *Time Out New York*, no. 268 (November 9–16, 2000) <http://www.tinyninjatheater.com/reviews/timeouttoytheater.shtml> Accessed July 15, 2005.
25. Quoted in Barlow, "Size Matters," p. 63.
26. Dan Bacalzo, "Tiny Ninja Theatre," *Theatremania.com* (April 9, 2003) <http://www.theatermania.com/content/news.cfm/story/3362> Accessed August 1, 2005.
27. Bacalzo, "Tiny Ninja Theater."
28. Barlowe, "Size Matters," p. 64.

2

"Smells Like Teen Shakespirit" Or, the Shakespearean Films of Julia Stiles

Robert L. York

The Inception: Luhrmann's *William Shakespeare's Romeo + Juliet* and the Teen Market

Baz Luhrmann's 1996 film *William Shakespeare's Romeo + Juliet* drew teenagers toward Shakespeare as no film had attempted before with a strikingly visual and aural adaptation of the most commonly studied play in American high schools, a play which had long been accompanied by a viewing of Franco Zeffirelli's 1968 film in the classroom. The newer film, with the appealing cast of Leonardo DiCaprio and Claire Danes, a soundtrack mixing hip-hop and alternative tracks (Butthole Surfers, The Cardigans, Des'ree, Everclear, Garbage, Radiohead, and others), and Luhrmann's distinctive, signature, MTV-style pacing and editing, transports Shakespeare's play and language to the mid-1990s Verona Beach—part Miami, part Mexico City, and part Vera Cruz. The film offered a fresh spin on the play in a format that was likely to usurp Zeffirelli's vision of Verona in the eyes of the era's freshmen in the classroom—and if not in the classroom at least in whatever hip collective psyche that prevailed among youth culture in 1996.

The film, with an estimated $14.5 million budget, opened in the United States to more than $11.1 million in box-office receipts on its opening weekend in November 1996. Over the next three months, the film grossed an overall $46.3 million in U.S. ticket sales; it also reached high figures in the United Kingdom, Italy, France, Germany, and Portugal as it ran until summer 1997.[1] Synergistic marketing of the film consisted of a best-selling soundtrack and editions of the original play paired with Luhrmann's script, published by Bantam/Dell/Doubleday, primarily an adolescent publisher. The paperback's cover displayed the two teen idols' face-to-face romantic pose, inviting young filmgoers with a newfound appreciation for Shakespeare to read the play. This selling of the play occurred about thirty-five years earlier, when *West Side Story* hit Broadway and then cinemas, the productions accompanied by soundtracks, paperback matchups of the play and Broadway script, and even a movie tie-in novelization. Luhrmann's film additionally prompted an official film Web site,[2] VHS sales and rentals (released in 1997), and a special edition DVD (released in 2002), all significantly contributing to the placement of this film in the mindset of the post Gen-X set.

Lynda E. Boose and Richard Burt state that Luhrmann's film, in "enunciating itself as a teen film," was market-tested among younger viewers and additionally attracted MTV news coverage, thus gaining the first place in box-office receipts the weekend of its release.[3] Counter to the tradition of "classical" Shakespearean films, they write,

[T]een-targeted, popular film has rocketed into the huge-budget model, while . . . anything considered "classical" had become equated with a kind of artsy-fartsy cultural elitism that was bound not to make money and was something thus left to the independent film producer aiming at the art houses or the Sundance film festival.[4]

Few popular or scholarly reviews or critiques have failed to mention the "MTV style" of Luhrmann's film, often pejoratively declaring it so. Roger Ebert calls the film "one grand but doomed gesture . . . that (a) will dismay any lover of Shakespeare, and (b) bore anyone lured into the theater by promise of gang wars, MTV-style." He adds, "This production was a very bad idea . . . The movie takes a 'Shakespeare's greatest hits' approach, giving us about as much of the original as we'd find in *Bartlett's Familiar Quotations*."[5] Gary Crowdus believes Luhrmann to be "more concerned about concocting a visual style that will pander to the tastes of young moviegoers" than remaining faithful to Shakespeare by projecting "blaring music" and performances "reaching the artistic level of a good high-school presentation." The filmmakers' "true passions lie . . . in the end credits," with too great an emphasis on special effects and other technical aspects. He concludes that the "MTV-like stylistic contortions" attempt "to suck up to its targeted youth audience rather than to offer a new experience that might require young viewers to stretch intellectually or artistically."[6]

And what defined *faithful*, according to the purists? Douglas Brode writes that critics were concerned that "the impressionable young audience witnessed an altered and diluted version, thus being misinformed and ill served by the film," though he argues that while "this might not be the stuff a purist's dreams are made of, it couldn't be denied that modern youth *did* turn out for Shakespeare, no mean feat in itself."[7]

Brode defends the film on the grounds that "It can . . . be appreciated as an important attempt to bring Shakespeare out of the elitist enclave of high culture, proving even in the MTV era of the oncoming millennium that the Bard's vision rings true."[8] He joins Francisco Menendez, who states that Luhrmann and co-screenwriter Craig Pearce "have married skillfully crafted images to the Elizabethan words in such a way that a contemporary text emerges from their script." Audience and critical misconceptions abound regarding a preconceived notion that productions should be "historically correct"—actually a nineteenth-century convention—while Shakespeare's own audience "would have been exposed to costumes of their own period, not of the play's setting."[9] Jonathan Bate states, "The best Shakespeare is always Shakespeare made contemporary," that Luhrmann's cinematic treatment, in keeping the authentic text but updating the setting, "makes Shakespeare familiar to a whole new generation."[10]

Peter Travers goes one further, calling the film "retrofuturistic" and citing Quentin Tarantino as equal an influence on the film as Shakespeare is. He states that the art design of the film, including costumes and settings, "is meant to make *Romeo and Juliet* accessible to the elusive Gen-X audience without leaving the play bowdlerized and broken." He draws the film in comparison to Zeffirelli's, applauding the new film for its more iambic-friendly casting of DiCaprio and Danes than the previous film had in leads Olivia Hussey and Leonard Whiting. He does note, however, that the two films' textual cuts, in Zeffirelli's case, "make up for the inadequacies of his otherwise appealing actors," and in Luhrmann's, "lead you to" Shakespeare's words. Luhrmann's lead actors, Travers writes, "speak the verse so naturally that the meaning registers."[11]

Luhrmann's greatest defender is Luhrmann himself. His premise that *Romeo and Juliet* meets the Hollywood formula of the "impossible love structure" led him to "reveal that myth anew or fresh." Romeo can be likened to tragic icons James Dean or Kurt Cobain, he says, "the individual against incredible odds, overcoming oppression."[12]

He adds, "One must simply address an audience at a particular moment in time and attempt to reveal the greater richness of the particular idea or story."[13] He argues that "truly great story telling defies time, geography and the so-called rules of right and wrong; the proof of its worth is that it lives on."[14]

Luhrmann does not eschew the MTV label, stating that "MTV provides a lot of cultural reference for young people at the moment."[15] Craig Pearce, Luhrmann's co-screenwriter, adds that presenting "these very recognizable characters in the modern world . . . help[s]" their audience access the play. The gun-wielding and fast-car-driving Capulets and Montagues, Pearce adds, "are the rich kids . . . they've got money, they've got cars. What do they do? They probably drive around in cars . . . slinging off at each other, biting their thumb at each other . . . armed to the teeth."[16]

Luhrmann's titling of the film *William Shakespeare's Romeo + Juliet* ironically captures the idea that while the play is Shakespeare's, this film belongs to Luhrmann. Luhrmann and Pearce selectively cut the text to facilitate tighter dialogue and flow. But this is not new, neither on film nor on stage. These screenwriters follow the traditional and widely accepted practice of deleting particularly antiquated references or abridging Shakespeare's longer lines. Various *Hamlet* films, for instance, even exclude references to Fortinbras, Reynaldo, Rosencrantz, and Guildenstern.

The elements *added* by Luhrmann make up the weight of content replacing any line excised, as he filters the play through the various cultural components of late twentieth century. Luhrmann notes that his use of pop music, for example, reflects Shakespeare's own practice of "[stealing] pop culture" in order to engage his audience.[17] Bridging the gap as the second installment in what would become known as the "Red Curtain Trilogy" (*Strictly Ballroom* being the first and *Moulin Rouge* the third), Luhrmann's inclusion of music in *William Shakespeare's Romeo + Juliet* (e.g., a Prince song sung by a boy's church choir) sets the template for what in *Moulin Rouge* becomes the model synthesis of existing material on film, the ultimate illustration of "stolen pop culture."[18]

Shakespeare's play itself was based on Arthur Brooke's *The Tragical Historye of Romeus and Juliet* (1562), which in turn was based on the Italian *Matteo Bandello* (1554). Luhrmann states that Shakespeare "just stole it—adapted it virtually in a few days. And the thing about it is, even then people were writing about how bad this nobody poet ripped off these great works of art and put them in his trashy theater."

Furthermore, he explains, Shakespeare made use of his own culture's "pop music" in his productions: "He would just stick the popular song of the day in the middle of the show. You know, to advance the story, but also to engage people through song."[19] Luhrmann claims to follow this suit in his own adaptation of the play, particularly allowing his cinematic influences to seep into the palate, ranging from *Rebel without a Cause* to *Giant*.[20] Shakespeare, he notes,

> had to arrest the attention of a very noisy, disparate, savage yet honest audience not unlike your local cinema. To facilitate this, he used all the devices at his disposal, the clash of low brow comedy with high tragedy, the use of popular song (pop music) etc. . . . [We] . . . transformed all of these devices into cinematic equivalents in order to achieve the same goal with our noisy, disparate, savage yet honest audience.[21]

Daggers and swords in this film are replaced by firearms; Queen Mab is a drug; and Romeo acquires drugs from a far seedier drug dealer than Shakespeare's Apothecary. All the modernized components, however, keep in check their Shakespearean counterparts. Luhrmann argues that the play represents the idea of

> the ugly duckling structure, or the transformation structure where you reveal that which you are, not that which you want to be.[22]

Luhrmann also used Latin American and African American actors because they took to Shakespeare's meter quite well, due to their knowledge of rap.[23]

The Popularlization of Will S. the Screenwriter

Luhrmann's film illustrates what 1990s critics termed the *popularization* of Shakespeare in the mass media—rooted in film but also finding ground in television (HBO's broadcast of the Russian television series, *Shakespeare: The Animated Tales*; NBC's Civil War-set *The Tempest*, starring Peter Fonda), CD-ROMS, Web sites, and the video transfers of films onto VHS and, later, DVD. Boose and Burt directly link popularization to youth culture. They identify existing reinforcements that distinguish, through "a cultural dichotomy," between "the popular" and "the classical" (i.e., the unstated "elite"). Additionally, they write, "In one widely held view, popularization functions as a vehicle for the transmission of subversive or transgressive recodings of

Shakespeare, whereas a film that is widely recognized as classical carries with it a kind of stable universality." Films in this era touch upon these considerations—youth appeal, movement from the classical, and, alas, some revolutionary filmmaking in comparison to any "stable universality" that (if it ever existed) is perceived.[24] This break from perceptions of "universality" might have started as a "stalwartly liberal tradition of noblesse oblige attempting to bring culture to the masses," but maybe it backfired in a sense, they write, because "popularization" resulted in Shakespeare's entry into "a strictly market-responsive milieu in which literary knowledge is in general a decidedly low capital, frequently mockable commodity, caught within the peculiarly American ambivalence about intellectualism, and therefore to be eschewed at all costs."[25]

Perhaps this explains the reworking of *Hamlet* in Disney's *The Lion King* (1994) or Showtime's post–Luhrmann made-for-cable *Ronnie and Julie* (1997), set in a high school with ice hockey as a backdrop for yet another *Romeo and Juliet*. Shakespeare's 1970s and 1980s visibility came mostly through the BBC's production of *The Complete Works of William Shakespeare* (broadcast in the United States on PBS) while the cinema simultaneously experienced a rather dry spell of Shakespearean adaptations. The 1990s boom of Shakespearean films dismantled audience's previous expectations of what Shakespearean films should look like, as their perceptions of the "classical" would have been formed by cinematic history and the BBC series. Boose and Burt argue that "the 'popular' must be thought through not only the media and institutions in which Shakespeare is not reproduced—mass culture, Hollywood, celebrity, tabloid—but above all, youth culture . . . an arena increasingly driven by a specifically youth culture, and Hollywood has clearly picked up on that fact."[26]

Brode echoes that

> While popular motion pictures based on Shakespeare's works seem unlikely candidates for a commercial trend in an era when wild teenage comedies and expensive special-effects extravaganzas dominate the studio's offerings, that's exactly what happened. The professionals and the public simultaneously rediscovered this enduring body of work, and, with Hollywood's help, Shakespeare is being rescued from the academics and returned to the masses, who have established Gentle Will as the most beloved author of all time.[27]

Luhrmann scoffs at the pejorative depiction of popularization, stating that Shakespeare was just as interested as anyone in reaching a wide audience and making money in the process: "At what time was

Shakespeare only interested in playing to a small elite? . . . It seems the antithesis of everything Shakespeare stood for is to treat his text as high culture."[28]

A Brief History of Film Adaptations of Shakespeare in the Sound Era, Sparse to Unabridged to Loose

The first Hollywood adaptation of Shakespeare in the sound era was the irreverent and campy *The Taming of the Shrew* (1929), directed by Sam Taylor, a film notorious for its brutal editing of Shakespeare's language; the *additional* comical dialogue to the script; and over-the-top performances by the era's biggest stars, the suddenly former-silent-film icons Mary Pickford and Douglas Fairbanks. Though the Shakespearean purists of the day balked, the film was successful and paved the way for a classic era of Shakespearean films, notably Max Reinhardt's whimsical, fantastical *A Midsummer Night's Dream* (1935), featuring the music of Felix Mendelssohn and the all-star cast of Olivia deHavilland, James Cagney, Mickey Rooney, and Joe E. Smith. Next came the triumvirate of plays filmed in England and other European outdoor locations by Laurence Olivier (*Hamlet*, *Henry V*, and *Richard III*) and two presentations by Orson Welles, *Macbeth* and *Othello*. Reinhardt's vision rode the fence between the classical and the popular through its Mendelssohn score and its stars—particularly Cagney's Nick Bottom and young Rooney's Puck, both challenging casting propositions; deHavilland, as Titania, is nothing short of "classic" in her characteristic performance.

Olivier's *Hamlet* (1948) addresses filming Shakespeare as a problem to be solved. Rather than indiscriminately cutting lines as Taylor had done or using the visual or fantastical effects of Reinhardt, Olivier seamlessly condenses word into action, with visible, physical activity accompanying or even replacing text, and presents soliloquy as voice-over commentary, showing the full potential of a medium that can show without always telling. Four years earlier, in *Henry V* (1944), he slowly moves the play from the Globe Theater to a studio soundstage and to exterior locations in Spain for his filming of the Battle of Agincourt. Ultimately, the metatheatrical and metacinematic tellings come full circle, as Olivier returns to the Globe for the finale.

The history of Shakespearean film, then, coincides with the history of film itself, and while there have been high points in this history—Olivier's films and later in the 1960s Zeffirelli's hugely popular *The Taming of the Shrew* (1967), with Elizabeth Taylor and Richard Burton, and *Romeo and Juliet* (1968)—Shakespeare's most prolific cinematic period was launched by Kenneth Branagh in his *Henry V* (1989), which was to be followed in the next decade by a rich, diverse array of adaptations—the diversities and departures slowly becoming the standard—that resulted in a greater exposure of the plays—hence, the popularization—previously unmatched in the cinema.

Setting *Romeo and Juliet* in a twentieth-century, multicultural, coastal hybrid, Luhrmann departs from the traditional and prevalent attempts at historically authenticating the story (or shortsightedly placing it in the Elizabethan era) through period costumes and visual designs. The first Shakespearean films of this recent era, Branagh's *Henry V* and Zeffirelli's *Hamlet* (1990) (or as it has come to be known, Mel Gibson's *Hamlet*), set the stories in believably medieval settings with period costumes, castles, and weaponry. Branagh's only historical adjustment, one fit to his medium of film, involves the Prologue character (Derek Jacobi), who, dressed in contemporary wardrobe, delivers the opening sequence on a soundstage crowded by film equipment; this is not unlike Olivier's own metacinematic movement in his *Henry V*. When Jacobi's Prologue reenters the film to comment on a battle scene, his contemporaneous and anomalous presence as a current commentator on medieval events richly contrasts with the mud and blood surrounding him. Zeffirelli's Freudian spin on Hamlet and Gertrude's mother–son relationship also invites speculation as to contemporary interpretation while maintaining a classic setting. However, Luhrmann and Pearce go even further in attempting more fully to "[build] a world of images and icons from the twentieth century to help illuminate Shakespeare's text,"[29] presumably for the younger movie-going public.

Luhrmann's film was not the first of the decade to update Shakespeare's setting. *Romeo + Juliet* follows a newer trend of time travel in filmed Shakespeare, a trend led again by Branagh in *Much Ado about Nothing* (1993), set in nineteenth-century Messina, a practice he would later employ in *Hamlet* (1996) and *Love's Labour's Lost* (2000), both set in alternative points in the nineteenth or early twentieth centuries. *Love's Labour's Lost* would follow *Romeo + Juliet* by merging Shakespeare with another era's pop culture, "stolen" songs by Irving Berlin, George Gershwin, Jerome Kern, Cole Porter, and others. Richard Loncraine and Ian McKellen transport

Richard III (1995) to the 1930s, attaching Richard to Hitler through imagery and costume. Trevor Nunn's *Twelfth Night* (1996) and Michael Hoffman's *A Midsummer Night's Dream* (1999) follow similar suits, both with nineteenth-century settings. Al Pacino's *Looking for Richard* (1996), half-documentary, half-performance, refreshingly alters the whole idea of adaptation through its own metacinematic design, while the performance segments involve a rather traditional wardrobe and setting. As the new millennium, century, and decade opened with Michael Almereyda's *Hamlet* (2000), set in a media-driven New York corporate setting, what might otherwise be regarded as unusual and radical in Shakespearean adaptations had by now become the expected. After a lapse in heavy distribution of Shakespeare, Michael Radford's *The Merchant of Venice* (2004) resumed the traditional approach, setting the play in Renaissance Italy, reminding viewers of a former era of adaptation.

Shakespearean film history also reveals an adjunct, tangential wing of adaptations, that is, "loose adaptations" that adapt *story* without *language*, that slightly alter characters' names for geographical or contemporary contexts, that transport every component of the play to a parallel placement without directly making explicit reference to the play itself, most times excluding the original's title. It is a subgenre of Shakespearean film most quickly and commonly affiliated with *West Side Story* (1961) but more penetratingly and dramatically engaged by Akira Kurosawa in *Throne of Blood* (1957), *The Bad Sleep Well* (1960), and *Ran* (1985)—versions of *Macbeth*, *Hamlet*, and *King Lear*—and by Paul Mazursky in *Harry and Tonto* (1974) and *Tempest* (1982), loose but bona fide deconstructions of *King Lear* and *The Tempest* that respectively address contemporary issues of aging and midlife crisis. *Throne of Blood* and *Ran* are set in historical periods, but they correspond with Japanese history, not Shakespeare's settings or Elizabethan history. These films also liberally re-create plot points, characters' names, and, obviously, the language of their "original" screenplays. The 1990s, a period already flourishing with Shakespearean cinema, also became fertile ground for a new batch of looser adaptations produced in proportion to the aforementioned films that more directly followed Shakespeare's text.

Leading the pack is the wildly popular, Oscar-winning *Shakespeare in Love* (1998), which works on a variety of metatheatrical and metaliterary levels, rooted in its parallel ties to *Romeo and Juliet*, *Twelfth Night*, and the sonnets. Lesser-known adaptations or modernizations include the punk-apocalyptic, irreverent *Tromeo & Juliet*

(1996), Abel Ferrara's Chinese American spin on *Romeo and Juliet*, *China Girl* (1987), his Mafioso take on *Macbeth*, *Men of Respect* (1991), and Gus van Sant's *My Own Private Idaho* (1991), homage to the *Henry IV* plays set among young runaways, orphans, and a rebellious heir.

If Shakespeare, then why not Shakespeare? As several of the preceding examples illustrate, the stories offer a firm basis for filmmakers to handle contemporary issues. Harry (Art Carney), in Mazursky's *Harry and Tonto*, reflects a modern Lear, a displaced senior citizen, evicted from an apartment building about to be torn down, hesitant to burden his adult son by moving in with him and his family, and resorting to cross-country travel with his cat Tonto as he seeks solace in old age. Kurosawa's Koichi Nishi (Toshiro Mifune), the "Hamlet" character in *The Bad Sleep Well*, concocts a plan to exact his revenge on the members of a corporate underworld who had his father, the former company president, assassinated. Van Sant's Mike Waters (Keanu Reeves) enjoys his time running with the homeless and homosexual hustlers, while his father, a governmental figure, holds high expectations over his head. Need one adopt Harold Bloom's argument that Shakespeare invented the human to see that, at the least, Shakespeare generated a fictional and thematic iconography from which contemporary filmmakers frequently draw?

If contemporary romance, punk aesthetics, Latino-Anglo relations, Asian culture, mobster tales, and homoerotic homelessness could be filtered through Shakespeare's works either directly or indirectly, another concern that filmmakers also took up was the youth culture at large, and the two most direct adaptations of Shakespeare geared toward this demographic, both in content and marketing, bridged the space between the 1990s and the new millennium—the first embracing the "teen-film genre" and the second attempting to reject the typical features of the genre. As a result, Shakespeare's service to these two films varies, as does their repayment to him for taking his works out on loan.

The marketing of films directly geared toward teens was most prominently practiced on a large scale in the early 1980s, with a string of slasher films, prompted by *Halloween* (1978) and *Friday* (1980) *the 13th*, and the coming-of-age sex comedies *Fast Times at Ridgemont High* (1982) and *Porky's* (1982) and their various clones. *Risky Business* (1983) helped to break the mold established by these films by presenting a more sophisticated, thought-provoking plot and an upscale setting—the affluent suburbs of Chicago. Filmmaker John

Hughes put these 'burbs on the map by producing, writing, and/or directing a group of films between 1984 and 1988 that brought to prominence a core group of actors, dubbed the "Brat Pack"— *Sixteen Candles*, *The Breakfast Club*, and *Ferris Bueller's Day Off* among them.

The 1980s teen films also introduced the synergistic practice of selling soundtrack albums, with songs from these films frequently in the top ten—Jackson Browne's "Somebody's Baby" (*Fast Times*), the re-release of Bob Seger and the Silver Bullet Band's "Old Time Rock 'n' Roll" (*Risky Business*), and Simple Minds' "Don't You Forget about Me" (*The Breakfast Club*). The VCR's advent in American homes during the period also led to large-scale repeated viewings of these films, a common weekend-night activity at teen gatherings. Socioeconomic class was a frequent subject matter, as images of cool cars, Sony Walkmans, and mall-purchased clothing filled the screen. Molly Ringwald's impoverished character in *Pretty in Pink* makes her own clothes, drawing ridicule from the richer girls.

Films of the 1990s reintroduced a new wave of teen films, again borrowing thematically from the 1980s films, ranging from the slasher homage *Scream* (1996) to the audacities of *American Pie* (1999), with turn-of-the-millennium teen-genre spoofs, *Scary Movie* (2000) and *Not Another Teen Movie* (2001), thus affirming the renewed vitality of the genre. Literary adaptations such as *Clueless* (1995, based on Jane Austen's *Emma*) and *Cruel Intentions* (1999, based on *Dangerous Liaisons*) also emerged, subtly recycling old plots but also introducing classic works to their audiences.

In the wake of *Romeo + Juliet*, loose Shakespearean adaptations arose among the teen-film genre, enabling filmmakers to comment on a broad array of contemporary interests among that demographic. The two most prominent entries in this subgenre are *10 Things I Hate about You* (1999), loosely based on *The Taming of the Shrew*, and *"O"* (2001), a modernized *Othello*. Like Luhrmann's *Romeo + Juliet*, these films target the teen market, with *10 Things* fully embracing the teen-film genre and *"O"* attaching *Othello* to contemporary teen social issues.

The Teen Genre Consumes Will: *10 Things I Hate about You*

10 Things I Hate about You offers a perfunctory presentation of *The Taming of the Shrew*. While screenwriters Karen McCullah Lutz and

Kirsten Smith owe Shakespeare for the general storyline, they and director Gil Junger hold more steadfastly to the teen-film genre. Shakespeare provides the template for a tale of polar opposite sisters (Kate and Bianca), vying suitors (Lucentio and Hortensio), a rule-oriented, doddering father (Baptista), and a man who will turn everything around (Petruchio), all directly mirrored in the film. Nonetheless, the filmmakers do not strictly adhere to Shakespeare's plot and sequence, leaning more heavily on the elements of the teen genre to design additional elements. Like Luhrmann's film, this movie also boasts a pop soundtrack, which includes contemporary songs by Barenaked Ladies, The Notorious B.I.G., The Cardigans, Semisonic, and Sister Hazel; retro material by Joan Jett, Madness, George Clinton, The Thompson Twins, and Joan Armatrading; and covers of Nick Lowe's "Cruel To Be Kind" (apropos to Shakespeare) and Cheap Trick's "I Want You To Want Me," both performed by Letters to Cleo.

But as soon as we see a sign for "Padua High School," the departures from Shakespeare ensue. For starters, there's no reference whatsoever to the Induction that opens Shakespeare's play, which features the prominent Christopher Sly. Neither Taylor's nor Zeffirelli's films employ the Induction. Diana E. Henderson, in reference to these earlier films, states that

> The erasure of the Christopher Sly induction from filmed versions of *Shrew* removes the play's most common theatrical "excuse" for its gender politics (i.e., it's all a prank, or a drunkard's wish fulfillment) . . . In choosing to erase the Sly frame and use actresses for the female roles, the filmmakers increase the inset story's claims to social reality, already abetted by the transfer to a normatively realist medium.[30]

Like earlier versions of *Shrew*, *10 Things* bypasses the commentary lying in Shakespeare's Induction. Set in a realistic present and loosely rather than literally adapted from the play, the film's main experiment is filtering the play through the strainer of youth culture. The setting forces all the other elements, all conventional to the youth market. L. Monique Pittman reinforces Henderson's aforementioned premise, suggesting that the film "offers simpler, more immediately satisfying answers to the problems of identity . . . the film's sheer popular appeal demands consideration as a reflection of contemporary tastes and as an interesting interaction with Shakespeare's text."[31] Ebert questions the wisdom in the filmmaker's construction: "The high school romance genre has become so popular that it's running out of new ideas and has taken to recycling classic literature," citing as examples *Clueless, Cruel Intentions, Great Expectations, Ever After*, and, of course, Luhrmann's film. Of *10 Things*, he writes, "It doesn't remake Shakespeare as much as evoke him as a talisman . . . the movie is charming, despite its exhausted wheeze of an ancient recycled plot idea (boy takes bribe to ask girl to prom, then discovers that he really likes her—but then she finds out about the bribe and hates him)."[32]

Set in Padua High School in Seattle, *10 Things I Hate about You* tells the story of the Stratford sisters, Kat (Julia Stiles) and Bianca (Larisa Oleynik). The younger sister draws the attention of Cameron (Joseph Gordon-Levitt), a transfer student who falls head over heels in infatuation upon seeing Bianca. Though he knows no French, he sets himself up to tutor Bianca in French to get close to her. However, Cameron learns that Bianca cannot date until the elder Kat does, a mandate laid out by their father (Larry Miller), a single father and obstetrician/gynecologist to teenage mothers—hence, his overly protective nature.

Michael Eckman (David Krumholtz), a "Media Geek" (i.e., member of the school's audiovisual club) assigned as school mentor to Cameron on his first day, cooks up a scheme to find someone to date Kat so Cameron can ask out Bianca. Eckman selects Patrick Verona (Heath Ledger), an Australian-born enigma, a tough guy swirling in rumors about his mysterious past (Did he eat a live chicken? Did he once burn a police officer?). However, since he is as allegedly unapproachable as the shrewish Kat, they decide to find a backer who will bankroll this endeavor. Michael boldly chooses as the backer another boy who has a well-known crush on Bianca, Joey Donner (Andrew Keegan), this teen movie's rich, snotty asshole (each teen comedy has one), a semiprofessional male model with a big tube sock ad coming out. To complicate things further, Joey and Kat hate each other for a compelling reason revealed during the course of the movie. The plot eventually turns to the vicissitudes of Kat's evolving relationship with Patrick, with a house party and prom to get through to reach the conclusion, and with as many addendums and striking contrasts to Shakespeare's original as these scarce similarities demonstrate.

Like the play, the film draws its main plot through a subplot; the main characters' involvement is attendant upon the second tier of characters' plight. To get to Kat and Patrick (read: Kate and Petruchio), we need to learn of Cameron and Bianca (read: Lucentio/Cambio and Bianca). *Shrew*'s first act opens with the introduction of Lucentio, accompanied by his servant Tranio. He declares, "For the time I study, / Virtue and that part of philosophy / Will I apply that treats of happiness / By virtue specially to be achieved" (1.1.17–20). Man, servant, and the intended devotion to study to be derailed by love were all common motifs in early Shakespeare, reflected one way or another in such plays as *The Comedy of Errors* and *Love's Labour's Lost*.

Whereas Lucentio has arrived at Padua from Pisa to pursue studies, the film's Cameron is introduced as a "military brat" who just moved to Seattle. Padua High School guidance counselor Ms. Perky (Allison Janney) meets with Cameron in her office on his first day. The teen-film genre's escapist ridicule of school figures begins here in *10 Things* as Ms. Perky tells Cameron that the school's student body consists of a bunch of "asswipes" and "deviants," not the standard fare in first-day orientation. Not only this, but she also secretly interrupts her discussions with students here and in other scenes to add an occasional line to her erotic novel, a work-in-progress appearing on her laptop screen that gives new meaning to the word "bratwurst." The later introduction of a militantly race-conscious African American teacher and pothead soccer coach who monitors detention exacerbates these reversals and stereotypes.

Michael Eckman gives Cameron a tour of the school, and for whatever descriptions Ms. Perky uses to refer to students, Eckman presents *prescriptive* labels and details, a wide array of high school cliques and stereotypes, including "Beautiful People," "Media Geeks," "Coffee Kids," "White Rastas," "Cowboys," and "Future MBAs," each group putting forth its signature demonstrative characteristic in its allotted space and time onscreen as Eckman and Cameron move through the courtyard. Of this scene, Pittman writes that director Junger

> [S]urely points to the heavily determined and socially constructed nature of young adult identity, but the camera movement implies a possible alternative to such limits on the self. Tracking alongside Michael and Cameron, the camera follows the two, creating energy and resistance to the categories. In contrast, the cliques remain static, sitting or standing in established quadrants of the courtyard.[33]

Upon first noticing Bianca, Cameron recites the lines of Lucentio in Shakespeare's first act: "I burn, I pine, I perish" (1.1.155). Cameron sees Bianca as "pure," reflecting Lucentio's description of her "mild behavior and sobriety," "sweet beauty," "sacred and sweet" character (1.1.71, 167, 176). Michael warns against her, informing Cameron of two essential points about Bianca, both conceived of in *The Taming of the Shrew*: Bianca needs a French tutor (in Shakespeare, it's Latin), and her father forbids her to date until her sister Kat chooses to date (in Shakespeare, it's marriage). Shakespeare's corresponding characters—Lucentio (later to be identified in disguise as "Cambio," a tutor) and Tranio (who will simultaneously pose as Lucentio to work on her father, Baptista)—map out a different plan than Cameron and Michael have, but in both cases, the objectives are the same.

Lucentio/Cameron's competition from other suitors varies between Shakespeare's tempestuous Hortensio and the film's Joey Donner, who strongly vies for Bianca's attention. Early in the film, Joey notices Bianca and boasts to his friends that he can get to her. Knowing Joey's interest, Michael believes he and Cameron can play this competitor for Bianca by getting him to commission a suitor for Kat, giving Joey the impression he can reach Bianca, while in the meantime Cameron can work the inside track by tutoring Bianca. In Shakespeare's play, while Lucentio/Cambio and Tranio/Lucentio follow through on their plot, Hortensio plans to disguise himself as schoolmaster "so I may, by this device, at least / Have leave and leisure to make love to her / And unsuspected court her by herself" (1.2.135–137). Never does Joey Donner don the role of tutor, thus striking the possibility of a scene analogous to Lucentio/Cambio's rivaling tutoring session with Hortensio/Litio. And whereas Hortensio is presented by his friend Petruchio to Baptista as a music tutor so the two of them can work toward marrying the two sisters, Joey's interactions with the film's Petruchio, Patrick Verona, are built upon confrontations over fees for dating Kat (first, $50, then $100, and finally $300). In other words, Joey, while fulfilling the role of Bianca's other suitor, is not rooted as deeply in Hortensio as the other characters are in their corresponding Shakespearean characters.

Shakespeare also presents Tranio disguised as Lucentio while the real Lucentio conducts the Latin lessons with Bianca, which enables them to have both direct effects on Baptista as Tranio competes on his master's behalf with yet another suitor, Gremio. Furthermore, the real Lucentio gets this competing suitor to present him to Baptista as "Cambio" while the disguised Tranio offers Baptista some books for Bianca's studies. The consolidation of this labyrinthine information in *10 Things* keeps the source at arm's length while simultaneously borrowing its basic skeletal structure. The improbability and comedy belying both narratives share qualities, and the factor of money, Petruchio's desired dowry and Patrick's acceptance of money to date

Kat, reinforces both a Shakespearean complexity and a teen-driven motivation—especially in an apparently affluent high school.

Ultimately, the suitor favored by Baptista and Bianca in the play is some version of Lucentio, the disguised Tranio winning over Gremio in Baptista's eyes while the disguised Lucentio beats out disguised Hortensio in Bianca's eyes. The same occurs in the film, but not with the father's favor, as the film's dad has no significant interaction with either Cameron or Joey, aside from brief meetings on prom night, wherein Cameron comes to pick up Bianca for prom (given that Kat, by the latter half of the film, is dating Patrick) and is threatened bodily harm if Bianca is violated. Joey, presuming Bianca will go with him to prom, also shows up after she has left with Cameron. The only reaction he gets upon announcing that he is there to pick up Kat is a closed door in the face from Dr. Stratford. This greatly contrasts with Baptista's summoning of Bianca through Cambio to let her know he has decided upon "Lucentio." Nor are we presented a version of Lucentio's father, Vincentio, or the play's traveling Pedant whom Petruchio convinces to portray him on Tranio/Lucentio's behalf, a subplot-within-a-subplot in Shakespeare—again, one too many for this consolidated version. While the disguises in Shakespeare serve to complicate the character's interpretations of events, the only disguises in this film are more literal forms of deception: Cameron's claim to tutoring French when not knowing French; Joey's bribes; and Patrick's acceptance of the bribes.

The film's Bianca is not far removed from her Shakespearean counterpart. Portrayed as equally intolerant of her sister's shrewness and also painted as a superficial beauty, her first lines, overheard by Cameron as he sees her for the first time, indicate such trivial concerns. She says to her friend Chastity, "Yeah, but see, there's a difference between *like* and *love*. Because I *like* my Skechers, but I *love* my Prada backpack." Chastity replies, "But I love my Skechers." Bianca concludes, "That's because you don't have a Prada backpack."

Later, as Bianca works with Cameron in the tutorial, we see comical scenes akin to Shakespeare's pleasant analogous scenes as Cameron struggles with the language he does not know, though he does so without Joey interrupting him as Hortensio does in *Shrew*. Hortensio/Litio observes that Lucentio/Cambio "looks as though he were in love" (3.1.88). Hortensio eventually observes Cambio and Bianca kissing, and he thus forsakes his attempts at her, choosing instead to pursue a wealthy widow to whom he already holds an open opportunity to marry.

The circumstances and motivations between the two fathers' shared dictate differ, too. In Shakespeare, Baptista's main motivation is to rid himself of the adult "shrew" of a daughter, which enables outside forces like Hortensio and Petruchio to act as catalysts to achieve this end. If anyone can be convinced to take Kate off his hands, he will then willingly make Bianca available to the proper suitor. Baptista declares, ". . . how I firmly am resolved . . . not to bestow my youngest daughter / Before I have a husband for the elder" (1.1.49–51). Yet in the film, we learn his greatest concern for protecting his younger daughter is rooted in his knowledge of teen pregnancy from his OB/GYN position. He tells his daughters early in the film about a 15-year-old whose twins he had just delivered. He later exacerbates this concern when forcing Bianca to put on the "tummy," a prosthetic device worn around the chest and stomach to simulate the pregnant body, before she attends a house party (which he only allows her to attend since Kat is going also).

When Bianca presses him to let her date, Dr. Stratford comes up with the arrangement that she can date when Kat does, fully confident that his eldest daughter's current hatred against boys will further ensure his motive to keep his youngest daughter home; in other words, he would likely have the same fears concerning Kat's dating, but he is so certain that with this arrangement and her seemingly irreversible hatred of boys, he's got all the bases covered. When Bianca urges him to let her attend prom, he maintains policy in what he calls language she will understand: "I've got news for you. I'm down, I've got the 411, and you are not going out and getting jiggy with some boy—I don't care how dope his ride is. My mama didn't raise no fool." Additionally, we learn in the film that Mrs. Stratford is an absentee, another addendum to film outside Shakespeare's scope, one which defies a common convention to Shakespeare's father–daughter-minus-unmentioned-absent-(we would naturally presume deceased)-mother relationships (Lear–Cordelia–Goneril, Polonius–Ophelia, Prospero–Miranda, and Baptista–Kate–Bianca).

Also contrasting to Shakespeare is the filmmaker's contention that Dr. Stratford wishes to keep Kat at home after she graduates from high school, though she is vying to attend Sarah Lawrence College across the continent. He fights her on this point intermittently throughout the film, but once she receives her acceptance letter, he does relent to her wishes, stating that when her mother left him, he feared being left alone. Baptista, on the other hand, seems highly motivated to get Kate wedded as quickly as possible so he can be rid of her tempestuous

presence. While Kat questions her father's clinging and his unwilling-
ness to see her grow up, Shakespeare's Kate, aware of Baptista's
motivation, says, "I pray you sir, is it your will / To make a stale of me
amongst these mates?" as she learns of his plans to find suitors for her
(1.1.57–58).

Padua's transformation into Seattle, with a good deal of the action
set in a high school, contemporaneously shifts us to the coffee capitol
during the opening credits of the film, when Junger opens with a wide-
spanning shot of coastal downtown, prominently displaying the Space
Needle in the far left of the screen's skyline to the tune of Barenaked
Ladies' "One Week." Seattle's earlier 1990s points of identity, the
Seattle of SubPop Records and Cameron Crowe's *Singles*—grunge and
the café scene—do not play a part in this film, though we are briefly
reminded (in case we forgot midway through) of the city in a scene
from MTV's Seattle season of *The Real World*. The Barenaked Ladies'
song, we soon learn, emanates from a contemporary Volkswagen
Bug's sound system while its teenage female driver and her three
passengers rock out. As they stop at an intersection, their joyous
moment is eclipsed and music is drowned out by the approaching vintage car playing Joan Jett's 1980s hit, "Bad Reputation." This is our
introduction to Kat Stratford. Both cars, we learn, are headed to
Padua High School, whose name is revealed on a prom poster attached
to a column of the school. Kat tears the poster down as she enters the
building, indicating early on her "shrewness."

As Kate was described in Shakespeare's play as "too rough . . . a
wildcat" (1.1.55) (Gremio), "stark mad or wonderful forward"
(1.1.69), "curst and shrewd" (1.1.180), and "wench" (1.2.196)
(Tranio), "shrewed ill-favored" (1.2.60), with a "scolding tongue"
(1.2.100), "Katherine the curst" (1.2.128), "a soldier" (2.1.145), "with
a most impatient devilish spirit" (2.1.151) (Hortensio), and an "irk-
some, brawling scold" (1.2.187) (Petruchio), the film's Kat is described
by various characters as "tempestuous," a "heinous bitch," a "wild
beast," the "muling Rampalian wretch herself," and a "shrew." The
Bianca of the film even describes her older sister as a "hideous breed of
loser." Kat's revulsion of the opposite sex, "the unwashed miscreants
that go to that school," invites wide speculation, as when Cameron
begins to ask Bianca, "She's not a . . .?," to which she quickly replies,
"k.d. lang fan? No." On her school discipline record, she has a prior
event of kicking a fellow student in the testicles. She defies attending the
typical high school party, depicting it as "a futile attempt for kids to get
together, drink beer, just to forget their meaningless existences."

Ultimately, we learn that at the core of Kat is a personal misgiving of having given up her virginity at a younger age, and, much to her regret, to Joey Donner. Sharply contrasting with Kate's physical attack on her younger sister in Shakespeare, the film's Kat, in her longest one-on-one scene with Bianca, states, "Everyone was doing it, so I did it . . . After that, I swore I would never do anything just because everyone else was doing it, and I haven't since." Pittman writes that "Kat has angrily retreated from expected high school girl behavior into a haze of grinding music and disdain . . . the film appeals to its target audience by retelling the myth of the independent subject—the young teenager capable of defying all social strictures and forging a self in complete freedom from the world."[34] Through this, Kat attempts to pass on an elder sister's wisdom to Bianca: "You don't always have to be what they want you to be, you know." Bianca's reply indicates the vanity bestowed upon her by the filmmakers: "I happen to like being adored, thank you."

Another side of Kat's character is reinforced by the recurring daily hostilities between Kat and her English teacher, Mr. Morgan (Daryl "Chill" Miller). When she protests the "patriarchal values that dictate our education" which force her to read Ernest Hemingway's *The Sun Also Rises* instead of Sylvia Plath (in one scene at her home, she is reading *The Bell Jar*), Mr. Morgan, an African American, argues that instead of focusing on the problems of "oppressed white girls," they should be wondering why no black writers are taught; he then kicks her out of class. On a day when he delivers up a rap rendition of a Shakespearean sonnet, Mr. Morgan concludes, "I know Shakespeare's a dead white guy, but he knows his shit." He assigns the class to write a sonnet, which Kat will deliver in a penultimate scene.

Coinciding with these slowly revealed insights into Kat is speculation surrounding Patrick Verona. Whereas Petruchio, who is visiting his friend Hortensio in Padua, is known and respected among Paduans, the rumors swirling around Patrick, an Australian in Seattle, settle on his coarser nature. No doubt, Shakespeare portrays a coarse character in Petruchio, but no points of mystery circulate around him. He attacks his servant Grumio, who deems him "quarrelsome"—"He wrings him by the ears" (1.2.13, 18)—and employs trickery and dogma to "tame" Kate, but no questions exist about his motive or his presence in Padua. In fact, he boldly announces upon his arrival that he has "thrust myself into this maze, / Happily to wive and thrive as best I may" (1.2.55–56). Patrick, on the other hand, is rumored to have attacked a police officer, done a year in San Quentin, sold his liver on the Internet, and eaten a live duck.

Also, Petruchio is more than willing to pursue Kate from the offset, given the likely lucrative nature of the dowry. Upon first hearing of Baptista's announcement about marrying off Kate, he declares to Hortensio that he will "wive it wealthily . . . I will not sleep . . . till I see her" (1.2.75,103). Unintimidated by her alleged shrewness, he asks, "Think you a little din can daunt mine ears?"(1.2.199). He boasts, "For I will board her though she chide as loud / As thunder when the clouds in autumn crack" (1.2.95–96). When meeting Baptista, he tells the father that he has heard of Katherina's "beauty and her wit, / Her affability and bashful modesty, / Her wondrous qualities and mild behavior" (2.1.48–50) on learning that he stands to score a dowry of 20,000 crowns and half of Baptista's lands.

Patrick, however, hesitates before asking out Kat, even with money as an object. When Cameron and Michael seek out Patrick in a biker bar to report that Kat hates smokers (Patrick smokes) and "pretty guys" (i.e., Joey) but prefers Thai food, feminist prose, and "angry girl music of the indie rock persuasion," Patrick retorts, "So I'm supposed to buy her some noodles and a book and sit around and listen to chicks who can't play their instruments, right?" The clincher that convinces Patrick, however, is inside information Cameron retrieved from Bianca that Kat wears black underwear.

In Shakespeare, Petruchio also boasts of his ability to tame Kate, telling Baptisa:

> [I]'ll attend her here
> And woo her with some spirit when she comes.
> Say that she rail, why then I'll tell her plain
> She sings as sweetly as a nightingale.
> Say that she frown, I'll say she looks as clear
> As morning roses newly washed with dew.
> Say she be mute and will not speak a word,
> Then I'll commend her volubility
> And say she uttereth piercing eloquence.
> If she do bid me pack, I'll give her thanks
> As though she bid me stay by her for a week.
> If she deny to wed, I'll crave the day
> When I shall ask the banns and when be married.
> (2.1.168–180)

The only such reference to *taming* made in the film, however, is when Patrick boasts to Cameron and Michael that he will "tame the wild beast."

And while Joey's offer of money tugs on Patrick's heart-strings, Petruchio does not hesitate in embracing Baptista's offer of dowry. Even after marrying Kate and setting up house with her at his own home, he presses to return to Padua to receive the dowry, stating to Kate:

> [A]nd now, my honey love,
> Will we return unto thy father's house
> And revel it bravely as the best,
> With silken coats and caps and golden rings,
> With ruffs and cuffs and fardingales and things,
> With scarfs and fans and double change of brav'ry
> With amber bracelets, beads, and all this knave'ry.
>   . . . The tailor stays thy leisure
> To deck thy body with his ruffling treasure.
>   . . . . we will unto your father's,
> Even in these honest mean habiliments.
> Our purses shall be proud, our garments poor,
> For 'tis the mind that makes the body rich,
> And as the sun breaks through the darkest clouds
> So honor peereth in the meanest habit.
> What, is the jay more precious than the lark
> Because his feathers are more beautiful?
> Or is the adder better than the eel
> Because his painted skin contents the eye?
> O no, good Kate, neither art thou the worse
> For this poor furniture and mean array.
> If thou account'st it shame lay it on me,
> And therefore frolic. We will hence forthwith
> To feast and sport us at thy father's house.
>   (4.3.52–60, 169–183)

But Patrick moves back and forth between accepting Joey's money and rejecting it, especially after complications arise in their relationship and he grows in love with Kat, a moral dilemma for the teen genre but not a viable point of guilt that we would find in Shakespeare.

In their earliest meetings, Kat remains true to her principles, blowing off his request for a date as he catches her in the school's multipurpose stadium after her soccer practice. This is their first conversation.

Patrick: Hey there, Girlie. How you doin'?
Kat: Sweating like a pig, actually. And yourself?
Patrick: Now, there's a way to get a guy's attention, huh?

Kat: My mission in life. But obviously, I struck your fancy, so, you see, it worked. The world makes sense again.
Patrick: Pick you up on Friday, then.
Kat: Oh, right. Friday. Uh-huh.
Patrick: Well, the night I take you places you've never been before.
Kat: Like where? The 7–11 on Broadway? Do you even know my name, Screwboy?
Patrick: I know a lot more than you think.
Kat: Doubtful. Very doubtful.[35]

He next catches her at a music equipment store, where she goes to play floor-model electric guitars; again, she brushes off his request. Later in the film, following her into a feminist bookstore does no good either, and she angrily reacts to his semi-stalking. Ultimately, his presence at Club Skunk, where the house band Letters from Cleo (her favorite band) performs, sets their relationship into motion. Stating that he likes the music and that he quit smoking, she reconsiders and begins to warm up to him.

Petruchio and Kate's first encounter, however, is far more volatile than the early interactions between Patrick and Kat. Scene 2.1 explores Petruchio's attempts to charm Kate while she thwarts him with utmost hostility. He first addresses her as

> [P]lain Kate,
> And bonny Kate, and sometimes Kate the curst.
> But, Kate, the prettiest Kate in Christendom,
> Kate of Kate Hall, my super-dainty Kate,
> For dainties are all Kates, and therefore, Kate,
> Take this of me, Kate of my consolation.
> Hearing thy mildness praised in every town,
> Thy virtues spoke of, and thy beauty sounded—
> Yet not so deeply as to thee belongs—
> Myself am moved to woo thee for my wife.
> (2.1.185–193)

Kate replies, "Moved! In good time, let him that moved you hither / Remove you hence. I knew you at the first / You were a movable" (2.1.196–197). She likens him to an ass, a jade, a swain, a buzzard, a fool, no gentleman, a crab, and a "Witless . . . son" (2.1.264). After their initial meeting, Baptista enters, and Petruchio contends to father and daughter that he was "born to tame you, Kate, / and bring you from a wild Kate to a Kate / Conformable as other household Kates" (2.1.276–278). Kate reprimands Baptista for setting her to wed "one half lunatic, / A madcap ruffian and a swearing Jack / That thinks with oaths to face the matter out" (2.1.287–289). Once it is established that she will marry him, Baptista refers to him as "mad-brain rudesby, full of spleen, / Who wooed in haste and means to wed at leisure" (3.2.10–11).

The familiar tête-à-tête and physicality surrounding Petruchio and Kate's first meeting in *Shrew* and Patrick and Kat's in *10 Things* sharply contrast. Demonstrative of the potential for physicality inherent in Shakespeare's play are the two previously mentioned film adaptations of *The Taming of the Shrew*, which both rely on the cinematic convention of physical action more akin to screwball comedies than anything implicitly Shakespearean. This physical comedy is accentuated in both films' treatment of scene 2.1.

The 66-minute 1929 version, directed by Sam Taylor and starring Mary Pickford and Douglas Fairbanks as Kate and Petruchio, as stated earlier, was the first adaptation of a Shakespearean play in the sound era. The film, sporting the new technology, enabled the artists to experiment within Shakespeare's text and simultaneously maintain the audience's usual expectations of physical comedy practiced in silent movies.

Any director taking on this play has to make up for the deficiency of stage directions, since Shakespeare provides only one single direction in the lines that encompass this first meeting. Taylor omits all of this bawdy dialogue:

> *Petruchio:*   Come, come, you wasp, I' faith you are too angry.
> *Kate:*   If I be waspish, best beware my sting.
> *Petruchio:*   My remedy is then to pluck it out.
> *Kate:*   Ay, if the fool could find it where it lies.
> *Petruchio:*   Who knows not where a wasp does wears his sting?
>   In his tail.
> *Kate:*   In his tongue.
> *Petruchio:*   Whose tongue?
> *Kate:*   Yours, if you talk of tales, and so farewell.
> *Petruchio:*   What, with my tongue in your tail? Nay, come again.
>   Good Kate, I am a gentleman.
> *Kate:*   That I'll try.
> *She strikes him.*
>
> (2.1.209–219)

In fact, Taylor's entire script only employs about 500 of Shakespeare's lines, a few from the working script of eighteenth-century actor David

Garrick, and his additional dialogue (which accounts for his notorious co-writing credit in the opening titles). In this scene, Taylor opts to have Pickford and Fairbanks spend the bulk of the scene not talking at all, instead relying on them to taunt each other physically instead of adhere to Shakespeare's 87 lines of dialogue. A mere fraction of this dialogue is presented, but careful physical choreography and visually rhetorical facial expressions substitute for dialogue.

The major sounds that dictate this scene are the cracking of whips and Fairbanks' larger-than-life laughter. As they face off, Petruchio chases after Kate, struggling with her down a staircase. Petruchio cleverly forces Kate to sit in a chair upon his command, achieved on film through a backward movement of the filmed exposures, giving the appearance that Kate is "sucked" into the chair.

Franco Zeffirelli, in his more complete 1967 adaptation featuring Elizabeth Taylor and Richard Burton, imbues the film with over-the-top physical antics that occasionally freeze the text long enough for comedic stunts and romps through elaborate sets.

In this version, Petruchio enters Kate's room while she busily throws furniture and vases across the room. He gains her attention by stating, "Good morrow, Kate." Since Burton was a more classically trained Shakespearean actor than Fairbanks, he easily runs through the famous lines that Taylor and Fairbanks had omitted from their film: "plain Kate . . . bonny Kate . . . Kate the curst," etc. (2.1.184–185). He next tells her he intends to "woo thee for my wife" (2.1.194). Taylor's Kate takes great offense at his presumption and then proceeds with her violent reactions.

Taylor secretly escapes her room into another part of the house where she lands gleefully on a pile of wool, invoking supposition in the viewer that she is actually *pleased* with Petruchio's proposal. But when he finds her, they battle again, this time with her escaping him and getting to an upper level that overlooks the pile of wool. Burton's Petruchio next does a parodic swashbuckling turn as he grabs a swing hanging from a ceiling and rides it up to Kate's position. As he approaches her a second time, she cuts one of the ropes, causing him to fall into the pile of wool. He stands up, grabs the remaining rope, and swings up to the second floor, this time crashing through a wooden railing. Kate runs out a window onto the roof of Baptista's house. Petruchio follows, and once he catches up with her, they fall through the roof and land onto the wool. Shakespeare's lines are presented at various moments throughout this struggle, but the scene more predominantly focuses on the physical choreography.

10 Things I Hate about You, however, relies less on physicality between the two leads and more on the early taunting dialogue between them.

Petruchio and Patrick both attempt to gain attention with over-the-top displays. Petruchio's well-known arrival at their wedding draws gasps from everyone. Biodello, one of Lucentio's servants, announces to the party that

> Petruchio is coming in a new hat and an old jerkin; a pair of old breeches thrice turned; a pair of boots that have been candle-cases, one buckled, another laced; an old rusty sword ta'en out of the town armory, with a broken hilt and capeless; with two broken points; his horse hipped (with an old mothy saddle and stirrups of no kindred), besides, possessed with the glanders and like to mose in the chine; troubled with the lampass, infected with the fashions, full of wind-galls, sped with spavins, rayed with the yellows, past cure of the fives, stark spoiled with the staggers, begnawn with the bots, swayed in the back, and shoulder-shotten; near-legged before, and with a half-cheeked bit and a head-stall of sheep's leather, which, being restrained to keep him from stumbling, hath been often burst and now repaired with knots; one girth six time pieced, and woman's crupper of velure, which hath two letters and her name fairly set down in studs, and here and there pieced with packthread. (3.2.43–63)

Patrick, instead, pays a marching band student to get the band to perform "I Love You, Baby," while the Media Geeks give him access to the stadium microphone, on which he sings the song during Kat's soccer practice. Knowing he is singing to her, she finally acquiesces to his attempts simply by smiling. As he sings, Patrick runs across the stadium stands, attempting to elude school security officials who are chasing him down.

Kat and Patrick's relationship takes an upward swing as they ditch school to run around Seattle, taking a paddle boat ride and enjoying an afternoon of paint ball. To start this sequence, Junger presents another bawdy and unlikely scene involving a teacher. Patrick, placed in Kat's soccer coach's detention hall, sneaks out the window while Kat distracts the apparently pot-headed, Cheeto's-munching teacher (implied by items he has confiscated from students in detention) with a flash of her naked chest (the PG-13 audience is spared; her back is to the camera as she lifts her shirt). Their idyllic day out takes the form of the music-video montage (set to such lyrics as "Fascinating . . . Somebody wants you . . . You're perfect . . . I'm surprised") and culminates in their first kiss on a bale of hay at the paint-ball facility.

The day promises to end perfectly as they return to Kat's house and sit on her front porch weighing in on their notorious reputations and the principles they hold. She argues, "Why should I live up to other people's expectations instead of my own?" Simultaneously, he denies all the rumors about himself that have been built up around the school. He musters up the courage to ask her to prom, but she calls prom a "stupid tradition." Patrick presses on, prompting Kat to bear her suspicion in his request: "Why are you pushing this? What's in it for you?" His integrity challenged, he lifts a cigarette in anger, provoking her to leave him hanging.

Petruchio and Kate's married life outside Padua is covered in two scenes, one in his country house and the other on the road back to Padua when he is intent on receiving his dowry. In his home, he rails at his servants Grumio and Curtis, attempting to prove his dominant nature in front of Kate. These charades carry an influence on her, though, as Curtis reports that he witnessed her in her chamber, "[sitting] as one new-arisen from a dream" (4.1.186). Meanwhile, Petruchio shares with his servants his plans to starve her, to complain, to keep her from sleeping, anything "to tame a shrew" (4.1.210). Kate eventually grows submissive to Petruchio, turning as agreeable here as she formerly was shrewish. On the road back to Padua, he convinces her to call the sun the moon and then turn around and call it the sun again. She states, "But sun it is not when you say it is not, / And the moon changes even as your mind. / What you will have it named, even that it is, / And so it shall be for Katherine" (4.5.19–22).

Community events yield further contrasts to Shakespeare's play. A typical high school house party, complete with fights breaking out, the glass patio door getting broken, and other shenanigans, tracks two situations unfolding, the Cameron–Bianca–Joey triangle and the Patrick–Kat situation. Upset over Bianca's interest in Joey and feeling pressure from Patrick to move forward, Kat drinks several shots of hard liquor, and the next thing Patrick knows, she is dancing provocatively on a dining room table. Spinning out of control, she hits her head on a chandelier, so Patrick swiftly carries her out to keep her awake. Meanwhile, Cameron becomes aware of Bianca's apparently greater interest in Joey than in him, so he hurtfully mopes around the party until catching Patrick. He tells him the deal is off because Bianca has no interest in him. Patrick encourages him to "go for it," to seek Bianca. At the same time, however, Bianca's interest in Joey diminishes when she realizes that he is nothing more than an arrogant braggart. He brags of his modeling resume—his Sears catalog shots, the forthcoming sock ad, and a hemorrhoid cream ad. By the time he starts posing his model stances for the crowd, Bianca appears disenchanted with him entirely. When Bianca tells Joey of her curfew, he chooses to take her friend Chastity home instead, which then leads her to ask Cameron for a ride home. After Cameron pulls his car in front of Bianca's house, he asks, "Have you always been this selfish?" He admits he learned French to become her French tutor, which awards him a spontaneous kiss goodnight. As she exits the car, he declares to himself, "And I'm back in the game!" Kat and Patrick's ride home ends less happily. She states that her father wishes she was more delicate, like Bianca, but Patrick declares that he prefers Kat to the likes of Bianca. This draws Kat to lean over and kiss Patrick goodnight; he declines because he is conflicted over his feelings for her while taking money from Joey. The scene ends in yet another angry departure between the two.

The other big event, the prom, opens with Kat meeting up with Patrick at the school, congenially telling him she is sorry for having ever questioned his motives. Kat's love for him is especially apparent as he directs her attention to the stage to catch the prom band kicking into "Cruel To Be Kind," with the Letters to Cleo vocalist joining the band, all arranged by Patrick. Both couples blissfully enjoy the prom until Joey comes between Patrick and Kat on the dance floor, upset over Bianca's choice of Cameron over him, and loudly reveals that he had paid Patrick to date Kat. Patrick now has to clear himself of the motive and explain to Kat that he has developed true feelings for her, which she is not buying, while Joey then confronts Bianca and Cameron, punching Cameron in the face. Bianca, learning from Chastity, Joey's back-up prom date, that he had laid wager with his friends that he had planned to take Bianca to prom and then have sex with her, retaliates by punching Joey's nose and kneeing him in the groin. Michael Eckman, witnessing the unfolding events, expresses, "The shit hath hitteth the fan!"

These events contrast to the public ceremonies in *The Taming of the Shrew*. Petruchio and Kate's wedding is not seen onstage, but Shakespeare chooses to narrate it through Gremio's recount to Tranio:

> [W]hen the priest
> Should ask, if Katherine should be his wife,
> "Ay by goggs woones!" quoth he and swore so loud
> That, all amazed, the priest let fall the book,
> And as he stopped again to take it up,

> This mad-brained bridegroom took him such a cuff
> That down fell priest and book and book and priest.
> "Now, take them up," quoth he, "if any list."
> . . . he stamped and swore
> As if vicar meant to cozen him.
> But after many ceremonies done
> He calls for wine. "A health!" quoth he as if
> He had been aboard, carousing to his mates
> After a storm; quaffed off the muscadel
> And threw the sops all in the sexton's face,
> Having no other reason
> But that his beard grew thin and hungerly,
> And seemed to ask him sops as he was drinking.
> This done, he took the bride about the neck
> And kissed her lips with such a clamorous smack
> That at the parting all the church did echo . . .
>   (3.2.158–165, 167–179)

Petruchio reenters the scene after his wedding, declaring that he will now return to his home. Kate pleads with him to stay for their reception, but he finally declares that they both will leave, referring to Kate as "my goods, my chattels . . . my house, / My household stuff, my field, my barn, / My horse, my ox, my ass, my anything" (3.2.230–232). Again, Petruchio establishes his dominance in the marriage. Patrick, however, never presents such a challenge and, despite his earlier claim, never overtly tries to tame Kat.

Shakespeare's final scene takes place at Lucentio's home during the feast commemorating the three weddings of Petruchio and Kate, Bianca and Lucentio, and Hortensio and his wealthy Widow. The new husbands wager 100 crowns that their wives will come attend to them at their beckoning. Neither Bianca nor the Widow come through for their husbands, but Kate famously does, giving Petruchio cause to boast his dominance over his new bride. When Bianca and the Widow reenter, laughing off the proclaimed "duty," Petruchio urges Kate to "tell these head-strong women / What duty they do owe their lords and husbands" (5.2.130–131). Kate delivers her famous speech:

> Fie, fie! unknit that threatening unkind brow,
> And dart not scornful glances from those eyes,
> To wound thy lord, thy king, thy governor:
> It blots thy beauty as frosts do bite the meads,
> Confounds thy fame as whirlwinds shake fair buds,

And in no sense is meet or amiable.
A woman moved is like a fountain troubled,
Muddy, ill-seeming, thick, bereft of beauty;
And while it is so, none so dry or thirsty
Will deign to sip or touch one drop of it.
Thy husband is thy lord, thy life, thy keeper,
Thy head, thy sovereign; one that cares for thee,
And for thy maintenance commits his body
To painful labour both by sea and land,
To watch the night in storms, the day in cold,
Whilst thou liest warm at home, secure and safe;
And craves no other tribute at thy hands
But love, fair looks and true obedience;
Too little payment for so great a debt.
Such duty as the subject owes the prince
Even such a woman oweth to her husband;
And when she is froward, peevish, sullen, sour,
And not obedient to his honest will,
What is she but a foul contending rebel
And graceless traitor to her loving lord?
I am ashamed that women are so simple
To offer war where they should kneel for peace;
Or seek for rule, supremacy and sway,
When they are bound to serve, love and obey.
Why are our bodies soft and weak and smooth,
Unapt to toil and trouble in the world,
But that our soft conditions and our hearts
Should well agree with our external parts?
Come, come, you froward and unable worms!
My mind hath been as big as one of yours,
My heart as great, my reason haply more,
To bandy word for word and frown for frown;
But now I see our lances are but straws,
Our strength as weak, our weakness past compare,
That seeming to be most which we indeed least are.
Then vail your stomachs, for it is no boot,
And place your hands below your husband's foot:
In token of which duty, if he please,
My hand is ready; may it do him ease.

                                        (5.2.136–178)

While the speech indicates Kat's "reform," staging that follows differs in productions; for instance, Pickford winks at the camera at the end of Sam Taylor's film, ironically hinting at her own trickery, while

Elizabeth Taylor quickly exits the feast out of Burton's reach as Zeffirelli's film closes.

In *10 Things*, though, Kat expresses sentiment through her sonnet assignment, which is neither iambic nor pentametric. Having learned of Patrick and Joey's deal, she writes of her disappointment in herself for falling for him in the first place. She rises before the class and reads the *sixteen*-line sonnet, delivering it directly to Patrick as he sits in the back of the room.

> I hate the way you talk to me
> and the way you cut your hair.
> I hate the way you drive my car.
> I hate it when you stare.
> I hate your big dumb combat boots
> and the way you read my mind.
> I hate you so much it makes me sick.
> It even makes me rhyme.
> I hate the way you're always right.
> I hate it when you lie.
> I hate it when you make me laugh,
> even worse when you make me cry.
> I hate it when you're not around
> and the fact that you didn't call,
> But mostly I hate the way I don't hate you,
> not even close, not even a little bit, not even at all.[36]

Yet ambiguity does not cloud *10 Things*' ending. Kat goes to her car after school, still upset over Patrick, to find a white Fender Stratocaster sitting in her front seat, one which Patrick had seen her playing in the music store. They renew their feelings for one another, and the film turns to closing credits, accompanied by Letters from Cleo's rooftop video of the song "I Want You To Want Me," followed by a blooper reel of the actors in various takes.

Aside from the loose adaptation and the sonnet assignment, the only other direct reference to Shakespeare is Michael Eckman's role as the school know-it-all; the establishment of the school's demographic rest on his word not only for Cameron but also for the audience. He serves as a surrogate for Shakespeare himself. He also builds a crush on Kat's friend Mandella (Susan May Pratt) and learns of a mutual interest they share in the Bard, prompted by her statement that Kat hates Patrick "with the fire of a thousand suns." This later leads Michael to invite her to prom by placing a Renaissance-era dress in her locker with a note attached requesting, "O fair one, Join me at the Prom. I will be waiting. Love, William S." While she reads and peruses the dress with adulation, the filmmakers insert Renaissance-era (or contemporaneously remodeled) harpsichord music in the soundtrack.

Michael also speaks "Shakespeare-ese" to Patrick while urging him to continue pursuing Kat even after she has given him one of her brush-offs. Michael says, "Sweet love, renew thy force," while Cameron stresses, "Sacrifice yourself on the altar of dignity and even the score." Patrick quickly scopes his surroundings and in his most macho tone snaps back at them, "Hey, don't say shit like that to me. People can hear you." Whether irreverent or not, the reaction to such "dialect" presupposes both the discomfort and even possible homophobia aligned in this episode with the elevated language and simultaneously reduces Shakespearean dialect to a patchwork of clichés. *10 Things'* universe is one whose parlance includes "crack whores," "skeezy boyfriends," and the clause "You suck." While this cursory adaptation of the play indicates that Shakespeare can offer credibility to even the slightest of ideas, the filmmakers' trivialization of their source contravenes any notion that their work does anything to repay the favor.

Othello, Like, Almost Literally

A reader or viewer scrambling around all parts of *10 Things I Hate about You* to discern which elements of *The Taming of the Shrew* weigh in at what time may easily track the linear coordinates of *Othello* in "*O.*" Director Tim Blake Nelson traces the source closely, telling the story of Hugo (Josh Hartnett), an overshadowed starting member of the Palmetto Grove High School Hawks, a South Carolina prep-school basketball team, who decides to exact revenge on Odin James (Mekhi Phifer), the team's star player and the school's only African American student. Hugo's father, the team's Coach Duke Goulding (Martin Sheen), awards Odin the Most Valuable Player award after the team wins a regional championship and announces at a pep rally that he loves Odin "like my own son." Adding insult to Hugo's injured spirit, Odin then publicly recognizes Michael Cassio (Andrew Keegan, *10 Things'* Joey Donner) and not Hugo for his contribution to the state-championship-bound team. Hugo confides in Roger (Elden Henson), a ridiculed rich kid who has an eye for Dean Bob Brable's (John Heard) daughter, Desi (Julia Stiles, formerly Kat of *10 Things*), that Odin has secretly been romantically involved with her. To try to break up Odin and Desi, Hugo urges Roger to call the dean to warn him of this disreputable match. The father's reaction in discovering the secret relationship matches that of the play's Brabanzio.

At a party following another basketball victory, Hugo next orchestrates a fight between Roger and Odin's right-hand man, Michael, whom Hugo has gotten intoxicated. After the fight, the Coach suspends Michael, and Odin dissociates himself from his once-favored teammate. Hugo now renews what was once a close friendship with Odin, suggesting to him that Michael and Desi seem to spend a lot of time together and are possibly having a relationship behind Odin's back. Odin, once on top of the world, now becomes consumed with jealousy. To accentuate the yet-to-be-confirmed possibility, Hugo puts his girlfriend Emily (Rain Phoenix) up to snatching a scarf from Desi, her roommate, one given to her by Odin, a keepsake from his deceased mother. The rest of "O" directly mirrors *Othello*, showing Odin's social breakdown, Hugo's manipulation of Michael, the passage of the scarf from Michael to his concealed girlfriend Brandy (Rachel Shumate), and Roger's involvement in Hugo's scheme. The film ends in a bloodbath claiming the same casualties as in *Othello*. When pressed to explain why he did what he did, Hugo, the true incarnation of Iago, states, "From here on out, I say nothing."

While the "MTV style" distinguished Luhrmann's *Romeo + Juliet* in critics' eyes, responses to "O" rested on the film's reflection of contemporary school violence, notably the shootings in Arkansas and Kentucky and most especially the meticulously orchestrated tragedy at Columbine. However, Kaaya's script and Nelson's filming of "O" pre-dated Columbine, and Nelson was working on postproduction when the event in Littleton, Colorado, took place. Hugo's closing monologue combined with the violent events of *Othello* too eerily reflected real events and headlines, so Miramax shelved the film for a couple of years, until the film was purchased by Lions Gate, who released it in 2001.

Ebert defends the film and criticizes Miramax's disinclination to release it. He writes,

> We have a peculiar inability in our country to understand the contexts of things; when it comes to art, we interpret troublesome works in the most literal and simple-minded way. In the aftermath of Columbine, Washington legislators called on Hollywood to police itself, and rumbled about possible national censorship. Miramax caved in by

suppressing this film. To suggest that "O" was part of the solution and not part of the problem would have required a sophistication that our public officials either lack, or are afraid to reveal, for fear of offending the bottom-feeders among their constituents.[37]

The film's structure, as stated earlier, almost exactly mirrors that of *Othello*, but it also offers some background information that helps feed Hugo's rage against Odin before he starts plotting. Iago's motive in the play is clarified when he states to Roderigo that Othello chose Michael Cassio as his first officer: "Preferment goes by letter and affection, / And not by old gradation, where each second / Stood heir to the first" (1.1.36–38). However, Othello's selection of Cassio may not be the only manifestation of his jealousy. Even Othello's top-line military position seems to be something he envies:

> I do suspect the lusty Moor
> Hath leapt into my seat, the thought whereof
> Doth, like a poisonous mineral, gnaw my inwards;
> And nothing can or shall content my soul
> Till I am evened with him.
>
> (2.1.295–299)

Camera shots of a flock of doves open the film, set to the tune of the aria from Verdi's opera *Otello*. Hugo's opening monologue joins the mix of cooing birds and the soprano's vocal: "All my life, I always wanted to fly. I always wanted to live like a hawk. I know you're not supposed to be jealous of anything, but to take flight, to soar above everything and everyone—now that's living." Steve Criniti sates that "the qualities of the hawk that are highlighted by the film's images and by Hugo's opening monologue are its freedom, originality, and high stature."[38]

The film then quickly makes transition to the sounds of contemporary hip-hop and a shot of a hawk, the basketball team's trained mascot, flying around the gymnasium during a divisional championship game. In a time-out prior to a last-second play, the coach assigns the team to set up either Odin or Michael to attempt the final shot, announcing that Hugo will act as decoy during the last play. It is Odin's final-second shot that wins the game and advances the team to the next level of play-offs. While the crowd rushes onto the court and gives the victorious Odin a ride on their shoulders after the final buzzer, Hugo watches on, ignored and disillusioned.

The pep rally that follows the next school day worsens Hugo's jealousy. His father states before the entire student body that he loves

Odin "like my own son." Odin, receiving a MVP award, further recognizes Michael as his "go-to guy," once again agitating Hugo. Criniti notes that the father–son relationship included by the filmmakers "heightens the intensity of Hugo's jealousy and provides a much clearer motivation for the ensuing crimes Hugo is supplanted in his role of son by Odin . . . assigning a clearer motivation . . . is most likely a practical attempt at maximizing audience comprehension." Having Hugo's father patronize Odin more than his own son gives the audience a viable "narrative consistency. If this comprehension is not established early, the power and message of the remainder of the film is lost."[39]

The film intersects with the play's first scene at a celebration party following the pep rally. While Odin and his girlfriend Desi dance in a bump and grind fashion, Hugo summons Roger, this film's Roderigo, and tells him he knows a way to break up Odin and Desi, thus freeing her up for Roger to pursue. Roger acts surprised, thinking Hugo and Odin are friends. Hugo counts this impression as "perfect, because if we're gonna do this, I gotta act like I'm cool with him anyway" a variation of Iago's confidence that "The Moor is of a free and open nature, / That thinks men honest that but seem to be so, / And will as tenderly be led by th' nose / As asses are" (1.3.399–402).

Hugo tells Roger that he is the team's "utility man" who rebounds and plays any position, useful to the team insofar as his being the one who sets up the stars of the team to gain their glory. "I'm the MVP on this piece of shit team," he declares. "I've been bangin' in the paint and settin' screens for the past four years and he [Odin] chooses Michael, a fuckin' sophomore—no way!" Hugo's motive, spelled out as distinctly as Iago's, is rooted in his desire for attention. Iago states that he will "follow [Othello] to serve my turn upon him . . . In following him I follow but myself" (1.1.42–44, 58), indicating how Othello's trust will serve his scheme: "Though I do hate him as I do hell pains—/ Yet for necessity of present life / I must show out a flag and sign of love, / Which is indeed but sign" (1.1.154–157).

He commands Roderigo to call out to Brabanzio to inform him of Desdemona and Othello's secret marriage. And while Roderigo does so directly, identifying himself to Brabanzio, Iago, tucked and hidden out of Brabanzio's sight, anonymously makes racist and racy remarks about Othello within Brabanzio's earshot: "an old black ram / Is tupping your white ewe" (1.1.88–89) and "your daughter and the Moor are now making the beast with two backs" (1.1.115–117).

In the film, we learn that Roger's father has endowed so much money to the school that the library is named after him, so Hugo uses this point to convince Roger of the possible influence he may carry with the dean in outing Desi and Odin. Standing outside Dean Brable's house, Roger places a cell phone call to the dean, waking him up in the middle of the night. Roger announces that someone has "stolen" his daughter. The scene ends with the dean angrily asking, "What about my daughter?"

Just as Brabanzio accuses Othello of using witchcraft and chemicals to seduce Desdemona away from him, Dean Brable brings Odin up before the coach and drudges up the student's past with drugs and the police as just cause for his suspicion that he poses danger to Desi. The coach defends Odin, just as the duke takes Othello's side against Brabanzio, an interesting reversal of power roles between the sources, wherein a duke is transformed into a school's coach while a duke's subject is analogous to the higher level administrator. In the play, Othello boasts his service to the state as justification for his marriage to Desdemona; the film's Odin has done a great deal for this school's basketball team, so he states to the dean and coach that he will leave the school if Desi says he has done anything out of line toward her.

Desi enters the coach's office and admits that she and Odin have secretly been together for four months. When the dean presses her for more information about their relationship, she tells her father that it's none of his business, a modern-day adaptation of Desdemona's speech regarding a daughter's shift of allegiance from father to husband after she marries. The meeting ends with Odin assuring the dean of his love for Desi, but the dean echoes Brabanzio's famous line, "Look to her, Moor, if thou hast eyes to see. / She has deceived her father, and may thee" (1.3.292–293), stating, "She deceived me. What makes you think she won't do the same to you?"

The Hawks' second game in the film opens with the team entering the high school's red, white, and blue gym amidst spotlights, dry ice, and loud hip-hop. Nelson states that the American flag's presence is prominent in film in order to create "an American version of Shakespeare's tragic tale." He also wished to emphasize the audacity of Americans' interest in high school sports, stating that his "cheesy introduction of the team" entering the gym meant to represent a "completely overblown and hilarious" display.[40] Ebert likens high school sports to "a kind of warfare," stating that sports in American high schools are "considered more important than study, generating heroism and resentment too powerful for most kids to cope with, and inspiring in their bitter backwash the kind of alienation we saw at Columbine."[41]

The game results in another victory for Palmetto Grove, but this time with Odin suffering an injury on the floor. As the coach, Hugo, Emily, Michael, and Desi meet him at the hospital, Odin enters the waiting area, catching Michael and Desi in an embrace as they express concern for Odin's well-being. Odin jokes, "What's the deal? Gone for a coupla hours, you already takin' my girl, Big Mike?" Hugo's attention is riveted to this statement and reminds the viewer of Iago's observation of Cassio and Desdemona's private conversations: "He takes her by the palm" (2.1.167). After Odin's release from the hospital, all the teen characters plan to attend an off-campus party, the film's version of Othello's homecoming celebration after returning from battle. Hugo goes to a pay phone and contacts Roger to set into motion in "O" what the play's Iago depicts as "double knavery" against Othello, Cassio, and Desdemona (1.3.394).

The film audience is not privy to this scheme until it is in progress as the play's audience is. While Iago delivers his plan to Roderigo to agitate Cassio, Nelson and Kaaya present Hugo commanding Roger to get going with the plan without revelation to the audience what that plan is. Shakespeare's Roderigo angers Cassio offstage, and when the two run onto the stage, Shakespeare has Montano intervene, which turns to swordplay between Montano and Cassio. This action disturbs Othello's homecoming bliss, and he dismisses Cassio from his ranks for his intoxication and involvement in the disruption.

In the case of the film, though, Roger annoys Michael on-screen by interrupting his conversation with a girl at the party, which gradually leads Michael to beating up Roger. The next day at school, the coach hauls Odin, Michael, and Hugo into his office and suspends Michael from the team for the next two games. Reprimanding Michael, he states that this suspension is going to disrupt the team's performance, which is especially shameful after Odin had held Michael up as a co-MVP. After they exit the office, Hugo overhears Odin say to Michael, "You fucked this up, Dogs. You fucked up." At dinner that night, Hugo hypothetically asks his father if Odin would have been suspended for the same behavior Michael had exhibited, which draws a dismissive response from the coach. Nelson reminds us that the father–son conflict in "O" reinforces Hugo's variation of Iago's motive.

After Cassio's dismissal, he bemoans, "Reputation, reputation, reputation—O, I ha' lost my reputation, I ha' lost the immortal part of myself, and what remains is bestial! My reputation, Iago, my reputation" (2.3.262–265). Iago claims reputation to be "an idle and most false imposition, oft got without merit and lost without deserving" and suggests that Cassio should attempt to gain Othello's favor by appealing to Desdemona and getting her to convince Othello to take him back (2.3.268–270). Confident that this may work, Cassio leaves the scene with this plan. Iago, in another soliloquy, expresses to the audience that he will subtly poison Cassio and Desdemona in Othello's eyes, knowing the Moor's reputed jealousy.

In "O," Hugo and Michael hold a similar conversation in the school library the day after Michael's suspension. Michael discusses how his parents, concerned with his reputation, will be disappointed with him over this situation. Hugo says that worrying about reputation are the concerns of a "Mama's boy." They then carry their conversation outside, and Hugo convinces Michael that to get to the coach's good side, he has to gain Odin's favor again, and by extention, the best way will be through spending a lot of time with Desi. "You gotta hang with her," he claims. "That's the only way this thing works. It's worth a shot, Bro." Like Cassio, Michael agrees.

At the third game in the film, Hugo begins to gain some of the praise usually reserved for Michael, thus placing him in Odin's favor. During a time-out, Hugo signals Michael, sitting on the bench, to go into the stands and accompany Desi. On the court, Odin and Hugo become the two-man powerhouse that once included Michael. The Hawks win again, but Odin's victorious spirit is briefly snuffed by his sight of Michael and Desi hugging in the stands.

The next scene in both play and film drives the remaining narrative. Three earlier sound-era film adaptations of *Othello* handle scene 3.3, lines 91 to 263 in disparate ways, and "O" is no exception. Shakespeare's scene involves Iago's first suggestion to Othello that Desdemona and Cassio might be intimately involved with one another, which is immediately followed by Desdemona's entrance and encounter with Othello. The films directed by Orson Welles (1952), Stuart Burge and Laurence Olivier (1965), and Oliver Parker (1995) differ in setting choices, textual omissions, film continuity cuts, and, most importantly, the emotive stances taken by the actors portraying Othello and Iago.

The scene greatly advances the story, with Iago's references and Othello's responses coming on the heels of each other, with a second speaker's lines often completing the iambic pentameter of a first speaker's verse. The passage exposes the reader to the major ideas that dictate the play, including Othello's steadfastness to Desdemona and an indication of how he would react were he not to love her.

> But I do love thee! And when I love thee not,
> Chaos is come again.
>
> (3.3.91–92)

Iago's speech on reputation:

> Good name in man and woman, dear my lord,
> Is the immediate jewel of their souls.
> Who steals my purse steals trash; 'tis something, nothing:
> 'Twas mine, 'tis his, and has been slave to thousands;
> But he that filches from me my good name
> Robs me of that which not enriches him
> And makes me poor indeed.

(3.3.155–161)

Iago's advice:

> Look to your wife; observe her well with Cassio;
> Wear your eyes thus: not jealous nor secure,
> I would not have your free and noble nature
> Out of self-bounty be abused. Look to't.

(3.3.197–200)

Iago's warning:

> She did deceive her father, marrying you;
> And when she seemed to shake and fear your looks,
> She loved them most.

(3.3.206–208)

Othello's first, short soliloquy:

> Why did I marry? This honest creature doubtless
> Sees and knows more, much more, than he unfolds.

(3.3.242–243)

and his second, longer one:

> If I do prove her haggard,
> Though that her jesses were my dear heartstrings,
> I'd whistle her off and let her down the wind
> To prey at fortune.

(3.3.260–263)

Lines 90 to 240 contain no stage directions. The first direction announced by Shakespeare comes very late in the scene, as Iago is directed to "go" the first time he announces his leave and then "returns" after Othello wonders, "Why did I marry?" Desdemona and Emilia's entrance is announced, and after Othello says to Desdemona, "Your napkin is too little," Shakespeare writes that "He pushes the handkerchief away, and it falls." Lastly, Shakespeare announces that Othello and Desdemona exit after she tells him that she is sorry he doesn't feel well.

Welles' *Othello* suffers from deep cuts into Shakespeare's text, a necessity given Welles' typically limited finances during productions. Approximately 200 measured lines between the two characters would normally take 15 to 20 minutes to perform in their entirety; Welles' cuts, however, shorten the scene to a fast-paced six-and-a-half minutes. Characterization and performance dictate the adaptation here. Micheál MacLiammóir's Iago, according to Roger Manvell, possesses "coldly cerebral villainy . . . he is quiet spoken, Elizabethan Machiavel, who knows how to set about his business."[42] MacLiammóir himself recalls Welles' interpretation of the part before production began.

> Iago, [Welles said], was . . . impotent; this secret malady was, in fact, to be the keystone of the actor's approach . . . "Impotent," [Welles] roared in (surely somewhat forced) rich bass baritone, "that's why he hates life so much—they always do," continued he (voice by this time way down in boots).[43]

Welles envisioned an acceptable "honest honest Iago reputation." Iago has no conscious villainy, he believed, but is instead a common man, with thoughts moving from one to the next: "a business man dealing in destruction with neatness, method, and a proper pleasure in his work."[44]

Welles' characterization of Othello seems to facilitate the theme of jealousy and rage very early on in this scene. With no time for the character to perform more slowly and deliberately the material that Shakespeare less succinctly presents, one might say that Welles' version, whether due to financing problems or a simple desire to condense the material, certainly exhibits a quick metamorphosis in Othello's character.

The scene opens with a tracking shot following Othello and Iago as they move along a castle terrace. Iago opens the dialogue, asking about Cassio, and Othello and the camera stop moving on Othello's line, "Nay, there's more in this?" Welles' grim countenance attests to Othello's instant suspicion. Two alternating cameras then jump back and forth between close-ups of both characters, during which time Iago tells Othello to "look to your wife."

They next enter an armory, wherein Iago says, "I see this hath a little dashed your spirits," to which Othello replies, "Not a jot, not a jot."

The camera captures the back of Welles' head as well as his distraught face in a mirror. After Othello states that he believes Desdemona is "honest," Iago states:

Iago: Long live she so. And long live you to think so.
Othello: And yet, how nature erring from itself—
Iago: Ay, there's the point . . .

The music rises as Iago speaks. Othello violently walks away, and Iago follows him as he continues to speak. At this point, Shakespeare calls for Othello to dismiss Iago, to which he says, "My lord, I take my leave." The play directs Iago to leave, but Welles chooses to include neither the direction to leave nor the gesture. Instead, he condenses the action and dialogue to have Iago conclude by asking Othello to "scan this thing no farther" and to "Leave it to time," after which he exits for good.

Next, Desdemona (Suzanne Cloutier) enters to join Welles' Othello. Seeing he is not well, she offers her handkerchief to him. Shakespeare's lines go as follows:

Desdemona: . . . Let me but bind it hard, within this hour
   It will be well.
Othello: Your napkin is too little;
   [He pushes the handkerchief away, and it falls.]
   Let it alone. Come, I'll go in with you.
Desdemona: I am very sorry that you are not well.

                              Exit [with Othello].

However, Welles completely revises this passage. His Othello vigorously snatches the handkerchief away from her, throws it to the floor, and steps on it as he exits the room into a hallway, in which he once again looks at his image in a mirror. Desdemona follows him into the hallway, and he moves toward her. He embraces her face, yet he is still horrified. Emilia (Fay Compton) is seen in a brief shot taking the handkerchief, thus advancing Iago's scheme. Othello next races from Desdemona to their bedchamber and violently pulls open the curtain to display the bed. Desdemona swiftly exits.

The 1965 version is a filmization of a production directed by Laurence Olivier at the National Theatre of Great Britain; the stage cast members appear under Olivier's direction, while Stuart Burge directs the soundstage cameras and other technical aspects. This production cuts nothing from the stage version, enabling the players to re-create their performances with little disruption by the cameras as possible.[45]

Manvell writes of this film, "The resources of the cinema are used with almost painstaking restraint, especially for a film of this length [three hours]."[46] Davies writes, "The cinematic dimension . . . tends to take the form of an overlay and to be, at best, unevenly integrated with the more dominant dramatic conventions and aesthetics of the theatre."[47] A distinction must be made, he states, between Shakespeare as filmed drama and as dramatic film. Burge switches between three Panavision cameras and uses television-style editing, while Olivier maintains his original stage blocking.[48] However, as Davies observes, the viewer must be aware that his or her concentration is restricted to only part of a theatrical presentation because of the medium of film.[49]

Scene 3.3, then, in its near entirety, runs thirteen and three-quarters minutes in this second film. The first shot after Desdemona and Emilia's departure is a close-up frame of Othello. He begins the speech ("Excellent wretch!") from this position, but a second shot follows him diagonally as he walks across the stage. As the camera moves and he speaks, Iago (Frank Finlay) is seen in the left side of the background.

Finlay reveals a more inquisitive Iago than MacLiammoír. Olivier's jovial Othello speaks loudly and assertively, and he animates the part by enacting such gestures as patting Iago on the shoulder while responding to the questions. When Iago says that Cassio is an honest man, he turns to walk away but is stopped in his tracks when Othello replies, "Nay, yet there's more in this?" Olivier's character detects wrongdoings without immediately giving in to jealousy; he even colors his phrases with chuckles and outbursts of laughter. When Iago warns Othello to "beware of jealousy," Olivier boastfully delivers Othello's self-defense:

> Think'st thou I'd make a life of jealousy,
> To follow still the changes of the moon
> With fresh suspicions? No! To be once in doubt
> Is to be resolved.

But once Iago commands Othello to "Look to your wife," all confidence is drained from Olivier's character. Finlay, upon his exit, hides in the background without leaving during Olivier's first, short soliloquy ("Why did I marry?"), a departure from Welles' film. He then regains Othello's attention and implores Othello not to worry about this, to which Olivier piercingly shouts, "FEAR NOT MY GOVERNMENT!" Iago then take his leave.

Olivier next launches into Othello's long soliloquy, which Burge captures in three shots. Olivier's treatment of the married couple's interaction also differs greatly from Welles'. Whereas Welles presents Othello as instantly repulsed by Desdemona's presence, Olivier responds gently to Desdemona (Maggie Smith). She stands behind him and puts her hand on his forehead. The viewer sees the terror disappear from his face and a charming expression emerge. He grabs her hand and adorns it with kisses, and the two of them laugh together. He pulls the napkin away gracefully, and the two kiss lightly and hug. Othello's face becomes one of grimacing denial, and he exits the scene arm and arm with Desdemona. Emilia (Joyce Redman) runs to the handkerchief and takes it.

Lastly, Oliver Parker's 1995 production eliminates nearly half of the play's lines, and sports Kenneth Branagh (Iago) and Laurence Fishburne (Othello) in the lead roles. A great variation lies in Parker's adaptation of act 3, scene 3 in ways that reinterpret the scene's pacing, both in terms of Iago's deliberations and the swelling of the seed planted in Othello's mind. The segment is actually broken into four scenes over eight and a half minutes, with time lapses between each setting, giving Othello time to digest the possibility of Iago's suggestions more deliberately.

The first scene occurs in a courtyard. Othello looks up at Desdemona (Irene Jacob) as she waves at him from a terrace, and he states the opening line of this sequence ("Excellent wretch!"). Iago opens the discussion as they stand in this position: "Did Michael Cassio, when you wooed my lady, / Know of your love?" to which Othello replies, "He did, from first to last," which is only half of Shakespeare's line. The film scene ends.

The continuity cut carries the viewer to the midst of a staircase where the men are washing after a session of sword sparring. The second half of Othello's line is completed here: "Why dost thou ask?" Several moments have passed since Iago's initial question and provides viewers with the impression that during the time it took the men to walk from the courtyard to the stairs, Othello had been wondering why Iago raised the question.

The film next cuts to the interior of an armory, where the men are dropping off arms and Othello is cleaning a pistol. Branagh's Iago revises both MacLiammóir's and Finlay's versions as he responds to Othello's questions in apparent afterthought, with quiet, uninquisitive replies, which increases Othello's attempts to get to the bottom of this. When Iago begins his famous speech on "Good name in man and woman," the scene is textured with music slowly rising and close-up shots of Othello's hands as he loads a pistol (setting this film well past the Renaissance). After the gun is loaded, Othello towers over Iago, who is seated, and presses the barrel into his chest: "By heaven, I'll know thy thoughts!" When Iago mentions jealousy, the music rises even more in volume and in movement, and Fishburne recites Othello's speech on jealousy. When Iago tells him to "Look to your wife," Othello stands, worried, and Iago apologetically says, "I see this hath a little dashed your spirits." When Othello utters, "Not a jot, not a jot," he is framed with his back to Iago, who is in the background.

The next bit, though, is the most extra-artistic of the three films, as Branagh's voice and the musical score accompany images in Othello's mind of Cassio and Desdemona dancing together, laughing, and smiling. Next is a close-up of Fishburne's head and Branagh's lips just inches from Othello's ear, with the lips moving but no words audible to the audience.

The scene is split to reveal one more location, as it cuts to the inside of Othello's hall, where Iago finishes the initial dialogue as he ties Othello's collar. Othello calmly dismisses Iago, who neither leaves nor is secretive about that fact. After Othello ponders why he married, Iago then asks him to "think not" on the matter and then merely pretends to exit. As Fishburne begins the longer soliloquy, he begins to experience a seizure. He pictures Desdemona and Cassio together in his mind's eye while Iago looks on and then finally exits. Othello sits on the side of the bed as Desdemona enters. She wipes his head with the handkerchief as they exchange dialogue, and they slowly stand together to leave. She leaves the handkerchief simply lying on the bed, so after they exit, Emilia (Anna Patrick) picks it up and holds it.

Despite these three variations, this scene provides the impetus for tragedy in the play, so its staging must be carefully selected. "O"'s corresponding scene takes place in the school's weight room, an appropriate setting for high school athletes, during a workout between Odin and Hugo. The scene, much shorter than Shakespeare's corresponding text and the aforementioned literal versions, begins with Odin entering the weight room and joining Hugo, who is already hard at work. This dialogue follows:

> Odin: Hey, bro. Y'know, I been thinkin', man. Think I'm gonna talk to Coach about Mikey. He should be a part of all of this, man.
> Hugo: Listen. Did Mike know that you and Desi were getting together?

Odin: Yeah, he knew. Why?

Hugo: I didn't think he knew.

Odin: Y'know, Mikey's the one that kinda hooked us up, man.

Hugo: You trust Mike?

Odin: I'm gonna tell you this: I trust him out there on that court. The man can play some ball.

Hugo: Yeah, but do you trust him?

Odin: Yeah, he's cool. [*Pause.*] What's up, man? Why you trippin'?

Hugo: It's nothin', man

Odin: C'mon, Hugo. Say what you gotta say, Player.

Hugo: You're not a jealous person, but I am. It's a weakness. You know, sometimes I see things that aren't really there.

Odin: Yeah?

[*Hugo hesitates.*]

Hugo: You don't want to hear what I have to say.

Odin: Let me be the judge of that, man.

Hugo: I can't help but think [*pause*] that you should watch your girl, bro. I mean, she and Mike spend an awful lot of time together.

Odin: Yeah, so what?

Hugo: So all I'm saying is that her and Mike are always together. And I know the dean would rather see Mike up in that piece.

Odin: You gonna say some shit like that to me, man?

Hugo: Y'see, you're right. I shouldn't have said nothin'. [*He pauses again.*] Forget about it man. Mike's a good guy.

Odin (approaching Hugo): Wait. Nah, man. You can't just say some shit like that an' just break out. What's goin' on, Dogs?

Hugo: Alright. You and Desi were going out for like four months before her father even had a clue. So obviously, the girl knows how to keep a secret. Now I know you grew up in the 'hood, so you've seen plenty of hustlers, but the one thing I do know better than you is white girls, man, and white girls are snakey. Alright. They're horny snakes. They act like we're the ones who want sex all the time, but they want it worse than us. They're just subtle about the way they go after it.

Odin: Hey, man. My girl's not like that, Dogs.

Hugo: But just think about the way she played her father when he found out about you and her.

Odin: What? Did Emily say something to you?

Hugo: No, no, but she wouldn't. Because they stick together, Bro. There is one way to find out, though.

Odin: Yeah, like ask Mike

Hugo: No, because if there is something goin' on—and I'm not sayin' that there is something goin' on—but if there is somethin' goin' on, they're not just gonna come clean. Watch her. If she keeps hanging out with Mike, if she keeps talking about Mike, then we got something to think about. We don't let on, bro. We just watch.[50]

And while this scene takes as much time onscreen as it takes to read the preceding transcription, Nelson follows it up by presenting a montage of quick scenes showing Odin sneaking around, witnessing Desi hanging out with Michael in various locations, and lastly catching his estranged teammate exiting her dorm as he arrives to take her away for a planned night off campus. Once in her dorm room, he asks her if she had ever dated Michael before he came along, which she dismisses by saying, "Michael? He's, like, my best friend, besides Emily." Odin states that he thought *he* was her best friend. They drop the subject and then exit for their night out, with Desi leaving behind on the floor Odin's great-grandmother's 100-plus-year-old scarf, a gift he had given her earlier in the film, which Emily sees. The scene ends there, and unlike *Othello*, the film at this point has yet to indicate the importance of the scarf in the plot.

Emily delivers the scarf to Hugo in the next scene, inviting a viewer unfamiliar with Shakespeare's plot to speculate how it will figure into his scheme. She asks him what he will do with it; he replies, "Just a little prank." Skeptical, she still succumbs to Hugo's charm as they go to bed together. Nelson states that Emily steals from Desi because of her own envy of her; hence, unwittingly, she participates in the larger scheme, and Hugo therefore does not work alone.[51] Can such an interpretation apply to Emilia's similar involvement in the play?

We learn that Desi and Odin have taken off for a night in a rented cabin at a lodge named the Willows, where they are planning to have sex, presumably for the first time. Beginning tenderly, Odin's mindset grimly turns toward images of Desi having sex with Michael, and a montage of the earlier scenes of her spending time with Michael ensues and leads to the gripping image of Odin looking at himself having sex with Desi in the mirror until his own image transforms into that of Michael, a haunting reminder of Parker's *Othello*, which presented a similar scene during an intimate moment between Othello and Desdemona. In this film, though, Odin violently accelerates the intercourse against Desi's protests, resulting in a de facto date rape. With no corresponding scene in Shakespeare, both treatments reveal a tangible manifestation of Othello's inner jealousy and rage. And while Parker's sex scene does not turn violent, the rape in Nelson's film adds another dynamic. Nelson marvels that while the Columbine event hung up this film's release, Miramax never scrutinized the film for its inclusion of date rape.[52]

Hugo next reveals to Odin that he has witnessed Michael with the scarf. The reality of how Michael received the scarf is shown in flashback as Hugo provides this information to Odin. As Hugo explains this to Odin, his voice is dubbed over flashes of him pulling Michael away from Brandy, this film's Bianca (not to be confused with the Bianca of *Shrew* and *10 Things*). He gives the scarf to Michael, and though we do not hear their dialogue, we see Michael happily take the scarf to Brandy as a gift, setting into motion the next part of the film's plot, revealed here for the first time, despite Shakespeare earlier revelation through Iago's soliloquies.

This sequence also contains the film's one overt reference to Shakespeare. As in *10 Things I Hate about You*, the conversation between Hugo and Odin is set in an English classroom, complete with illustrations of iambic pentameter printed on the chalkboard and the distant sounds of a teacher's lecture on the Bard. The teacher interrupts Hugo and Odin's conversation to regain their attention and asks if either of them can identify a single one of Shakespeare's poems, to which Hugo humorously replies, "I thought he wrote movies," a tongue-in-cheek reference to the wave of films to which "O" belongs and even a viable perception that teen viewers of the era might hold of the filmmaker named William Shakespeare.

In the play, Iago lies to Othello about overhearing the mutterings of Cassio's dream while the two had recently slept in the same quarters: "Sweet Desdemona, / Let us be wary, let us hid our loves . . . O, sweet creature! . . . Cursed fate. / That gave thee to the Moor!" (3.3.419–420, 422, 426); according to this false account, Cassio also kissed Iago and threw his leg over Iago's thigh while uttering these words. Iago also mentions seeing Cassio with the handkerchief, and Othello grows convinced that there is now no choice but to kill both Desdemona and Cassio.

Othello next confronts Desdemona about the handkerchief, and she comes up empty yet starts campaigning for Cassio, further agitating Othello. In the same scene (3.4), Cassio gives Bianca the handkerchief, and though it is a copy patterned after the original (Emilia's contribution), Bianca is suspicious that it came from another lover.

In the film, when Odin goes to Desi's room to inquire about the scarf, she also turns up empty-handed. She begins pressing Odin about Michael. He asks, "Hey, D, um, you'd' never give out no love behind my back, now would you? I mean, maybe I'm not enough for you, y'know, especially, with you being all hot and shit?" His reference to their night together at the Willows takes place in front of Emily, angering Desi and embarrassing her roommate. He asks her point blank if she is cheating on him with Michael, which she denies. He leaves without a word. The scene consolidates 3.4, mentioned above, and 4.2, in which Othello refers to Desdemona as a "whore."

At the practice prior to the final championship, the coach sees Odin's diminished performance and replaces him with Michael, who has been warming the bench since his suspension. Odin attacks Michael as he comes on the floor and leaves the gym, despite the coach's summoning him back. Nelson's additional scene here reflects Othello's gradual downfall that ensues in the play, especially as it is witnessed by a superior—in Othello's case, Lodovico and the party from the Venetian duke visiting Othello in Cyprus.

"*O*" interjects another new scene next, possibly the most subtly dramatic of the film and one which advances Kaaya's father–son motif. Nelson frames the scene at a distance from the Coach's office door, which the audience peers through to witness Hartnett speaking to an offscreen Sheen. Hugo enters his father's office, and the viewer listens to their conversation as he sits in the chair across from his unseen father's unseen desk. A slow tracking shot starts wide and closes in gradually on Hugo as they talk. The father–son dimension, an extra-artistic influence on the filmmakers' part, lends more credibility to Hugo's motive, stressing the familial dilemma within him as opposed to the strictly political and military ambitions of Iago in the play.

In this scene, after Hugo enters the office, this dialogue follows in a slowly paced pattern, heightening the familial drama:

Hugo: Hey, Pop.
Coach: Have a seat.
Hugo: It's been awhile since you invited me in here for dinner.
Coach: What is going on with Odin?
Hugo (hesitating): I don't know. I saw him in class today. He seemed alright. [*He pauses.*] By the way, I'm getting an "A" in English again.
Coach: That's great, son. Congratulations. You know I don't ever have to worry about you, thank God. I mean, you've always done well, and you always will, but Odin is different. He's all alone here. Hell, there's not even another black student in this whole damn place, and we're his family. I want you to keep an eye on him and find out what's going on.
Hugo: Sure, Pop.
Coach: All right. Because if he's got a problem, we've got a problem.
Hugo: All right, Dad.
Coach: You know, your mother just doesn't understand us. [*He clears his throat and appears onscreen long enough to pat Hugo on the head and move to exit the office.*] You stay here and finish your supper.

[*The shot changes to the interior of the office, where Hugo puts his dinner tray on the floor and zips his jacket up to his neck, leaning against the wall of the office, alienated.*][53]

Odin later tells Hugo that he must concretely prove that Michael and Desi are getting together; not knowing for certain is driving him crazy. Hugo tells Odin that Michael told him the two had been together the night before. Odin says, "They don't know who they fuckin' with!" To present Odin learning of visible "proof," Nelson and Kaaya adapt scene 4.1 to take place in Hugo's dorm room, where Hugo is feeding Odin cocaine and alcohol. Odin's intoxicated shape reflects Othello's epileptic seizure in the scene, and Cassio and Iago's discussion on Bianca, overheard by Othello, is demonstrated throughout Hugo's leading questions and Michael's coarse descriptions of sex with Brandy. Odin's interpretation matches Othello's, as he is certain that they are speaking provocatively of Desi. Brandy's sudden entrance and accusation that Michael had given her some other "bitch's" scarf provides Odin with the proof he needs, a direct adaptation of Bianca's entrance in the play. To further poison Odin's ears, Michael also states that the "ghetto" came out of Odin recently. After Michael leaves the room, Odin asks Hugo, "How we gonna kill this motherfucker, Hugo?" Hugo's reply ends the scene: "That's a big step. What about Desi?"

In *Othello*, this question is answered immediately after Cassio's exit in scene 4.1, as Iago relays the firm plans to murder the two: "Strangle her in bed, even the bed she hath contaminated . . . And for Cassio, let me be his undertaker" (4.1.207–208, 211). But the film's next sequence begins in a pawn shop, where Hugo trades a pricey watch for a pistol. And then he next appears with Odin at the top of a spiral staircase, stating his plan in a monologue style as Odin listens on. The camera snakes itself upward in a spiral pattern matching the staircase's design:

> *Hugo:*   You've been everything to me, O. To me, you're not my friend, man; you're my brother. And when a brother is wronged, so am I. I'm you, O. I'm a part of you. The plan I've come up with is flawless—planned down to the minute. I spent the last few days going over every possible detail, every angle. All we have to do is set this thing in motion and never look back.
>
> [*The camera switches to a close-up of Hugo as he leans on the top banister and continues relaying the plan. As he speaks, grainy images of the "flawless" plan are presented, supposedly in his and/or Odin's imagination.*]

Hugo: Tomorrow, I'm going to talk to my dad. I'm gonna tell him me and Michael will find our own way to the game. I'll say we want to get there early. We'll take Roger's car. [*Odin is seen crossing the schoolyard toward Desi.*] You're gonna talk to Desi. You're gonna tell her you want to make up—a little love session before the game. [*Odin and Desi are imagined jovially interacting.*] She should be alone in her room. Emily will go on without her. Now if this is gonna work, we have to make sure it looked like Michael did it. [*Images of Michael and Hugo drinking alcohol shots are followed by the camera's focus on Michael's glass.*] We'll leave behind a little present. [*Odin is seen entering Desi's dorm room and attacking her.*] At exactly 7 p.m., you take out Desi, and you plant Michael's glass. [*Odin is presented delicately placing Michael's glass on Desi's table; he is then shown on her phone.*] When that's all done, you call me on Roger's cellular. [*Hugo is shown driving Michael on a deserted road; Roger lies in the front seat of another car, leaning over the wheel as if he has been in an accident.*] We'll have a rental car waiting on the side of the road. When Mike gets out to help, we'll make it look like suicide. [*Roger rises when Michael approaches the rental car and shoots him with the pistol; Michael's dead body is shown lying on the ground with the pistol in his hand.*]

[*The camera returns to the top of the stairwell, focusing back and forth on Hugo and Odin, as Hugo concludes.*]

Hugo: Then we all make our way to the game on time. I know my dad. Without Mike, he's got to play you. So we win the game, and we all swear we never saw Mike or Desi at all. If we stick to the timetable, this will work.

Odin: What about Roger?

Hugo: Roger thinks you and Desi are just breaking up. But after it's all over, I'll tell him. He'll be so scared, he'll go along with whatever I say.

Odin: And if he doesn't?

Hugo: You said you're going all the way with this thing, right?[54]

Nelson states that the "plot [takes] its final turn as these two high school students, like Harris and Clebold of Columbine, decide that they're going to commit murder."[55] Once the plan is set into motion, Odin hides outside Hugo's room while Hugo convinces Michael to have a liquor shot before the game. After they leave, Odin enters Hugo's room to collect Michael's shot glass. Meanwhile, Emily leaves Desi, and Roger is seen waiting on the road in the rental car. The game warm-ups begin without Hugo, Michael, or Odin.

In the final act of *Othello*, Iago reveals his need to employ Roderigo and then dispose of him, as his presence has become both an asset and a liability. Roderigo is both a potential instrument for Iago's scheme, yet he complains and knows too much for Iago to allow him to live. Roderigo first attacks Cassio but gets stabbed himself. Iago secretly wounds Cassio in the leg and exits. Lodovico, the duke's envoy, arrives with company in tow and investigates the incident. Roderigo, calling out for help, is met by Iago's own edged weapon and killed. Bianca enters, and Iago additionally accuses her of conspiring to kill Cassio. Grasping for straws now that his plan has gone partly awry, Iago realizes, "This is the night / That either makes me or fordoes me quite" (5.1.128–129).

In "O," Nelson goes back and forth between Odin's and Hugo's ends of the plan, the second of which goes completely awry, as Roger hesitates long enough for Michael to pull the gun away from him. Hugo intervenes by attacking Michael from behind with a crowbar. Roger retrieves the gun but only manages to shoot Michael in the leg. Knowing now that it will not look like suicide, Hugo uses the gun to kill Roger, while Michael lies on the ground suffering from his wound. Brandy drives by, but when she assesses the scene, she quickly departs, leaving behind a befuddled Hugo, who retrieves his crowbar and the scarf from Roger's body.

Shakespeare has Othello wake Desdemona from a slumber, accusing her of the affair, offering her time to pray before he kills her, but Odin's approach differs here, too. He goes to Desi's room, climbing up the ladder on the side of the house into her window, planting the shot glass, and waking her up. Odin apologizes to Desi for how he has recently acted toward her. They begin kissing, lying on the bed; Odin towers over her and then starts to choke her. "I saw Michael with the scarf. He's dead." She struggles. "Go to sleep . . . please," he pleads. Emily returns to the room after she dies, just as Emilia had entered upon Othello's murder of Desdemona. Yet unlike Desdemona's brief resurrection before finally dying, Desi is left limp. The aftermath that follows, though condensed in comparison to Shakespeare's version, faithfully follows the original: Emily's confrontation with Odin; Hugo's entrance on the scene; Emily's revelation of the truth about the scarf; and Hugo's murder of Emily to get her to be quiet about the scarf.

However, Odin does not wound Hugo as Othello does Iago. Yet the verbal confrontation is equally mirrored. Othello asks Lodovico to demand of Iago why "that demi-devil . . . hath thus ensnared my soul and body." Iago famously responds, "Demand me nothing. What you know, you know. / From this time forth I will never speak word"

(5.2.203–204). Hugo's variation conveys the same: "You're gonna ask me nothing. I did what I did, and that's all you need to know. From here on out, I say nothing."

In the play, Othello contends that he has served the state well, but that

> [I]pray you, in your letters,
> When you shall these unlucky deeds relate,
> Speak of me as I am. Nothing extenuate,
> Nor set down in malice. Then must you speak
> Of one that loved not wisely but too well,
> Of one not easily jealous but, being wrought,
> Perplexed in the extreme; of one whose hand,
> Like the base Indian, threw a pearl away
> Richer than all his tribes; of one whose subdued eyes,
> Albeit unused to the melting mood,
> Drops tears as fast as the Arabian trees
> Their medicinable gum. Set you down this,
> And say besides that in Aleppo once,
> Where a malignant and a turbaned Turk
> Beat a Venetian and traduced the state,
> I took by th' throat the circumcised dog
> And smote him thus.
>
> [*He stabs himself.*]
> (5.2.340–356)

Odin, waving Hugo's gun and surrounded by police, delivers his final speech, placing blame on Hugo and declaring his own self-defeat:

> My life is over. That's it. But while all of y'all are out livin' yours, sittin' around talkin' about the nigger that lost it back in high school, you make sure you tell them the truth. You tell them I loved that girl. I did. But I got played. He twisted my head off. He fucked it up. I ain't no different than none of y'all. My moms ain't no crackhead. I wasn't no gangbanger. It wasn't some hood rat drug dealer that tripped me up. It was this white, prep-school motherfucker standin' right there. You tell them where I'm from didn't make me do this.
>
> [*He aims the gun and shoots toward his chest; the frame freezes after the blast.*][56]

Upon Odin's death, the Verdi aria plays again, filling the soundtrack as the cameras display Odin's dead body on the porch swing and Hugo being carted off by the police in handcuffs. Dean Brable arrives, running inside the dorm. In addition to the police, multiple ambulances and the news media are both on the scene; student witnesses speak before the press; reporters are delivering their stories; groups of girls are seen shocked and crying. The scene switches to the site of Roger and Michael's shootings, and despite Cassio's survival in Othello, Michael's body lies dormant on the ground. Then Nelson goes to the gym, where the coach learns of the events and then rushes out of the gym. Back at the dorms, bodies are carted onto ambulances; Odin's body is photographed by crime scene investigators; and Hugo is driven off from the scene, looking out the back window of the police cruiser. Nelson says that it was news footage from the five nationally reported shootings that occurred *before* the Columbine event, including images of crying students, interviews, ambulances, and police cars carrying off perpetrators that made him want to direct the film.[57]

As these images go across the scene, set again to the Verdi aria, Hugo's voice-over from the first of the film is presented again: "All my life, I always wanted to fly. I always wanted to live like a hawk. I know you're not supposed to be jealous of anything, but to take flight, to soar above everything and everyone—now that's living." Yet this time, the script provides coda to the original monologue: "But a hawk is no good around normal birds; they can't fit in. Even though all the other birds probably want to be hawks, they hate them for what they can't be: proud, determined, dark. Odin is a hawk. He soars above us. He can fly. But one of these days, everyone's gonna pay attention to me because I'm going to fly, too."[58] Criniti writes that though Iago swore to never utter another word, Hugo's final voice-over enables him to

> ponder his doings and ultimate undoing . . . Hugo reinforces that a quest for attention is his motivation . . . [reiterating] his determination to achieve that attention. One must wonder whether he has truly learned from the tragic happenings—it would appear from his final line that he has not. This is a key departure from the Shakespearean original, as Iago is merely carted off the stage in silence.[59]

The film's stringent adaptation of *Othello* to tell this contemporary story draws the attention of critics and scholars. Ebert draws comparisons between "O" and Luhrmann's *Romeo + Juliet*. While "O" is not a "line-by-line update" like Luhrmann's film, it does represent

> an attempt to reproduce the passion of the original play, and for younger viewers new to Shakespeare, it would only enhance a reading of the real thing . . . True, some of the plot threads seem unlikely. Is it

that easy to overhear and completely misunderstand crucial conversations? How much more use can a scarf be put to? But those are problems in Shakespeare, too—or perhaps simply plot mechanisms that allow the characters to arrive at their tragic destinations.[60]

Criniti echoes this assessment, stating that the film "is a complex and powerful one owing much of its success to its very adherence to Shakespeare's ingenious rendering of human evil and jealousy."[61]

"O" provides instruction on teen issues, reflecting Boose and Burt's emphasis on the pedagogical implications of such works designed for the youth culture:

> Students in today's average, college-level Shakespeare course are now more often shown select scenes from two or more versions of a given play than they are a single production in its entirety . . . Shakespeare's accessibility is guaranteed, but along with this move to film comes a perhaps inevitable new sense of Shakespeare's reproduction, one which offers certain challenges to cultural criticism of Shakespeare as is now practiced.[62]

Aside from the issues of date rape and school violence, "O" also deals with the explosive matters among American teens concerning racial conflict and illegal drug use.

Race is handled cautiously at first, first during a light conversation between Odin and Desi involving the "N" word. When he refers to himself as "that kind of nigger," Desi shows her discomfort with the word. He explains that he can say "nigger" because he is a "nigger". When she asks why she can't say the word, he tells her she better not even "think" the word. She says, "You said that I was so fine you'd let me dress you up and play 'Black Buck Got Loose in the Big House.' " He jokes back that if any other black person knew he had said that, he would have his "suffering Negro card revoked." That this dialogue generates laughter between them attests to their personalized light-hearted regard for the epithet. But the same word gets more charge when Odin is in a completely other state of mind later in the film, particularly when under the influence of cocaine and alcohol. Hugo falsely tells Odin that Michael told him that he and Desi use the epithet when talking about Odin, telling him they refer to him as "The Nigger."

Drugs are another concern of the film, particularly steroids and cocaine, both supplied by an African American dealer Dell (Anthony Johnson). Nelson states that he was concerned over Kaaya's inclusion of this factor in the script, but the screenwriter, an African American, argued the connections between African Americans and drug dealing were a "sad reality that he wanted the film to examine." Whereas in *Othello*, only jealous rage drives the action, he states, drugs bring forth "a social reality" of high schools and teens' actions that equally influence Odin's decisions and actions.[63] Obviously, Hugo's administration of drugs to Odin, both directly and indirectly, are essential to his larger scheme. But Hugo, too, is a regular customer of Dell.

In Hugo's first interaction with Dell early on in the film, the drug dealer warns him of the dangers of steroids. Hugo states that it is enhancing his athletic performance, and for that, he is pleased with the product. Dell chats with Hugo about his athletic future: "When you start playin' for North Carolina, don't forget about me. Shoot a nigger some tickets. I'm talkin' about courtside." While injecting Hugo with the steroids, he says, "I know you're all into this basketball stuff, but if it don't work, don't trip. I'm sayin', 'cause there are some things in life we weren't meant to have. I mean, don't go out there makin' yourself all crazy and shit." Hugo replies, "How can I go crazy when I got you selling me dream in a bottle, man?"

Dell appears a second time in the movie in the boiler room of the gymnasium, where Hugo has arranged for him to provide Odin with cocaine before he participates in a slam-dunk competition with students from other schools. Odin's coke-driven performance begins with his sight of Desi and Michael sitting together in the gym. He starts dribbling the ball against the floor, preparing for his shot, and the audience begins clapping and shouting "Odin! Odin!" in unison with the ball's contact with the floor. He next launches into the slam-dunk attempt, moving toward the basketball goal and jumping toward the hoop. He lands the ball in the rim so hard that he shatters the glass backboard and breaks off the rim, drawing unanimous applause from the crowd. However, when a much younger ball boy comes to retrieve the ball from Odin, he pushes the boy to the floor, picks the rim up, and tosses it across the court. The audience boos him this time, which corresponds with the scene in *Othello* when the duke's representative Lodovico expresses incredulity at witnessing Othello's treatment of Desdemona during their initial meeting. After this event, the coach meets with Dean Brable over whether Odin can play in the state final. Hugo, listening in, quietly says to himself, "Yeah, Dad. Who's your favorite now, Dad?" The same night, Hugo and Odin get together, and he "consoles" him with more cocaine and alcohol to help him "make it through."

The film does not proselytize on these social issues, and it offers no solutions; nor does Shakespeare's play. But the film does boast a hyperrealistic presentation, down to the issues, the setting, the situations, and the characters. Nelson states that he wanted to cast the film with

> young actors who would radiate intelligence, who would seem smart. I didn't want to talk down to the audience with stupid or shallow characters who seem to populate most teen-genre films. And it really mystified me when some critics . . . chided us for creating characters who seemed too smart or too sophisticated for high school. Not only did I want to say, "Well, what country have you been living in for the last ten years?" but I wanted to ask, "Well, why can't young actors in a film about young people seem smart?" Kids in this country are now more sophisticated and smarter. That's simply true.[64]

He adds that most teen-genre films would have changed Shakespeare's ending instead of having students murder each other. Hugo is a good student, he states, who departs from the cliché of who might commit such acts in the same way that the perpetrators in the widely reported high school shootings defied such clichés.

Nelson also sets up other volatile behaviors among the teens. He states that he wanted to explore the "cruelty . . . between good-looking, socially popular high school students toward a less popular student whom they're trying to ostracize."[65] Roger suffers the role of the less popular student. After Odin's early meeting with the dean concerning Desi, he and Michael beat up Roger on the school grounds for telling the dean about Desi and Odin. Later, during the slam-dunk contest, Michael and a friend sit behind Roger and taunt him by flicking the back of his ear until it brings tears to his eyes. While Roger holds the same crush for Desi as Roderigo does for Desdemona, his involvement in Hugo's scheme is likely solidified by wanting to retaliate against Michael for these various acts of abuse.

Criniti writes that the film is "a comment on the dark and tragic behaviors that often plague contemporary high schools and the time-lessness of such primal human emotions like jealousy and rage."[66] Ebert writes that Hugo is a "psychopath" and that his "allies are victims of that high school disease that encourages the unpopular to do anything in order to be accepted. Those who think this film will inspire events like Columbine should ask themselves how often audiences want to be like the despised villain." Due to high school violence, Nelson states, the high school "is not only a credible place to tell the story but the most appropriate one as well."[67]

End of a Trend?

10 Things I Hate about You and "*O*" both turned profits well exceed-ing their initial budgets. In the United States alone, *10 Things* grossed more than double its $16 million budget, while "*O*" exceeded its $5 million budget on its opening weekend, ultimately grossing over three times that.[68] Both films, like Luhrmann's *Romeo + Juliet*, did well overseas. How much of this was due to Shakespeare's appeal rather than Stiles' or Ledger's or Hartnett's or Phifer's or the other young stars' is inestimable, but exposure to the Bard is a similar outcome both films generate, even if by varying degrees. Like Luhrmann's film, the films do indirectly invite the viewers to survey the original sources. The DVD release of "*O*," in fact, carries a bonus disc featuring the 1922 silent adaptation of *Othello* directed by Dimitri Buchowetzki and starring Emil Jannings.

The period since "*O*"'s release has been less fruitful in such teen-marketed adaptations. While two other 2001 films, *Get over It* and *The Glass House*, possess overt references to Shakespeare, neither are actually full-scale adaptations. R. Lee Fleming, the screenwriter of *Get over It*, wrote an original script titled *Getting over Allison* that contained neither mention nor reference to Shakespeare. Harvey Weinstein, chief of the film's distributor—Miramax once again—wanted to ride the crest of success he had with *Shakespeare in Love*, so he demanded that Fleming and director Tommy O'Haver place the characters in a high school musical version of *A Midsummer Night's Dream*.[69] Various fantasy sequences loosely based on the production design of Reinhardt's Hollywood version of the 1930s permeate the film. Otherwise, the film's plot is hardly reminiscent of *Midsummer*.

However, the original script of *The Glass House*, written by Wesley Strick, incorporated a good deal of direct references to *Hamlet* to relay the story of the recently orphaned Ruby, whose suspicions surround-ing her parents' mysterious death leads to her realization that her cur-rent guardians, once close friends of her parents, were responsible for their fatal auto accident, their motive being a takeover of the children's inheritance. Strick states the film would have been three hours long had he and director Daniel Sackheim kept the Shakespearean allusions, but their studio, Columbia Pictures, wanted to appeal to the teen-genre-thriller set and forced cuts that resulted in a 106-minute running time.[70] The few remaining contents parallel to *Hamlet* include Ruby's mother's "ghost" appearing in her dream and an essay assignment on

Hamlet that Ruby must complete for English class that includes a reference to Harold Bloom's *Shakespeare: The Invention of the Human.*

As of this writing, filmmakers have ceased producing these teen-marketed loose adaptations of Shakespeare. Michael Almereyda's *Hamlet* (2000), casting Stiles as Ophelia to Ethan Hawke's Dane, follows an abridgement of Shakespeare's text and is set in the corporate, media-driven world. Jet Li and Aaliyah star as another variation of the star-crossed lovers in the martial arts film *Romeo Must Die* (2000), with the African American and Asian mob conflict in full force. Another spin on *Shrew*, the L.L. Cool J. showcase, *Deliver Us from Eva* (2003), hardly qualifies either, as the film involves characters in their twenties and thirties involved in marriages and other adult contexts. At best, these films might appeal to an aging Luhrmann audience who has stuck with Shakespeare. But as Shakespearean film history has repeatedly demonstrated, the ebbs and flows of possibilities will occur in waves attendant to filmmakers' ongoing employment of a William Shakespeare who "writes movies." With teen audiences always a premium target for the studios, a resurgence of such adaptations seems likely at any point.

Notes

1. *Internet Movie Database,* "*Romeo + Juliet,*" <http://www.imdb.com/title/tt0117509/>
2. <http://www.romeoandjuliet.com>
3. Lynda E. Boose and Richard Burt, "Totally *Clueless?*: Shakespeare Goes Hollywood in the 1990s," in *Shakespeare the Movie,* edited by Lynda E. Boose and Richard Burt (New York: Routledge, 1997), pp. 17–18.
4. Lynda E. Boose and Richard Burt, "Introduction: Shakespeare, the Film," in *Shakespeare the Movie,* edited by Lynda E. Boose and Richard Burt (New York: Routledge, 1997), p. 2.
5. Roger Ebert, review of *Romeo & Juliet, Chicago Sun-Times,* November 1, 1996 <http://rogerebert.suntimes.com/apps/pbcs.dll/article?AID=/19961101/REVIEWS/611010304/1023>
6. Gary Crowdus, "Words, Words, Words: Recent Shakespearean Films," *Cineaste* 24, no. 4 (1998), p. 15.
7. Douglas Brode, *Shakespeare in the Movies: From the Silent Era to Shakespeare in Love* (New York: Oxford University Press, 2000), p. 56.
8. Ibid., p. 57.
9. Francisco Menendez, "Redefining Originality: Pearce and Luhrmann's Conceptualization of *Romeo and Juliet,*" *Creative Screenwriting* 5, no. 2 (1998), pp. 36–37.
10. Jonathan Bate, "Commentary," *William Shakespeare's Romeo + Juliet,* special ed. DVD.

11. Peter Travers, review of *William Shakespeare's Romeo + Juliet, Rolling Stone* (1996) <http://www.rollingstone.com/reviews/movie/_/id/5949093>

12. Baz Luhrmann quoted in Erik Bauer, "Re-revealing Shakespeare: An Interview with Baz Luhrmann," *Creative Screenwriting* 5, no. 2 (1998), p. 33.

13. Luhrmann quoted in "Shakespeare in the Cinema: A Film Directors' Symposium," *Cineaste* 24, no. 1 (1998), p. 53.

14. Luhrmann quoted in "Shakespeare in the Cinema," p. 55.

15. Luhrmann quoted in Bauer, "Re-revealing Shakespeare," p. 35.

16. Craig Pearce, "Commentary," *William Shakespeare's Romeo + Juliet*, special ed. DVD.

17. Luhrmann, "Commentary," *William Shakespeare's Romeo + Juliet*, special ed. DVD.

18. See Kevin Wetmore's chapters on popular music and Shakespeare in this volume.

19. Lurhmann quoted in Bauer, "Re-revealing Shakespeare," pp. 32–33.

20. Ibid., p. 35.

21. Luhrmann quoted in "Shakespeare in the Cinema," p. 48.

22. Luhrmann quoted in Bauer, "Re-revealing Shakespeare," p. 33.

23. Ibid., p. 35.

24. Boose and Burt, "Introduction," p. 2.

25. Boose and Burt, "Totally *Clueless?*" p. 12.

26. Ibid., p. 13.

27. Brode, *Shakespeare in the Movies*, p. 241.

28. Luhrmann quoted in "Shakespeare in the Cinema," 54.

29. Pearce, "Commentary," *William Shakespeare's Romeo + Juliet*, special ed. DVD.

30. Diana E. Henderson, "A Shrew for the Times," in *Shakespeare the Movie: Popularizing the Plays on Film, TV, and Video*, edited by Lynda E. Boose and Richard Burt (New York: Routledge, 1997), pp. 149–150.

31. L. Monique Pittman, "Taming *10 Things I Hate about You:* Shakespeare and the Teenage Film Audience," *Literature/Film Quarterly* 32, no. 2 (2004): 144–152 <http://80proquest.umi.com.allstate.libproxy.ivytech.edu/pqdweb?RQT=305&querySyntax=PQ&searchInterface=1&moreOptState=CLOSED&TS=1124691219&h_pubtitle=&h_pmid=&clientId=54498&JSEnabled=1&SQ=L.+Monique+Pittman+Taming+10+Things+I+Hate+about+You&DBId=1&date=ALL&onDate=&beforeDate=&afterDate=&fromDate=&toDate=&pubtitle=&author=&FT=0&AT=any&revType=review&revPos=all&STYPE=all&sortby=REVERSE_CHRON&searchButtonImage.x=0&searchButtonImage.y=0>

32. Ebert, review of *10 Things I Hate about You, Chicago Sun-Times*, March 31, 1999 <http://rogerebert.suntimes.com/apps/pbcs.dll/article?AID=/19990331/REVIEWS/903310301/1023>

33. Pittman, "Taming *10 Things.*"

34. Pittman, "Taming *10 Things.*"

35. My transcription from *10 Things.*

36. My transcription from *10 Things.*

37. Ebert, review of "*O*," *Chicago Sun-Times*, August 31, 2001 <http://rogerebert. suntimes.com/apps/pbcs.dll/article?AID=/20010831/ REVIEWS/108310302/ 1023>

38. Steve Criniti, "Othello: A Hawk among Birds," *Literature/Film Quarterly* 32, no. 2 (2004), pp. 115–121 <http://80 proquest.umi.com.allstate. libproxy. ivytech.edu/pqdweb?index=0&did=653729321&SrchMode=1&sid=1& Fmt=4&VInst=PROD&VType=PQD&RQT=309&VName=PQD&TS= 1124691219&clientId=54498>

39. Ibid.

40. Tim Blake Nelson, "Commentary."

41. Ebert, review of "*O*."

42. Roger Manvell, *Shakespeare and the Film* (New York: Praeger, 1971), p. 62.

43. Micheál MacLiammóir, "Put Money in Thy Purse," in *Focus on Shakespearean Films*, edited by Charles W. Eckert (Englewood Cliffs, NJ: Prentice Hall, 1972), p. 81.

44. Ibid.

45. Manvell, *Shakespeare and the Film*, p. 118.

46. Ibid.

47. Anthony Davies, "Filming *Othello*," in *Shakespeare and the Moving Image: The Plays on Film and Television*, edited by Anthony Davies and Stanley Wells (Cambridge: Cambridge University Press, 2004), p. 196.

48. John Simon, "Pearl Throwing Free Style," in *Focus on Shakespearean Films*, edited by Charles W. Eckert (Englewood Cliffs, NJ: Prentice Hall, 1972), p. 157.

49. Davies, "Filming Othello," p. 200.

50. My transcription from "*O*."

51. Nelson, "Commentary."

52. Ibid.

53. My transcription from "*O*."

54. My transcription from "*O*."

55. Nelson, "Commentary."

56. My transcription from "*O*."

57. Nelson, "Commentary."

58. My transcription from "*O*."

59. Criniti, "Othello: A Hawk among Birds."

60. Ebert, review of "*O*."

61. Criniti, "Othello: A Hawk among Birds."

62. Boose and Burt, "Totally *Clueless*?," pp. 18–19,

63. Nelson, "Commentary."

64. Ibid.

65. Ibid.

66. Criniti, "Othello: A Hawk among Birds."

67. Nelson, "Commentary," "*O*" deluxe edition DVD.

68. *Internet Movie Database, 10 Things I Hate about You* <http://www.imdb. com/title/tt0147800/>; s.v. "*O*" <http://www.imdb.com/title/tt0184791/>

69. R. Lee Fleming, "Commentary," *Get over It* DVD.

70. Wesley Strick, "Commentary," *The Glass House* DVD.

3

"Are You Shakespearienced?" Rock Music and the Production of Shakespeare

Kevin J. Wetmore, Jr.

All the world's indeed a stage, and we are merely players,
Performers and portrayers, each another's audience
Outside the gilded cage.

—Rush "Limelight" after Shakespeare,
As You Like It 2.7.139–140

I loved Macbeth—*a gorgeous piece of nastiness, that.*

—Johnny Rotten of The Sex Pistols

"Hair, Prince of Denmark": Rock-and-Roll Shakespeare, an Introduction

In 1966 Gerome Ragni and James Rado teamed up with a composer named Galt MacDermot. MacDermot had composed some songs for a few revues in Montreal, but his work with the two young actors, a "free-form musical" titled *Hair*, designed to transform theatre and provide a new model for musicals, was his first full-length effort. *Hair*, called "The American Tribal Love Rock Musical" by its creators, was one of the first American musicals to use rock and roll as its dominant musical style.[1] It was also one of the first plays to combine an Americanized Shakespeare with rock and roll.

The play tells the story of Claude Hooper Bukowski, a hippie who has been drafted to go to Vietnam, and his friends Berger, Hud, Woof,

Crissy, Sheila, and "the Tribe."[2] The first version of the play featured Berger and Claude speaking Hamlet's "What a piece of work is man!" speech as a dialogue. In later versions, the speech then became a song.

In the Broadway production, the cast sang "Three-Five-Zero-Zero," an antiwar song, after the stage was littered with the bodies of dead soldiers and dead Native Americans from historic wars. Two cast members then walked among the dead bodies singing "What a Piece of Work is Man," a song which slightly alters the original text. Rado and Ragni begin the song with *Hamlet* 2.2.303: "What a piece of work is man . . ." and continue through line 307, "the paragon of animals." The song then returns to an earlier point in the speech, editing the text for rhythm and rhyme:

> I have of late—but wherefore I know not—lost all my mirth.
> This goodly frame the earth seems to me a sterile promontory;
> this most excellent canopy, the air, look you;
> this brave o'erhanging firmament, this majestical roof fretted with
> golden fire, why it appears no other thing to me than a foul and pestilent
> congregation of vapors.
>
> (2.2.295–296, 298–303)

The piece then concludes by repeating the first two lines now in the original place: "What a piece of work is man, how noble in reason." The authors intend, as Hamlet did, for the words to be taken ironically—as Hamlet then confides, "to me what is this quintessence of dust? Man delights not me . . ." (2.2.308–309). Whereas Hamlet is disgusted with what is rotten in the state of Denmark, the authors of *Hair* use Shakespeare's words to decry what is rotten in the state of America in the Vietnam era.

At the conclusion of the musical, Claude has passed his medical exam, been sent to basic training and then on to Vietnam, where he is killed. At his death, Claude sings a song called "Eyes Look Your Last," taken directly from Romeo's death speech in *Romeo and Juliet* (5.3.112).[3] Claude's last song, "The Flesh Failures," features a chorus that sings after he dies, following his last lines with a repetition of the phrases "Seal with a righteous kiss" (*Romeo and Juliet* 5.3.114—taken from the same speech as the previous reference) and "The rest is silence" (*Hamlet* 5.2.358), the final words of Romeo and Hamlet.

Ragni and Rado sought not to create a rock-and-roll Shakespeare, but rather to use familiar lines from the plays to link their tragic young heroes with Shakespeare's. Hamlet and Romeo are, apart from Troilus, Shakespeare's only youthful tragic male protagonists. They both die because of conflicts with the older generation. *Hair* places Claude into the same tragic model—a young man born "to set things right," and, while only desiring to love and live free, dies in a conflict not of his own making, but a fight among members of the older generation. In the 1960s in the United States, Hamlet and Romeo had become figures of youthful rebellion, and the music of youthful rebellion was rock and roll. Shakespeare's plays do not have to be presented in their entirety, using the original texts the experiment seemed to say, but rather can serve as intertexts, mixed with rock-and-roll music to develop theatre for a younger generation.

In this essay, the mutual expropriation of Shakespeare and rock and roll in American production will be considered. Rock music-centered adaptations of Shakespeare not only appropriate the texts of the plays (in fact, in some cases the text is not appropriated at all, but erased!), they also exploit and explore what "Shakespeare" represents. In other words, they explore the idea of Shakespeare, not just as a playwright but as a cultural phenomenon occupying a singular place in American culture. In doing so, the author argues that such productions adapt the concept of Shakespeare as much as the actual texts for the paradoxical purposes of both legitimizing contemporary alternative performance through the use of alleged "high" culture and creating an accessible, demystified Shakespeare for contemporary audiences through familiar cultural referents. This use of Shakespeare's plays begs the larger question of what is "Shakespearean" about Shakespeare, which is also considered later. Last, the author will contextualize such productions as adaptations, rock musicals, and a return to earlier constructions of "American Shakespeare."

Rock Shakespeare could not exist until the 1960s nor could it have developed without the United States, quite simply because rock music is an invention of the United States in the mid-to late 1950s. Even as Shakespeare served as the synecdoche for elite culture, rock music stood for (and stands for) youth culture, antiauthoritarianism, and freedom. The expropriation of Shakespeare by rock music and of rock music for productions of Shakespeare blend worlds that seem at opposite ends of the cultural spectrum, and often times the elements serve to question assumptions about both Shakespeare and the music, while simultaneously using each other in order to gain market share.

Hair was produced by Joseph Papp, the creator of Shakespeare in Central Park. In 1969, Papp commissioned Galt MacDermot to write the rock-and-roll score for his *William Shakespeare's "Naked" Hamlet*, staged at the Public Theatre in New York. The production, starring a young Martin Sheen, was a collage of the original text, designed to deconstruct audience assumptions about Shakespeare and his most famous play.

The production handbook begins by noting a series of actions designed to prompt "guesses" by the audience as to what the production might be. "The Third Guess" consists of "a minute of rock music" designed to make the audience ask, "Is this going to be a rock *Hamlet*? . . . And what is a rock *Hamlet* anyway?"[4] In Scene XXX, all of Ophelia's songs are performed at once, as a "vaudeville/rock show," with original rock music by MacDermott. Papp argues that the music grew organically out of the company's exploration of the text: "We found . . . rock music in the play, so we put [it] in the production."[5]

The production was loudly decried by many critics and many older audience members. The *New York Times* critic referred to the production as "a *Hamlet* for the Philistines."[6] Yet, as Joseph Papp observes in his preface to the production handbook, "the Public Theatre was jammed every night" with an audience mostly in their teens and twenties.[7] The loud rock music and the deconstructive nature of the production, which rearranged Shakespeare's text and added new elements, such as Hamlet disguising himself as "Ramon the Puerto Rican Janitor" demonstrated that the target audience was not one that favored traditional readings of the text or standard (for the time) interpretations of the meaning.[8] Everything about the play was loud and rebellious, arguably the very qualities that define rock and roll.

We should note that both Papp and MacDermott continued blending Shakespeare and rock and roll. Papp used rock music in numerous productions of Shakespeare in Central Park. In 1973, MacDermot teamed up with John Guare and Mel Shapiro to create a rock-and-roll musical version of *The Two Gentlemen of Verona*.[9] By the end of the decade, "Rock Shakespeare" was hardly a novelty anymore.

Shakespeare very quickly found his works linked to rock and roll in a variety of manners. In the same year that Papp presented his rock-and-roll *Hamlet*, Tony Richardson cast Marianne Faithful, famed groupie and rock artist in her own right, as Ophelia in his *Hamlet*. The same year that MacDermott rocked Verona, Patrick McGoohan directed *Catch My Soul*, a rock-opera adaptation of *Othello*. The BBC, when creating its complete works of Shakespeare on video, cast The Who's Roger Daltry as Dromio in *The Comedy of Errors*. Very quickly Shakespeare's plays have come to occupy the same cultural space as rock-and-roll music through the expropriation of Shakespeare (the man and the plays, characters, and words) by rock music and through the use of rock music in American productions of Shakespeare.

Similarly, other productions of Shakespeare were simultaneously being read in terms of youth culture during the same period. Writing in 2004, Deanne Williams sees Roman Polanski's 1971 film *Macbeth* as a "period piece" that situates the story not in medieval Scotland (as the mise-en-scene of the film suggests) but in "the sybaritic world of the late sixties and early seventies."[10] In particular, Williams cites the similarity in appearance between Jon Finch, who played Macbeth, and Mick Jagger, in order to posit the film as rock Shakespeare. She sees Macbeth and Lady Macbeth, played by atypically young performers, as a "good-looking" celebrity power couple.[11] Though some have seen in the film an echo of Polanski's own history, given the Tate/LaBianca murders of 1969, during which Charles Manson's followers killed Polanski's pregnant wife, Sharon Tate, which some see referenced in the murder of Lady MacDuff and her child, Williams sees the film as "a study in the loss of the ideas of sixties youth culture," and that Polanski's *Macbeth* ultimately concerns "an untimely decline from starry-eyed youth to disillusioned maturity, the movement from high hopes and great expectations to jaded dissipation."[12]

In other words, even when actual rock music is not appropriated into a production of a Shakespeare play, the culture of rock and roll can still be present and influence the perception of the play or film. Though no music is played, Finch's "uncanny" resemblance to Mick Jagger, argues Williams, connects the film to the Rolling Stones and the associations that the band's presence brings with them. Just as music creates a sense of identity among youth, it also creates a sense of community and a sense of connection. "Mick Jagger Macbeth," without using any music, links Shakespeare's play to the world of 1960s rock excess and creates a discourse with a community of viewers that might otherwise have avoided the film. Audience expectations are generated by the appearance of the familiar (a Jagger-like figure), who behaves in a manner that does not seem at odds with the public perception of that figure. In the wake of Altamont and such songs as "Sympathy for the Devil," the lead singer of the Rolling Stones could be seen connected to murder and the occult. The world of rock shapes the reception of the Shakespearean text.

Rock and Roll Expropriates Shakespeare

If rock and roll shapes production and reception of Shakespeare, it is only fair to observe that Shakespeare has also shaped rock and roll, at least the lyrical content. In particular, Shakespeare's Romeo and Juliet (the characters, not the play) are perhaps the bard's greatest contribution to rock and roll. If, as Paul Friedlander argues, "the dominant topic in rock music lyrics has always been romance," then Romeo and Juliet, as the archetypical romantic couple, have served as the ultimate rock-and-roll reference for young love.[13]

Stephen Buhler has thoroughly documented the transformations of Romeo and Juliet in pop music and catalogued their presence in pop lyrics.[14] A random, and far from complete sampling would include "(Just Like) Romeo and Juliet" by The Reflections (1964), "(Don't Fear) The Reaper" by Blue Oyster Cult (1976), "Romeo is Bleeding" by Tom Waits (1978), "Romeo and Juliet" by Dire Straits (1980), "Romeo Had Juliette" by Lou Reed (1989), two direct references by Madonna (in "Cherish" in 1989 and "Fever" in 1992), in three direct references by Bruce Springsteen alone (in "Incident on 57th Street" in 1973, "Fire" in 1979, and "Point Blank" in 1980), and songs by Ratt, Alanis Morisette, Aerosmith, Elvis Costello, Michael Penn, Bob Dylan, and the Indigo Girls. Romeo and Juliet are referenced in rock lyrics hundreds of times more than the next most popular character, Ophelia, who has been mentioned in songs by such artists as the Indigo Girls and Natalie Merchant (both of whom have also invoked Polonius's much put-upon daughter in album titles, *Swamp Ophelia* [1994] and *Ophelia* [1998], respectively), and in the names of such bands as San Francisco-based The Ophelias and Boston-based Ophelia Rising.[15]

Pop-music Romeo and Juliet references, however, reinscribe not Shakespeare's play, but the characters themselves as pop-culture celebrities, leaving them with more in common with "Bogey and Bacall" (Bertie Higgins, "Key Largo" 1981), Bette Davis and her eyes (Kim Carnes, 1981), Captain Jean-Luc Picard of the United Federation of Planets (Refreshments, "Bandito" 1997) or, perhaps most accurately, Superman (take your pick: The Kinks, Donovan, R.E.M., Roy Gaines, Eminem, Three Doors Down, Spin Doctors, Five for Fighting, Alanis Morissette (again), The Flaming Lips, and the Ominous Seapods, among others) than with the characters of Shakespeare's plays.[16] As a result, it is not Shakespeare's play that is being referenced, but the idea of romantic love as embodied in the characters, and they are the equivalent of any other pop culture figure—real or fictional. One need not be familiar with Shakespeare's play—only the idea (or ideal) of the characters.

In much the same way, Shakespeare the man, or perhaps more accurately, Shakespeare the concept, lent his name to rock and roll in the

1980s. Robbie Shakespeare, the well-known reggae producer and bass player took his name from the swan of Avon. In the mid-1980s, Minneapolis-based "Trip Shakespeare" formed, titling their second album "Are You Shakespearienced?" a play on Jimi Hendrix's "Are You Experienced," and the source of the title for this essay. Forming in 1989, "Shakespeare's Sister," consisting of Siobhan Fahey and Marcella Detroit, released two albums before breaking up. Although not well known in the United States, they achieved great popularity in Europe and England. The name "Shakespeare" is synonymous in American society with high culture, British cultural superiority, "drama," and great writing. Bands that employ his name in theirs seek to define themselves, sometimes ironically, in terms of Shakespeare.

The name "William Shakespeare" is used not only by bands but by directors who seek to shape the plays but retain a sense of authority and authenticity, in much the same way that rock musicians seek through the use of the name to establish their own artistic skills and authenticity. Papp's titling his production *William Shakespeare's "Naked" Hamlet* serves the same purpose as Baz Luhrmann's titling his film *William Shakespeare's Romeo + Juliet* nearly three decades later.[17] In both cases, the product was aimed at a youth market, and Shakespeare's name was placed in front not only in order to assert the primacy of the author, but to buttress the new work by ascribing it to Shakespeare, giving the work a gloss of authenticity that the textual and visual deconstructions of Papp and Luhrmann do not always have.

Lynda E. Boose and Richard Burt note in their introduction to *Shakespeare: The Movie* that "youth culture" by and large dominates the milieu of most current films based on Shakespeare (vis-à-vis "*O*," *10 Things I Hate about You*, *William Shakespeare's Romeo and Juliet*, *Clueless*, etc.) and that "major Shakespearean critics are turning their talents to the reading of MTV videos."[18] The largest (at least in terms of attention given by the media) of these is Luhrmann's film, which many critics felt was as much rooted in rock culture as it was in Shakespeare.[19] Not one but two soundtrack CDs were issued.[20] MTV did a half-hour special on Baz Luhrmann's *William Shakespeare's Romeo + Juliet*, further linking that film to the world of rock and roll. One critic complained the film was "more concerned with its rock / hip-hop soundtrack than with any Shakespearean verse."[21] Yet James Loehlin sees the rock soundtrack as being "sonic flair," which is used to "balance out the weaknesses in the film, notably the vocal shortcomings of the cast."[22]

Where teen heartthrobs Leonardo DiCaprio and Clare Danes fail to do Shakespeare's verse justice, One Inch Punch, the Butthole Surfers, and Stina Nordenstam support the text by referencing it in the music and, arguably, serve as a more poetic interpretation of some of the lines. Many of the songs on the sound track echo lines from *Romeo and Juliet*, placing Shakespeare's text into a rock context. For example, almost all of the lyrics from "Pretty Piece of Flesh" by One Inch Punch come from the opening scene between the servants of the two households:

> "I strike quickly being moved" (1.1.6)
> "The weakest goes to the wall" (1.1.13–14)
> "I am a pretty piece of flesh" (1.1.29)

Similarly, lines from the play occur in "Local God" by Everclear, "To You I Bestow" by Mundy, and "Whatever" by the Butthole Surfers, all contemporary American alternative rock bands invited to contribute to the sound track. For Lurhman, it was not enough to have rock music in the Shakespearean film, it was necessary to have Shakespearean verse in the rock sound track.[23]

Mary Lindroth takes this argument even further by stating that the soundtrack of Luhrmann's film serves the same purpose in the movie that music did in Shakespeare's play: to entertain the audience, to "shape the audience's experience," "to signal a change in scene, a change in tone, [or] a change in pace," and works with the camera to tell the story.[24] In other words, just as the music in Shakespeare's original production served a variety of purposes, but was inarguably "contemporary music," Luhrmann's film uses contemporary music of the present (i.e., rock and "pop") to serve the same purposes in his film version. Luhrmann, clearly directing for a youth audience, relies upon a heavily edited text, a strong popular music sound track, and, in Loehlin's words, "MTV-style camera work and editing" to recreate Shakespeare's play for generations X and Y.[25] *William Shakespeare's Romeo + Juliet* is the most obvious example, but neither the first nor last film to cinematize Shakespeare for the alternative pop and hip-hop generations.[26]

We might note in closing this section that it was The Beatles, arguably one of the greatest and most popular rock bands of all times, who were among the first to expropriate Shakespearean text for use in a song. A year after Rado, Ragni and McDermot began work on *Hair*, John Lennon wrote a song titled "I Am the Walrus," which has become a cultural touchstone in many ways. While recording the song on September 29, 1967, the engineer had a radio turned to the BBC's production of *The Tragedy of King Lear*. Lennon chose to end the song with a section of text from the production.

As the final "Goo Goo Goo Joob" blends into a cacophony of sound, under the noise and music is the following exchange from *King Lear*:

> *Oswald:*   Slave, thou hast slain me. Villain, take my purse.
>   If ever thou wilt thrive, bury my body
>   And give the letters which you find'st about me
>   To Edmund, Earl of Gloucester. Seek him out
>   Upon the English party. O, untimely death!
>   Death! [He dies].
> *Edgar:*   I know thee well: a serviceable villain,
>   As duteous to the vices of thy mistress
>   As badness would desire.
> *Gloucester:*   What, is he dead?
> *Edgar:*   Sit you down, father. Rest you.
>
> (4.6.246–255)

Ironically, this first use of Shakespeare's text was neither for the purposes of demystifying Shakespeare nor for connecting the Beatles's music with high culture, which Lennon notoriously (yet playfully) dismissed. Rather, Lennon used the Shakespearean expropriation in the service of his desire to mock and "take the piss out of" those who found literary references, allusions to the band's personal lives, and deeper philosophical and poetical meanings in Beatle's lyrics than John believed were actually in them.

Pete Shotton, John Lennon's good friend and biographer reports that Lennon was both displeased and amused that teachers at his former school were having students study Lennon's lyrics to see the poetry and deeper meanings. Upon recording the song for *Magical Mystery Tour*, Lennon remarked, "Let the fuckers work that one out."[27] "I Am the Walrus," including the *King Lear* text, was written solely to string together a series of nonsense words and images in order to see what meaning might be found by fans, scholars, and teachers. Lennon had no intention to link the song to high culture by using Shakespeare: he thought those who studied his lyrics as poetry were already quite foolish. Lennon had no intention to popularize or make Shakespeare accessible. That the text of *King Lear* is in the song at all is part coincidence and serendipity and part practical joke. If anything, it proves how much humor plays a role in rock Shakespeare.

Expropriation of Rock Songs in Productions of Shakespeare

If productions of Shakespeare in the 1960s used rock to rebel, as argued above, productions in the 1980s, 1990s, and the current decade have used rock nostalgically. This fact may be partly attributable to the aging of the baby boom generation, in their teens and early twenties in the 1960s, but significantly older in the latter era, and to the trend to commercialization in contemporary rock music. As Dennis Hopper has stated, "The counterculture has become the culture."[28]

In every period since the Elizabethan, the production of Shakespeare's plays has expropriated contemporary music from the period. Shakespeare has always been "adapted" by using the popular music of the day, whether operatic adaptation, the addition of songs and/or dances, and incidental music. Nineteenth-century America saw burlesques, vaudevilles, and even minstrel show pastiches/adaptations of Shakespeare. The twentieth century saw numerous Broadway-style adaptations of Shakespeare's plays, renegotiating American cultural space through this indigenous dramatic form.[29]

Unlike earlier adaptations of Shakespeare into musicals, such as *Kiss Me Kate* and *The Boys from Syracuse*, which had original songs, and *Hair* and *"Naked" Hamlet*, which gave a rock soundtrack to Shakespeare's text, the new American Shakespearean adaptations use songs from popular music alongside Shakespeare's prose to develop new pieces, or, perhaps more accurately, new pastiches, not unlike the nineteenth-century variation. The first adaptation to do so was actually a British production based on *The Tempest*, titled *Return to the Forbidden Planet*. First performed in May of 1983 by the Bubble Theatre Company in England and revised and performed all over the world with extended runs in London and New York, Bob Carlton's rock-and-roll musical blends Shakespearean text with the 1956 film *Forbidden Planet*, itself adapted from Shakespeare's *The Tempest*.[30] The play also uses sections of text from *Romeo and Juliet* and *A Midsummer Night's Dream* and incorporates the 1950s and 1960s rock-and-roll music to induce nostalgia as well as to advance the plot: Jerry Lee Lewis's "Great Balls of Fire," "Please Don't Let Me Be Misunderstood" and "We Gotta Get Out of this Place" by the Animals, "Why Must I Be a Teenager in Love?" by Frankie Lymon and the Teenagers, "Who's Sorry Now?" by Connie Francis, and Bobby "Boris" Pickett's "Monster Mash." The songs were not original to the show. The pleasure (and meaning) for the audience came from the use of a familiar song in a different context—in this case, Shakespeare's play via a science fiction film.

Presaging Baz Luhrmann by a decade and a half, Carlton's play opens with a television newscaster on a video screen reciting a parody of the opening chorus of *Romeo and Juliet*:

> Two parents, both alike in dignity
> In outer space where we our play locate
> From ancient grudge break to new mutiny
> And on a forbidden planet meet their fate.[31]

The chorus evokes both a Shakespearean sense and the original science fiction film upon which the play is based, equating the two and relying upon the audience's awareness of the double reference to create nostalgia, both for Shakespeare and 1950s science fiction films.

The play tells the story of Captain Tempest, whose ship lands on the forbidden planet where Dr. Prospero has been raising his daughter Miranda, since having been marooned by his wife. His experiments have created an "Id Monster," that attacks the group, and Captain Tempest, who has fallen in love with Miranda, rescues her and the ship escapes just in time.

The play blends familiar Shakespearean reference with familiar rock-and-roll songs from the 1950s and 1960s, often changing words to make them more relevant to the situation in the drama. The crew sings Jerry Lee Lewis's "Great Balls of Fire" when the ship encounters the asteroid storm that forces them to land on the forbidden planet. Prospero sings "Don't Let Me Be Misunderstood" by the Animals when he first encounters the crew. Miranda, being accused by her father of having an interest in Captain Tempest, sings "Why Must I Be a Teenager in Love?" by Frankie Lymon and the Teenagers. Overhearing this, Captain Tempest belts out "Young Girl" by Gary Puckett and the Union Gap. As Tempest and Miranda flee, Ariel sings Connie Francis's "Who's Sorry Now?" to Prospero. As the Id Monster attacks, the crew sings "We Gotta Get out of This Place" by the Animals. The ship takes off from the forbidden planet to the tune of "Wipe Out," which then segues into "Telstar." Lastly, for the curtain call, Prospero and the Id Monster sing Bobby Pickett's "Monster Mash" as a duet.

The play closes with the epilogue from *A Midsummer Night's Dream*, "If we shadows have offended . . ." with a few changes from the Shakespearean original. The play places classical drama and classical rock music side by side in both importance and sites (and cites) both referentially. As cited in the last chapter, in most productions of Shakespeare expropriating popular music, audiences must be familiar with both the world of popular music and the texts of Shakespeare, and it is the interplay between the two that generates the meaning within production. In other words, double reference. If rock-and-roll Shakespeare relies upon double reception—audiences recognizing both what is Shakespearean and what is rock-and-roll nostalgia—then *Return to the Forbidden Planet* uses triple reception, ideally aimed at an audience that recognizes all sets of references: rock and roll, 1950s science fiction, and Shakespeare.[32] The new play is rewritten with the codes of rock and roll and the new text refers to three sets of source material. Some audience members might know one text referenced, some might know two, some might know all three, and some might not know any.

The different levels of reference are blended, sometimes within the same instance, linking the world of rock music to the worlds of Shakespeare. For example, going mad, *Return*'s Prospero recites Lear's "Blow winds and crack your cheeks" speech to the tune of Elvis's "All Shook Up." Both Elvis and Lear are signified and referenced at the same moment in the production.

The Troubadour Theatre Company of Los Angeles has taken the model of *Return to the Forbidden Planet* and created a style of adaptation and production from it.[33] Blending contemporary clown and commedia dell'arte techniques with the philosophy of Brecht and the plays of Shakespeare, the "Troubies" as they call themselves have deconstructed several of Shakespeare's plays through blending the narrative with the songs of a particular 1970s or 1980s rock group. These productions, including *Twelfth Dog Night*, *A Midsummer Saturday Night's Fever Dream*, *Romeo Hall and Juliet Oates*, *All's Kool That Ends Kool*, *Fleetwood Macbeth*, *The Comedy of Aerosmith* and, most recently (as of this writing) *Hamlet, The Artist Formerly Known as Prince of Denmark* have been critical and popular successes for their reliance on double reference—both familiarity with Shakespeare and popular music—to tell the story in an entertaining way. The improvisational and interactive sections of each show blend with the set pieces of Shakespeare and rock songs to create something not quite Shakespeare and yet wholly dependent on the plays and one's perception of them.[34]

The Troubadours were founded in 1993 and presented a pair of clown-based Shakespearean adaptations in the mid-1990s: *Clown's*

Labour's Lost, a circus version of *Love's Labour's Lost* and *Shrew!*, a clown *Taming of the Shrew*. Beginning in 1999, however, the company (through the lead of its artistic director Matt Walker) began to blend 1970s rock and roll with Shakespearean texts. The first such production was *Twelfth Dog Night*, a blending of Shakespeare's *Twelfth Night* with the music of Three Dog Night.[35]

The program of the show states that the play was written by "the Company (with add'l material by William Shakespeare)." This credit, while humorous, is also indicative of the focus of the company: not on preserving the Shakespearean original, but reshaping the entire experience by the actors for the audience. We might also note that the Troubadours are based in Los Angeles, the same city that produced the infamous credit "By William Shakespeare, with additional dialogue by Sam Taylor" for the 1929 film version of *Taming of the Shrew* starring Douglas Fairbanks and Mary Pickford, the same city that earlier inspired Anita Loos, screenwriter of *Gentlemen Prefer Blondes*, to credit her 1916 screenplay of *Macbeth*, "Written by William Shakespeare and Anita Loos." The program credit may further be a parody of these famous attributions. After *Clown's Labour's Lost* and *Shrew!*, which were very loosely based on the originals, this production was, in the words of one reviewer, the "Troubadour's most faithful production of a Shakespeare play," although he does admit "it still won't satisfy the purists."[36]

When Orsino, stating that "music be the food of love," asks the musicians to "play on," they perform "Just an Old Fashioned Love Song." When Malvolio is locked up for being mad by Toby, Andrew, Feste, and Maria, he sings "One Is the Loneliest Number." Viola sings "Mama Told Me Not to Come" in response to Olivia's attempted seduction, and the whole company rejoices at the end with "Joy to the World."[37]

Over and above the musical additions, the actors metatheatrically engage the fact that they are performing not Shakespeare, but a pastiche of Shakespeare. For example, at one point the characters, desiring to check the Shakespearean original to see how far away from it they have come, pull out not Shakespeare's text but the *Cliffs Notes* for the play. Nonsensical choices are commented upon by the performers: Viola is played by an African American woman, while Sebastian is played by a Euro-American man, prompting the characters to ask why anyone is confusing the twins at all. As with Lennon and "I Am the Walrus," a sense of humor inspires the company to explore the Shakespearean convention of twins in *Twelfth Night* that challenges modern audiences to accept that a man and a woman can be confused for the same person and to take it to a humorous extreme.

Other popular culture references abound, further removing the play from the realm of high culture. The re-enactment of the shipwreck is accompanied by the theme from *Gilligan's Island*. In response to Malvolio's threats to his mistress's uncle and his friends, one of them remarks, "You look like a Klingon." The topical references of Shakespeare's day are replaced with contemporary topical references.

The consultation of the *Cliffs Notes* by the characters indicates that this particular type of "Shakespearean offshoot," to use Ruby Cohn's term, is not merely an attempt to replicate Shakespeare's original texts in new contexts. The Troubies's show is also as much about the idea of Shakespeare and the popular cultural concept of Shakespeare as it is about the original text. Double reference is employed, but it is not even necessary to know the original; one need only know "Shakespeare." The productions are not concerned with authenticity of text, which raises questions of what is being "lost" in such adaptations and to what end, to what extent contemporary audiences have actual knowledge about Shakespeare, and what such experiencing such productions teaches the audience (and the scholar) about Shakespeare and the Elizabethan theatre. As with other youth-culture Shakespeares, the Troubies reduce and translate Shakespeare to the language of youth culture.

The following year, 2000, the Troubadours opened *A Midsummer Saturday Night's Fever Dream*, setting Shakespeare's play in the world of disco. They were not the first to do so. At almost the same time, Project 400 Theatre Group in New York created *The Donkey Show*, a version of *Dream* set in the 1970s in New York at Club Oberon, based on Studio 54. The fairies are gay clubgoers, and Bottom and company are replaced with "the Vinnies, a twin pair of Travolta-ish goon wearing giant afros and leisure suits."[38] Randy Weiner, cocreator of the piece observes, "*Midsummer Night's Dream* is about drugs, love, and sex, and disco is about drugs, sex and love."[39] Like the Troubadours, Project 400 Theatre Group used songs from the era, such as "Ring My Bell," "Knock on Wood," and "You Sexy Thing," performed by the actors, in lieu of some of Shakespeare's text. The same group, it should be noted, previously did *Club 12*, a hip-hop version of *Twelfth Night*. Their goal is to "connect . . . theatre culture with club life, pop culture, and pop music."[40]

In the Troubadour production, Bottom and the mechanicals are presented as the Village People. The play has moved from Athens to the San Fernando Valley, Theseus is "Duke of Burbank," and the play-within-the-play becomes a drag show to the tune of "More than a Woman," yet retaining all of Shakespeare's original lines, referencing both gay culture and the Renaissance tradition of boys playing women. This last is an example of the double reference present in every moment of Troubadour's productions. Again, the local reviewers concur: "this is not pure Shakespeare" (whatever that is), but "the world needs more such Shakespeare," because it tells the story, has lots of laughs, and is accessible to all ages.[41] "Youth culture Shakespeare" triumphs over "boring Shakespeare" every time.

A *Midsummer Saturday Night's Fever Dream* was followed by *Romeo Hall and Juliet Oates* in 2001. A local critic referred to the growing body of the Troubadour's work as "mutilations of Shakespeare," even as he recognized that they were "honest attempts to channel the playwright's original intent. Between goofball parody and historical accuracy, the group drew a very fine line."[42] Again, popular rock songs, this time from the 1970s and 1980s duo Hall and Oates, replace or augment Shakespeare's text. The Queen Mab speech becomes "Man Eater," the fairy queen that "driveth o'er a soldier's neck, / And then dreams he of cutting foreign throats," (1.4.82–84) is now one that one must "watch out for her, she'll chew you up / wo-oo here she comes, she's a man eater." The Nurse admonishes Juliet with "Rich Girl." At the Capulet's party, as Romeo and Juliet spy on each other, even as Tybalt watches them, the company sings "Private Eyes." The balcony scene closes with "Kiss on My Lips." Of course, when Romeo comes to Juliet's tomb he sings "She's Gone." One critic observed "Strange as it may sound, vintage Hall and Oates hits . . . dovetail perfectly with Shakespeare's tragedy."[43]

The Comedy of Aerosmith presents Shakespeare's comedy as literal rock concert. Rather than ushers, the production featured security and bouncers. A band called "The Rag Dolls" form the backing group (as well as a play on Aerosmith's song "Rag Doll"). Twin Antipholi, dressed like Stephen Tyler, the lead singer of Aerosmith, and followed by twin Dromios, dressed as roadies, are mistaken for one another throughout the concert. As with *Midsummer*, the references are topical. The duke becomes "The Duke of San Fernando Valley," who opens the show with Aerosmith's "Home Sweet Home," and sentences Egeus to death. Dr. Pinch sings "Livin' on the Edge." Antipholus attempts to sooth his angry wife with "Cryin'." In short, many well-known Aerosmith songs are used to replace Shakespeare's monologues and dialogues.

The key difference between *Aerosmith* and the previous offerings was the age appropriateness of the material. Whereas in previous productions the Troubies had kept the adaptations family friendly, *Aerosmith* (in keeping with the music of the band) was bawdy, at times verging on the pornographic. Reviews, press releases, and the program all mentioned that the show was intended "for adults."[44] The change in approach also entailed a change in venue. In addition to performing in the Los Angeles area theatres the company ordinarily performed in, the show premiered at the Roxy on the Sunset Strip, a club known for the performances of some of the most famous rock-and-roll performers.

Most recently, as of this writing, the company performed *Hamlet, the Artist Formerly Known as Prince of Denmark*, "an experiment in excess," according to Walker that combines the story of Hamlet with the music of Prince.[45] The company even used a line from Prince's "1999" to promote the play: "Tonight we're gonna party like it's 1599," parodying Prince's tribute to the pre-millennial celebrations (written in 1984), as well as emphasizing the period when the play was written.

Prince's music is used throughout the play to replace lines or explicate scenes. "Sign 'o the Times" is used to give the back story of the play. Ophelia's madness is summed up when she sings "Delirious." Hamlet's scene with Gertrude in her closet featured "I Feel for You" (written by Prince, but covered by Chaka Khan), which replaced the lyrics of the cover "Chaka Kahn, Chaka Kahn, let me love you, that's all I want to do," of the original with "Hamlet's mom, Hamlet's mom, let me love you, that's all I want to do," thereby implying the relationship between Hamlet and his mother as expressed in the Olivier film.

That same subtext is also raised in the "Get thee to a nunnery" scene, which devolved from Shakespeare's dialogue into Prince's "When Doves Cry." Hamlet sings to Ophelia, "Maybe I'm just too demanding, maybe I'm just like my father—too bold," and the Ghost danced through the scene. This bit was followed by the next lyric, "Maybe I'm just like my mother. She's never satisfied," and Gertrude followed the ghost through the scene. The song itself is from the record and film *Purple Rain*, Prince's semi-autobiographical story of a young musician who leaves a difficult home life to become a famous musician. In the Troubie production, the story of Hamlet becomes overlaid with the story of Prince and the story of "The Kid," Prince's character in *Purple Rain*.

The scene is made more complicated by the fact that Ophelia is played by a young man in drag, which is consistent with English

Renaissance practice, although certainly not modern practice. The young man and Hamlet also echo the questionable masculinity of Prince, who is known for his own androgyny. In short, the Troubie's version of *Hamlet* conflates the Shakespearean character with the contemporary rock musician and uses the audience's knowledge of each to inform the performance.

The killing of Claudius is carried out (ironically?) to "I Would Die 4 U," another song from *Purple Rain*. Hamlet "dies" by putting on makeup that allows him to resemble the Ghost while the company sings "Purple Rain," a song about "the afterlife" and the wishes one has for those left behind. Again, Hamlet, Prince, and "The Kid" are conflated, or "ghosted" in Marvin Carlson's sense—the figure of Hamlet is haunted not only by other Hamlets one has seen, but now by the figure of Prince and a character that Prince has played.[46] The recognizable lines of Shakespeare's play are conflated with recognizable lines of Prince music, forming not only an intertext, but a dialogue between the two. The rest is not silence; it is a party in the afterlife with funky music.

It is not only the use of Prince music that transforms *Hamlet* into youth culture, but the manner in which that music is used. The Troubies use Prince's music (and their own rewrites of the script) to transform *Hamlet* into a teen drama. Not only does Hamlet have a nasty stepfather, friends he cannot trust and friends he can, and a crazy girlfriend, he also has the ghost of his dead father telling him to avenge his father's murder. The Nunnery scene is transformed though the use of a "flashback curtain" (behind which, Hamlet puts on a huge blonde afro while Ophelia puts on orthodontic headgear), to show what Hamlet's senior prom was like. Ophelia was his date, and the two of them slow dance awkwardly while discussing what they want to be when they grow up.

When Hamlet stabs Polonius through the arras, the Ghost appears to him. Hamlet apologizes, "Sorry, Dad." Rather than telling Hamlet to leave his mother alone and get revenge on Claudius, as in the original, the Ghost calmly states, "Hamlet, I'm not angry. I'm just disappointed," to which Hamlet drops to his knees, crying out, "That's so much worse," as any teen can relate. The Troubies reduce *Hamlet* to *Dawson's Creek* or *The O.C.*, reduces the metaphysical uncertainties of the play to moments of teen angst, and conflates Hamlet, Prince, and The Kid, so that Hamlet is just that—a kid.

Lastly, the Troubies reduce, translate and openly refer to "Hamlet," *Hamlet*, and Hamlet. The production consciously acknowledges the audience's idea (and ideal) of *Hamlet*. As is standard for the Troubies, *Hamlet* enters reading the *Cliffs Notes* to the play, informing his mother, "You do not want to know what's going to happen." Horatio begins writing down the famous lines from the play when Hamlet says them. "You've got to write these things down when you hear them," he tells the audience. "That's another good one," he tells Hamlet in response to a line. "It's like you're quoting something!" he excitedly tells Hamlet at one point. Finally, when Hamlet is alone on stage with Ophelia, after telling her to get herself to a nunnery, he calls out, "Ooooh, Horatio," to which Horatio, backstage, yells back, "Got it!" The "To Be" soliloquy is moved to the end of the play, where the gag then plays out. As Hamlet finishes the speech and looks expectantly at Horatio, who has been writing furiously, Horatio intones, "or not to be . . ." and then tells Hamlet that he got "the important bit." As noted in the introduction, *Hamlet* is reduced down to a series of recognizable quotations: the important bits.

In yet another bit that deconstructs "Hamlet" and the image of Hamlet in the popular culture, Hamlet holds up the skull in the gravedigger scene and asks who it is. The gravedigger responds, "This same skull, sir, was Yorick's skull." "Yorick!" exclaims Hamlet, who is immediately undercut by the gravedigger grabbing the skull back and saying, "Whoops, no. Wait! His is down here somewhere." The gravedigger then throws around several skulls before holding one up to Hamlet. Hamlet takes the skull, but the spinal column of vertebrae is still attached to it. Thus, the audience sees not just the iconic image of a young man dressed all in black holding a skull, but also holding a spine. There is also no guarantee that the skull is, in fact, Yorick's, as the audience has just seen several in the grave. What seems initially a series of sight gags ultimately serve to destabilize the popular, iconic image of Hamlet as the young man contemplating the skull of his beloved jester. Instead, the audience sees a young man unsure of whose skull he's holding and with the rest of the skeleton partly attached. The iconic image is undermined and satirized, reminding the audience that they are watching *Hamlet*, but not really *Hamlet*.

Walker promises to continue the rock and Shakespeare blend through the canon until audiences lose interest. Future possibilities include *Queen Lear* (*King Lear* with the music of Queen), *Little Richard III*, *The Merry Wives of Earth, Windsor, and Fire*, *As U2 Like It*, *Much Adoobie Brothers about Nothing*, and even some of the lesser-seen works of the canon, such as the proposed *Timon and Garfunkle of Athens*.

Bad puns aside, the suggested titles each link one of Shakespeare's plays with the music of a specific popular singer or group. The actual linkage is not made because of the appropriateness of the specific music for the play: there is nothing inherent in either *King Lear* or the music of Queen that links the two together. Nor does the pastoral comedy of *As You Like It* find an automatic correspondence in the often politically charged music of Irish band U2. Instead, the connection is made by the compatibility of the title of the work and the title of the band, allowing the two to form a punning title, and requires that the band have a familiar enough and large enough catalogue of music available to fill two hours traffic on a stage. As a result, the songs make sense, but they are often linked to the show in a tenuous manner at best. I shall return to this idea later. Likewise, the Troubies rely upon nostalgia for rock and roll from the 1970s, 1980s and 1990s and nostalgia for Shakespeare, an idea that I shall explore in depth later as well.

The series of similar productions has also resulted in a following for the Troubies in Los Angeles, which has lead to further "hauntings" in Marvin Carlson's sense. Carlson writes that individual companies build up a "bank of remembered previous work."[47] Not only is *Hamlet, The Artist Formerly Known as Prince of Denmark* haunted by Prince and "The Kid," it is haunted by ten years of other productions. "The primary haunting," as Carlson puts it, "has become the artist's own previous work."[48] The Troubies certainly repeat elements form show to show, including the use of a trampoline, a "penalty flag" for forgotten lines or missed cues, singing to latecomers, as well as the presence of company members. The idea of Troubie-style rock Shakespeare also haunts their work. Reviewers are quick to criticize if a show does not match previous levels of professionalism or silliness, and equally quick to compare the current production with past ones in a manner that they might not had the Troubies not developed such a distinctive approach to Shakespearean appropriation through rock music.

Finally, I would like to focus on the idea that "rock-and-roll Shakespeare," whether practiced by the Troubies or by Baz Luhrmann, translates Shakespeare by adapting not only the texts of the plays and linking nostalgic rock music to it, but also by adapting the idea or concept of Shakespeare. In popular culture, Shakespeare is often presented as "high culture," even though the very presence of Shakespeare in popular culture indicates a far more complex relationship between the canon, the playwright, popular, high, mass and mass produced culture, or what Michael Bristol terms "Bardbiz."[49] Shakespeare as cultural icon serves multiple functions in these productions.

First, Shakespeare as the embodiment of "high" culture can be invoked in production to grant legitimacy to performances and productions equally yoked to mass or popular culture. Rather than rock music serving Shakespeare, the Shakespeare in the piece serves the rock music. Second, as Shakespeare the concept is a distant and scary thing, served up in high school as part of education and "culture," he is "bad" and boring. In order to rescue the plays from this context, the rock-and-roll adapters attempt to demystify Shakespeare by making his plots, characters, and occasionally language, accessible and not too distant from more contemporary entertainments. In other words, the rock music serves the Shakespeare as a vehicle.

These contrasting uses of Shakespeare the concept raise the larger issue of what is "Shakespeare" about Shakespeare? The Troubies consult the *Cliffs Notes* rather than the actual text. They replace Shakespeare's poetry with more familiar rock songs. Shakespeare's plays are rooted in his language and poetry, and yet that is precisely what many of the adaptations listed here remove and/or replace with rock music. What remains are Shakespeare's plots and characters, which were borrowed in the first place. When Shakespeare is expropriated through rock music (or rock music expropriated to serve Shakespeare) in American cultural space, more often than not what is being adapted is Shakespeare the concept as much as the play itself.

For example, in 2002, *All's Kool That Ends Kool* blended the plot of *All's Well* with the funk music of Kool and the Gang.[50] Unlike the previous three shows, the Troubies were attempting to produce a lesser-known play, leading one to ask what, precisely, is being decontextualized here: the Shakespearean play or the popular music? Arguably, both are being recontextualized. Again, Shakespeare's plotline stays intact, but well-known rock songs are introduced to the narrative. When the songs work, they really work, such as when the lords, Bertram, and Parolles prepare for Bertram's wooing of Diana by singing "Ladies Night," or when "Cherish" is sung ironically at the wedding of the unwilling Bertram and Helena in II, iii, or (the rather obvious) singing of "Celebration" at the conclusion of the play when Bertram agrees to remain with Helena. Some of the song choices, however, seem random and arbitrary, such as when the company sings "Jungle Boogie" as Helena cures the King in II, i. This production perhaps best showcases the strengths and weaknesses of the approach.

Perhaps the most telling moment in the production is when Bertram (played by artistic director Matt Walker) woos the widow and her daughter and actually uses the exact lines from the Shakespearean original. The lines flow and sound remarkably smooth, even as we recognize their heightened artifice. After a beat, Walker turns to the audience and says, "That's what this is all supposed to sound like— pretty good stuff, huh?" Walker does not, however, drop character at that moment as he does at other times in the play, instead keeping his Bertram voice and demeanor. We become aware of the numerous levels of reference, for example, a character, aware that he is a character, not in a Shakespeare play, but a play based on Shakespeare, and aware of the difference between the audience's Shakespearean expectations and Troubadour expectations. The fact that the performer delivers the original Shakespearean lines so well further blurs the reality of the show. The performers could perform Shakespeare as written, had they chosen to, says Walker, even as he acknowledges that the stuff is "pretty good." He also acknowledges that the original is how *All's Well* is "supposed to sound." But this production is not *All's Well*, it is *All's Kool*—the change in name connoting more than a change in text, but rather a change in attitude. Yet, interestingly, Walker argues that what the Troubies do is Shakespeare, at least as Southern Californian audiences understand him.

"Each production," Walker asserts, "involves the awareness that you must keep the familiar things."[51] The "familiar things" refers to both the familiar in Shakespeare ("But soft, what light through yonder window breaks?") and the familiar rock songs associated with the band of the title. As Walker puts it, "You can't do a show about Fleetwood Mac and not do 'Landslide,' " referring to one of the best known hits of the band. In the Troubie production, the dead Macbeth gets up after being killed by Macduff and sings the song, which is a rather bizarre choice—not corresponding to anything in the Shakespearean original but needed as the familiar things must be kept.

The familiar things do not even need to be related to the production at hand. For example, in *Fleetwood Macbeth*, Macbeth stands on the castle battlement contemplating killing the king, when a man in tight black pants, t-shirt with the Rolling Stones's lips logo on it, and large lips dances up to him. A look of horror crosses Macbeth's face and he asks, "Is this a Jagger I see before me?" The line only works if one knows both Mick Jagger and the original Shakespeare line about a dagger, otherwise the pun is lost. The pun is there, however, for its own sake. Jagger has nothing to do with Fleetwood Mac, nor with

Macbeth. His "presence" is an incorporated reference designed solely for humorous effect, without any other meaning intended.[52] However, simply because meaning is unintended does not mean that none is generated. Audiences read into the presence of Jagger beyond the pun.

Walker further asserts that American culture is all recycled: "Our television shows and movies are remakes; our music is sampled," and thus, our Shakespeare is merely an amalgam of other Shakespeares we have encountered. The role of the Troubies, he asserts, is to create a Shakespeare for popular audiences in Southern California. They translate Shakespeare using the popular music more recognizable to the audience that the Elizabethan texts.

The use of youth music, however, does not necessarily indicate a limitation of the ages of the audience to only those who are currently young; the Troubadours are interested in appealing to all ages. The use of classical rock provokes nostalgia for the older members of the audience. The combination of clowning and rock music is to provide mediation for younger audience members. Walker claims, "If we can help them to become interested in Shakespeare at a young age, hopefully they will appreciate good theatre as adults."[53] The presumption behind Walker's remark is that the Troubadours's version of Shakespeare is not only "good theatre" but also an authentic Shakespeare in which young audience members might become interested. He may be right (his productions, after all, are always critical and popular successes), but any audience member who looks to the original text to see what was present in a Troubie production will find the two are remarkably different. What has been offered up on stage is an approximation of Shakespeare the concept as much as (if not more so than) an adaptation of the original play.

It is ironic and appropriate that the Troubadour productions are hailed as innovative, considering that they link two cultural pasts—the Elizabethan/Jacobean theatre and classic American rock and roll. A double nostalgia is thus evoked, both for the rock and roll of the audience member's youth as well as for the theatre considered to be one of the greatest in the history of the English language. These productions are also reflective of similar cultural trends. The predominance of music video in the last decades of the twentieth century and the first decade of the twenty-first means music has become more visually oriented, even as productions of Shakespeare move further away from text and more toward the visual. The Troubadours displace the text of Shakespeare with references to Shakespeare and create a new visual narrative for the popular song.

The Troubie productions are not so much adaptations as pastiches. They do not so much adapt Shakespeare as mediate between the text, the idea of Shakespeare, and American popular culture. The rock music becomes a mediating device that bridges the gaps of high and popular culture, old and modern, British and American. In their discussion of Shakespearean films of the 1990s, Lynda E. Boose and Richard Burt observe that Shakespeare "is such a signifier for British cultural superiority."[54] Yet rock and roll is as American as the proverbial apple pie. The use of Three Dog Night, Hall and Oates, Kool and the Gang, and disco hits Americanizes Shakespeare, making his work only 20 years distant in the past, rather than 400, and removes the language by which youth audiences are typically challenged. Dennis Kennedy observes that translations of Shakespeare into foreign languages make the texts closer to the contemporary language of London (or Los Angeles, for that matter) than to the original English.[55] "Foreign Shakespeare" tends to be much more accessible to the audience, linguistically speaking. Rock-and-roll Shakespeare treats the texts as foreign works to be translated into modern American English. While Kennedy observes that "modernist high culture and the entrenched position of the Shakespeare industry" indicates that no translations of Shakespeare's plays into modern English will gain wide currency, production can and will do just that.[56]

One might look at these productions of rock-and-roll mediated Shakespeare in different contexts, observing different possible ways in which they reinscribe the plays, the man, and the concept of Shakespeare. First, all of the plays considered in this study fall into the category of adaptations of Shakespeare, just like Nahum Tate's *King Lear* or Tom Stoppard's *Rosencrantz and Guildenstern Are Dead*. While knowledge of the original provides a different understanding of the play in the case of the latter, in the case of the former Tate does not care if his audience knows the original (and arguably would prefer that they did not). The Troubadours use music as a double referent that moves the plot, but also substitutes for the original Shakespearean verse for the purpose of making, as Tate did, a Shakespeare that is to the taste of a contemporary audience. Authenticity and faithfulness to text or original conditions of production are not prioritized (although the issue of "authenticity" is more complex, and will be noted later)— playing to a popular audience on its own level through its own taste is.

Second, one might see the plays as rock musicals, particularly given the recent trend of pop musicals. In a recent article in *American Theatre*, John Istel noted that for much of the twentieth century "popular music *was* theatre music"—Irving Berlin, George M. Cohen, even Rodgers and Hammerstein's music was the pop music of its day.[57] Recently, musicals have been created around the music of Abba, Billy Joel, and Randy Newman, to name but three. Baz Luhrmann's follow-up to *William Shakespeare's Romeo + Juliet* was *Moulin Rouge*, an "original" musical that used pop songs from Nirvana, T-Rex, Madonna, The Police, David Bowie, Elton John, and dozens of others. Productions such as *All's Kool That Ends Kool* or *Hamlet, the Artist Formerly Known as Prince of Denmark* simply does the same thing with Shakespeare.

Third, Troubadour Theatre Company productions represent a kind of American Shakespeare, one perhaps more original than more straightforward, high productions and predating the Poel-inspired Elizabethan revival. Lawrence Levine tells of a nineteenth-century American production of Shakespeare's first comedy titled *Ye Comedie of Errours, a Glorious Uprorious Burlesque, Not Indecorous nor Censorious, with Many a Chorus, Warrented Not to Bore Us, Now for the First Time Set Before Us*.[58] Levine argues that the idea of Shakespeare as so-called high culture is a fairly recent invention in the history of Shakespearean production, the product of Victorian attitudes toward culture. Until the twentieth century, Shakespeare was popular culture, and was frequently adapted into American milieus. One might consider the Troubadour productions as a return to a genuinely American way of approaching Shakespeare.

Fourth, reviews of the productions discussed in this article argue rock Shakespeare is offensive to "purists" and lack the authenticity of a "straight" production of Shakespeare. Yet, one might read rock productions Shakespeare via Baudrillad's theories of simulation. In *Simulacra and Simulation*, Baudrillard argues that Shakespeare is no longer real. Shakespeare is a "simulated environment" much like the Cloisters in New York, taken out of its original context and presented as if real, though not—it is the idea of a "real" Shakespeare that is a "total simulation."[59] Critics who dismiss youth-culture Shakespeare, including rock Shakespeare, dislike its "simulation of the third order," a reminder that ALL Shakespeare is appropriation, is imaginary, is not real, or authentic, or canonical, in any sense of the word.[60] Which *King Lear* is real? Is Hamlet's flesh solid or sullied? The more one strives for authenticity, such as at the Globe in London, the more the experience is actually simulation. *Hamlet, The Artist Formerly Known as Prince of Denmark* is neither Prince concert nor Shakespeare play; it is a simulation of both, one designed to amuse, delight, and evoke nostalgia. And, as Baudrillard writes, "when the real is no longer what it was, nostalgia assumes its full meaning."[61] In other words, since no Shakespeare is real, all Shakespeare is nostalgia and the Troubadours, among others willingly embrace the simulacrum, even as they indicate to the audience that it is a simulacrum, via the use of *Cliffs Notes* on stage or the metatheatrical knowledge of the characters.

Shakespeare and rock-and-roll music are now permanently mixed in American production culture, and what was so shocking to audiences in 1969 has become commonplace and even expected.[62] Rock-and-roll rebellion has become nostalgia. The music of rebellious youth is now hip-hop and rap, although these forms, too, are becoming rapidly mainstream and commercialized. In the future it is altogether possible that so-called ad-rap-tations of Shakespeare will be equally as nostalgic and commonplace. If each generation must rediscover the classics, then one of the standard methods of rediscovery and exploration of Shakespeare's plays will be to filter the texts through the popular music of those generations yet to come. While this author will not predict how soon we might see Britney Spears as Ophelia, or hear King Lear rap out Eminem's "My Name Is . . . ," yet it will come: the readiness is all.[63]

Notes

1. Information about *Hair* is taken from both the published text (Gerome Ragni and James Rado, *Hair* [New York: Pocket Books, 1969]) and from the liner notes of the re-release of the original Broadway cast recording on compact disc (*Hair: The Original Broadway Cast Recording*. RCA Victor 1150–2-RC, 1968, 1988). See also Barbara Lee Horn, *The Age of Hair* (Westport: Greenwood, 1991).
2. Note the similarity between "Claude" and "Claudius." Yet Claude is the Hamlet figure in this play.
3. All quotations from Shakespeare are taken from *The Riverside Shakespeare*, edited by G. Blakemore Evans (Boston: Houghton-Mifflin, 1974).
4. Joseph Papp and Ted Cornell, *William Shakespeare's "Naked" Hamlet: A Production Handbook* (New York: Macmillan, 1969), p. 40.
5. Ibid., p. 41.
6. Quoted in the Preface to Papp and Cornell *"Naked" Hamlet*, p. 9.
7. Papp and Cornell, *"Naked" Hamlet*, p. 9.
8. Interestingly, a similar situation evolved out of the 1999–2000 production of *The Bomb-itty of Errors*, an "ad-rap-tation" of *The Comedy of Errors*, in which *New York Times* critic Bruce Weber slams the play as doing "damage to Shakespeare." See the next chapter (chapter 4) for an analysis of both that production and hip-hop and Shakespeare in general.

9. John Guare, Mel Shapiro, and Galt MacDermot, *Two Gentlemen of Verona* (New York: Holt, Rinehart and Winston, 1979).

10. Deanne Williams, "Mick Jagger Macbeth," in *Shakespeare Survey 57: Macbeth and Its Afterlife*, edited by Peter Holland (Cambridge: Cambridge University Press, 2004), p. 145.

11. Williams, "Mick Jagger Macbeth," p. 147.

12. Williams, "Mick Jagger Macbeth," pp. 148, 147.

13. Paul Friedlander, *Rock and Roll: A Social History* (Boulder: Westview, 1996), p. 285.

14. Stephen M. Buhler, "Reviving Juliet, Repackaging Romeo: Transformations of Character in Pop and Post-pop Music," in *Shakespeare After Mass Media*, edited by Richard Burt (New York: Palgrave, 2002), pp. 243–264.

15. The rise of pop Ophelia references may be directly related to the increased connection between Ophelia and disenfranchised and alienated teenaged girls in such works as *Reviving Ophelia* by Mary Pipher (New York, 1994) and the other volumes on the topic that have followed, although The Ophelias and *Swamp Ophelia* predate those books. See chapter 6 in this book for an analysis of the "Ophelia-ization" of American adolescent girls.

16. See B. Lee Cooper and Wayne S. Haney, *Rock Music in American Popular Culture: Rock "n" Roll Resources* (New York: Haworth, 1995) for the leveling of references within pop lyrics. They observe, "Sources such as The Holy Bible, Shakespeare's plays, and books by Lewis Carroll and Charles Dickens are freely intermingled with popular culture references" (p. 192).

17. The irony is, of course, that the film is so much the product of Luhrmann's vision that many reviews and articles referred to it as "Baz Luhrmann's *William Shakespeare's Romeo + Juliet*."

18. Lynda E. Boose and Richard Burt, "Totally *Clueless*? Shakespeare Goes Hollywood in the 1990s," in *Shakespeare: The Movie*, edited by Lynda E. Boose and Richard Burt (New York: Routledge, 1997), p. 17. See Robert L. York's chapter on Shakespearean youth films in this volume for more information.

19. *William Shakespeare's Romeo + Juliet*, prod. Gabriella Martinelli and Baz Luhrmann, dir. Baz Luhrmann, 120 minutes, Twentieth Century Fox, 1997, DVD.

20. *William Shakespeare's Romeo + Juliet: Music from the Motion Picture*, Capitol Records CDP8 37715 0, 1996 and *William Shakespeare's Romeo + Juliet: Music from the Motion Picture: Volume 2*, Capitol Records CDP72438 55567 2 2, 1997.

21. Donald Lyons, "Lights, Camera, Shakespeare" *Commentary* (February), pp. 57–60.

22. James N. Loehlin, " 'These Violent Delights Have Violent Ends': Baz Luhrmann's Millenial Shakespeare," in *Shakespeare, Film, Fin de Siècle*, edited by Mark Thornton Burnett and Ramona Wray (New York: St. Martin's, 2000), pp. 123–124.

23. Yet we might also note that the vast majority of music used in the film is not rock but opera, classical music (Wagner, Faure, Mozart, etc.), Gregorian chants, and other forms of music. The film sites itself in the rock world, and

the focus by critics and MTV, not to mention that the rock music is on the sound tracks, while the classical music is not, makes Luhrmann's film seem much more rock-oriented than it actually is. Mozart and Wagner have as much to do in shaping the soundscape of the film as One Inch Punch and the Butthole Surfers.

24. Lindroth, Mary, "The Prince and the Newscaster: Baz Luhrmann Updates Shakespeare for a Y2K Audience" <http://www.mtsu.edu/~english/lindroth. html> Accessed September 27, 2000.

25. Loehlin, "Violent Delights," p. 123.

26. Luhrmann's film attempts to site Shakespeare not in high culture but in popular culture. Yet even then it is seen as high popular culture. Troma Entertainment, a low budget studio known for such films as *The Toxic Avenger, Class of Nuke 'Em High, and Sgt Kabukiman, N.Y.P.D.*, produced *Tromeo and Juliet* (prod. Lloyd Kaufman and Michael Herz, dir. Lloyd Kaufman, 100 minutes, Troma Entertainment, 1997, videocassette), featuring "all the body-piercing, dismemberment, and car chases Shakespeare always wanted, but never had." Like the sound in Luhrmann's film, this sound track is filled with songs from rock groups such as Sublime, Motorhead, the Ass Ponys, and Unsane. Whereas Luhrmann's film is musically located in alternative pop and dance music, Troma's film is clearly in the world of punk and heavy metal. This fact is underscored by having Lemmy Killmeister, lead guitarist and singer of the heavy metal band Motorhead, as the chorus. Like Luhrmann's film, this film uses written text to identify the members of the cast as they are shown. As the chorus, speaking obviously in Times Square, intones his speech, the onscreen text states "Lemmy: House of Motorhead," equating the band with the Capulets and Montegues. Much of the Troma film parodies the Luhrmann film, where Baz seeks seriousness in his employment of popular culture, Troma revels in b-movie excesses of sex and violence and showing far more edge than *William Shakespeare's Romeo + Juliet*, even as it is as equally distant from mainstream culture.

27. Pete Shotton and Nicholas Schaffner, *John Lennon in My Life* (New York: Stern and Day, 1983).

28. Quoted in Jon Lewis, *The Road to Romance and Ruin: Teen Films and Youth Culture* (New York: Routledge, 1992), p. 100. In the case of the commercialization of rock and pop music, we might note that all 18 tracks of Moby's techno-pop album *Play* were licensed for commercial usage before the album was even released. The acquisition of the Beatles catalogue by Michael Jackson was followed by the licensing of "Revolution" for use by Nike Shoes in its commercials. Both classical rock and new rock music are rapidly being used to endorse products and services.

29. I am in debt to one of the anonymous readers for pointing out this context.

30. Bob Carleton, *Return to the Forbidden Planet* (London: Metheun, 1985).

31. Ibid., p. 7.

32. *Return to the Forbidden Planet* is similar in this fashion to *The Rocky Horror Show*, and the film based upon it, *The Rocky Horror Picture Show*, both of which reference the tropes of rock and roll and 1950s horror/science fiction films. *RTTFP*, however, adds the original Shakespearean references missing from the film *Forbidden Planet*.

33. Which is not to say the Troubadours were directly inspired or influenced by the British show. They developed their style independently out of working on productions of Shakespeare for young audiences at the Grove Shakespeare Theatre in Southern California (Matt Walker, Interview, November 20, 2003). Unless otherwise noted, all quotations from Walker come from this interview.

34. Much information on the group can be found on their Web site <http://www. troubie.com> including the group's mission statement, a history, and several reviews (accessed February 15, 2003).

35. It should be noted that even in their non-Shakespearean productions, the bard is never far from the Troubies's stage or rock culture. In *Funky Punks with Junk in Their Trunks*, a circus-based piece that features clowning, acrobatics, and sketch comedy, one sketch, entitled "The Funky Punks Watch TV," channel surfing clowns switch back and forth between "Masterpiece Theatre's *Romeo and Juliet*" and MTV's *TRL* (although both are performed by the same set of clowns) until the two begin to blend.

36. Joel Beers, "And Now for Something Completely Different," *Orange County Weekly*, July 16, 1999, p. 29.

37. Some material about the production comes from reviews. See Richard Schulenberg, "Troubadour's 'Twelfth Dog Night' at Miles Is 'The Funniest Show in Town'," *Santa Monica Mirror*, August 18–24, 1999, n.p.; Terri Roberts, "Twelfth Dog Night," *Daily Variety*, December 21, 1999, p. 14; and Beers, "Completely Different," p. 29.

38. Isaac Guzman. "Boppin' with the Bard: A Pair of Plays Raps on the Shakespeare Thing," *Newsday*, January 27, 2000, p. C1.

39. Quoted in Guzman, "Boppin," p. C1.

40. Quoted in Guzman, "Boppin," p. C1. It is interesting that two groups, one on each coast in the two largest cities in America, have dedicated themselves to creating accessible productions of Shakespeare through contemporary pop music and both, independently, perform *Twelfth Night* first and *Dream* second. There are, no doubt, reasons for the similar choices, particularly a disco *Dream*, but as such speculations are beyond the scope of this writing; the author simply draws the reader's attention to them.

41. Michael M. Miller. "Shake, Rattle, and Roll Speare," *Orange County Weekly*, July 14, 2000, p. 21.

42. Joel Beers. "Romeo Hall and Juliet Oates," *Orange County Weekly*, July 6, 2001, p. 29.

43. F. Kathleen Foley, " 'Romeo' Forms a Happy Union," *Los Angeles Times*, June 7, 2001, F40.

44. See F. Kathleen Foley, "Sex, drugs and Shakespeare," *Los Angeles Times*, January 1, 2005, E5.

45. Quoted in Dany Margolies, "Bard to the Future." *Backstage West*, August 4, 2005, p. 14.

46. See Marvin Carlson, *The Haunted Stage*: Theatre as Memory Machine (Ann Arbor: University of Michigan Press, 2001).

47. Ibid., pp. 103–104.

48. Ibid., p. 106.

49. Michael D. Bristol, *Big-Time Shakespeare* (London: Routledge, 1996).

50. See Julio Martinez, "All's Kool That Ends Kool," *Daily Variety*, May 23, 2002, p. 12.

51. Walker, Personal Interview, November 20, 2003.

52. Unless, of course, one has read Deanne William's article, cited earlier, "Mick Jagger Macbeth," in which case yet another level of reference, this time academic, is generated. Walker had not heard of the article, the pun was happy coincidence.

53. Quoted in Clara Sturak "Shakespeare's Stayin' Alive with New Production at Miles Playhouse," *Santa Monica Mirror*, July 19–25, 2000, p. 12.

54. Boose and Burt, "Totally *Clueless?*" p. 13.

55. Dennis Kennedy, "Shakespeare without His Language," *Shakespeare, Theory and Performance*, edited by. James C. Bulman (London: Routledge, 1996), pp. 136–137.

56. In fact, one can argue that all productions, even those that use the original texts unedited, "translate" the original language by adding other semiotics (set, costume, video, music, gesture, tone, etc.) to signify in a manner that alters the meaning of the original text. One might not understand the exact meaning of a particular phrase, but in production the meaning (original or new) is made clear as a result of additional signs.

57. John Istel, "Pop Goes the Musical," *American Theatre* 20, no. 3 (March 2003), pp. 21–25.

58. Lawrence Levine, *Highbrow/Lowbrow: The Emergence of Cultural Hierarchy in America* (Cambridge: Harvard University Press, 1988), p. 14.

59. Jean Baudrillard, *Simulacra and Simulation*, translated by Sheila Faria Glaser (Ann Arbor: University of Michigan Press, 1994), 11.

60. Ibid., p. 12.

61. Ibid., p. 6.

62. The author himself, it should be noted, is guilty of employing rock music in academic and professional productions of Shakespeare's plays, from *Richard III* to *The Tempest* to other Elizabethan and Jacobean productions. And he'll do it again, too.

63. An earlier version of this chapter was published in *Theatre Symposium: Elizabethan Performances in North American Spaces* (Tuscaloosa: University of Alabama Press, 2004). The author is grateful for permission to reprint (and greatly expand) it here.

4

"Big Willie Style" Staging Hip-Hop Shakespeare and Being Down with the Bard

Kevin J. Wetmore, Jr.

Is it drama? Is it tragedy?
It's whatever we want it to be.

—The Bomb-itty of Errors

What I do—that's poetry.

—*KRS-ONE*

Sampling Shakespeare

In 1990 Malcolm McLaren, best known as the founder and manger of the Sex Pistols, developed "The World Famous Supreme Team," a group of American hip-hop and dance performers for his CD *Round the Outside! Round the Outside!* Among those gathered was MC Hamlet, a "Dancin' Black Indian Poet" whose name played on then-popular MC Hammer's, as well as the Shakespeare play. MC Hamlet rapped a track entitled "II Be or Not II Be," which played on the famous soliloquy. The first verse of the song began:

> To be or not to be that is the question
> Is it more noble of mind this decision
> To die and lie still for life's ills and torture

The slings and arrows of outrageous fortune
Much more important than winning is trying
Life should be more than just living and dying
Dare I bare arms against troubles I see
Opposing—to end them—to die—to sleep.[1]

This expropriation of Shakespeare into a hip-hop song demonstrates what Henry Louis Gates Jr. terms "signifyin(g)." Signifyin(g) is an African American literary tradition rooted in "repetition and revision, or repetition with a signal difference."[2] Gates argues for the model of "the Trope of the Talking Book"—the "double voiced texts that talk to other texts."[3] This process of signifyin(g) underscores the relationship between texts, works as "an act of homage" to previous texts, and bases its meaning on willful manipulation of the signifiers. In other words, the traditional paradigm in African-derived cultures, argues Gates, is "metamorphosis rather than metaphor"—transforming what already has been referenced into another reference on a multitude of levels.

"The impetus of African-American signifying," reports James R. Andreas, Sr. after Gates, "is the search for the 'black voice' in the 'white written text'."[4] Hip-hop Shakespeare is thus signifyin(g) on Shakespeare—setting up a complex interplay between the original Shakespearean text, elements of hip-hop culture, and the performers' own identities—finding a "black voice" in the "white text" of Shakespeare.

All cultural production is reproduction, but Western critics and scholars seem to especially savage two cultural products as particularly unoriginal: adaptations of Shakespeare and hip-hop "music." Both cultural products frequently find their authenticity questioned as they are derivative of works of others and seen as inferior to the original works. Yet hip-hop expropriations of Shakespeare (and Shakespearean appropriations of hip-hop!) might be seen as part of the larger tradition of signifyin(g)—rewriting through reference, repetition, and revision for the purpose of creating new levels of meaning. Hip-hop Shakespeare "samples" Shakespeare like hip-hop musicians sample previous works of music. Sean "Puff Daddy" Comb's "Come with Me" samples a riff from Led Zepplin's "Kashmir," Vanilla Ice's "Ice Ice Baby" simply looped a hook from Queen's "Under Pressure," Ice T's "The Tower" uses the theme from the film *Halloween* to present a portrait of prison life, etc. The sample not only provides the music and the beat, it is also referential—it refers to the earlier song and the meanings associated with it, building on the previous meaning and juxtaposing the new lyrics in order to generate meaning.

Shakespearean adaptation works in the same way. One can "understand" *Rosencrantz and Guildenstern are Dead* without knowing *Hamlet*, but entire levels of meaning would be missing. Likewise, *Desdemona, a Play about a Handkerchief* works best when the audience knows *Othello*. Hip-hop Shakespeare samples Shakespeare—building a new work by signifyin(g) on the old, and adds new levels of meaning and reference, and above all, play.

In the case of MC Hamlet, for example, the Shakespearean original ("Or to take arms against a sea of troubles") is transformed into "Dare I bare arms against troubles I see," engaging in wordplay with the homonyms "bare" and "bear" and "see" and "sea." The line puns on "bearing arms," that is, carrying weapons, and "baring arms," that is, pushing up one's sleeves and getting to work. It finishes with Shakespeare's original "to die—to sleep," without continuing the line as Shakespeare does. The original text is metamorphosed, Shakespeare's words "signified" upon and played with to generate new and different levels of meaning while still evoking the original. This song might serve as a model for hip-hop productions of Shakespeare's plays.

Following "II Be or Not to Be" was a Grandmaster Caz-rapped track entitled "Romeo and Juliet" that plays on the story of Romeo and Juliet, describing their first sexual encounter from the point of view of a young, urban, African American male. This track is followed by "Wherefor Art Thou?" which samples British voices reciting lines from Shakespeare's *Romeo and Juliet* to a drum machine and the scratching of a hip-hop DJ. The entire album *Round the Outside! Round the Outside!* centers on signifyin(g) on Shakespeare and opera.

Play That Funky Music, White Bard

The problem with contextualizing hip-hop Shakespeare as rooted in the African American literary tradition of signifyin(g) is that Malcolm McLaren, much like many of the creators of much hip-hop Shakespeare, is white. We might interpret this as exploitation as much as expropriation—Europeans using African-derived culture that has proven popular (and profitable) to make money. But there is more going on in hip-hop that has proven a complex site for cultural negotiation, embracing binary dualism on the surface (black/white, male/female, urban/suburban, art/commerce, young/old, etc.), yet on another level rejecting such a simple structuring of the world and examining and working out identity and culture on a much more complex matrix.

One of the top hip-hop artists in America at the time of this writing, for example, is Eminem, who is white. Both Malcolm McLaren and the creators of *The Bomb-itty of Errors* (arguably the most successful appropriation of Shakespeare and hip-hop, discussed later) are white, which can be problematic, especially when signifyin(g) is rooted in the attempt to find a black voice in a white text. Armond White argues that "White . . . appropriation . . . may look like a form of tribute, but it preys more than it praises."[5] He goes on to argue that all too often, especially as witnessed in the case of Vanilla Ice, "white appropriation [of hip-hop] attempts to erase the culture it plunders. . . ."[6] When white artists "rap" Shakespeare, they are essentially removing all African American cultural influences, according to White. Yet, at the same time, Chuck D and Ice T both argue that "hip-hop is at its most revolutionary when it enters the ears of white teenagers."[7] Hip-hop is not only about who produces it, but also who listens to it and who then incorporates its culture into their own identity. Hip-hop, as Potter observes, "invites identification across forbidden lines" of race and class, challenging notions of identity.[8]

Hip-hop sites itself as the product of African American urban cultures. That product has been commodified and used to enrich the corporations of the primarily white-owned music industry, and yet the works themselves also allow, as Potter argues, for the consumer to become a producer. The DJ purchases and plays records, but in playing them, the DJ becomes a producer who remixes, adds new sounds, and works with an MC to create a new product that signifies on the earlier work(s) and also establishes its own identity.[9] Similarly, hip-hop adaptation of Shakespeare turns the artists into producers, who take the Shakespeare (the ultimate dead white male) which was imposed upon them in school and make his works their own. Andre Lefevere notes that, "Rewriting, then, in all its forms, can be seen as a weapon in the struggle for supremacy between various ideologies, various poetics. It should be analyzed and studied that way."[10] Hip-hop Shakespeare asserts the superiority of hip-hop and subjugates the language of the dead, white male with the playful urban vernacular of hip-hop.

African American-derived and pop musics have informed the adaptation of Shakespeare for much of American History. Lawrence Levine and Errol Hill outline how the minstrel tradition shaped nineteenth-century presentation of Shakespeare. The twentieth century has seen Broadway-style musicals such as *Kiss Me Kate* and *The Boys from Syracuse*.[11] African American music forms have also been expropriated to rewrite Shakespeare: *Swingin' the Dream* with Louis Armstrong presented a swing *Midsummer Night's Dream*, *Catch My Soul*—a Jazz version of *Othello*, and, most recently, *All's Kool That Ends Kool*, an adaptation of Shakespeare's *All's Well That Ends Well* by Los Angeles's Troubadour Theatre Company set to the music of Kool and the Gang.[12]

The Shakespearean musical meets with an emerging form, hip-hop theatre, to create hip-hop Shakespeare. Hip-hop theatre, according to Danny Hoch, founder of the New York Annual Hip-Hop Theatre Festival and a hip-hop theatre pioneer, is any theatre aimed at the hip-hop generation (defined as people between 12 and 35 years of age) that utilizes hip-hop culture. More and more within the past few years, hip-hop theatre has turned to classical European works for source material. In 1996 Ifa Bayeza won acclaim for *Homer G. and the Rhapsodies in The Fall of Detroit*, a hip-hop retelling of *The Iliad* and *The Odyssey*. Michael Henry Brown's *Generations of the Dead in the Abyss of Coney Island Madness* is a Greek tragedy-derived hip-hop play that was mounted at Long Wharf Theatre in Connecticut and Minnesota's Penumbra Theatre. 2001 saw Will Power's award-wining *The Seven*, a hip-hop retelling of *The Seven Against Thebes* commissioned and performed by San Francisco's Thick Description Theatre Company. The following year Rickerby Hinds developed *Keep Hedz Ringin'*, "a hip-hop tetralogy freely adapted from Richard Wagner's Ring cycle."

The larger question that one may ask is who is doing what to whom? Is hip-hop theatre appropriating/expropriating Shakespeare or is Shakespearean theatre appropriating/expropriating hip-hop? The answer is: both. It depends on who is doing the appropriating and from which point do they start.

An example of producers of Shakespeare using hip-hop can be found in *The Complete Works of William Shakespeare* by the Reduced Shakespeare Company, already discussed in the introduction. In the original performances the cast made a big deal about being unable to perform *Othello* as "the part is written for a black man" and the members of the company are "Southern California white trash surfer dudes . . . we're honkies."[13] Thus, they decide to rap the play instead:

> Here's the story of a brother by the name of Othello
> He liked white women and he liked green Jell-O
> And a punk named Iago who made hisself a menace
> 'cause he didn't like Othello, the Moor of Venice.[14]

Note that the cast immediately drops into African American vernacular English, the language of rap: "hisself" instead of "himself." Later, Cassio becomes a "chump sucka."

This passage is an example of the expropriation of rap, done tongue-in-cheek style, in reference to Shakespeare. The "Other RSC," as they call themselves, make a big deal of performer's ethnicities. A footnote in the published text notes that the rhythm of the piece was always questionable because "the performers are all extremely white."[15] They posit themselves as white boys rapping Shakespeare. This tactic, by the way, creates another problematic formulation: as Russell Potter states, hip-hop becomes "a simple synecdoche for 'blackness'."[16] *Othello* is rapped because the main character is a Moor, that is, is black. Hip-hop equals blackness in the RSC equation, and the "extremely white" performers use it to tell Shakespeare's narrative about a black character. Tellingly, a footnote in the published text indicates that "Rap Othello" is "one of the most consistently crowd-pleasing parts of the show."[17]

The Reduced Shakespeare Company use rap several times in their reductions of Shakespeare, most notably on the BBC radio program that ran for six episodes in 1994. Two of the episodes end with rap songs: "Rap Your Willy," a word play on both the suggestion that Shakespeare is more accessible when rapped, and with a line suggestive of advertisements encouraging young people to use condoms in order to avoid sexually transmitted diseases, and "OTT," a play on Naughty-by-Nature's "OPP," also referenced in *The Bomb-itty of Errors*, later, and on the phrase "over the top," referring to the RSC's (Reduced Shakespeare Company's) tendency to overplay the humor of the scene. Similarly, in the episode that explored the tragedies, Adam Long, one of the performers kept attempting to rap *Anthony and Cleopatra* ("by my main man Willie, so I'm gonna rap it at ya . . .") because it's set in Egypt, which is in Africa, which means that everyone in it, according to Long, is black. Thus, as with their Rap *Othello*, the RSC equates all things of African origin with blackness and therefore rap music. Rap becomes the means by which Shakespeare's "black plays" can be reduced. The popularity of rap demonstrates the "hipness" of the RSC, who use it as a tool to further demonstrate their commitment to making Shakespeare accessible through reduction. I shall return to the issues of race, rap, and Shakespeare later.

Reducing Shakespeare through Rap

In any case, rap music can (and has been used to) serve as a means of reducing, translating, and referencing Shakespeare, as noted in the introduction, for the purpose of making the plays accessible to a modern audience. Shakespeare's plays can be summarized through hip-hop, which plays on language, rhythm, rhyme, and reference, as well. The RSC's *Othello* is one example. The film *Renaissance Man* also features a rap summary of a play, *Hamlet*.

The film tells the story of an unemployed advertising executive, played by Danny Devito, who accepts the only job he can find: teaching literature to a group of soldiers in danger of flunking out of basic training in the army because they are all "dumb as dogshit." Initially, Devito's character encourages the soldiers to read whatever they want, but they grow interested in *Hamlet* when they see him reading it. They all read the play and demonstrate their understanding of it by performing a rap, which translates the plot into rap slang:

> This shit's iller than *Cape Fear*, the Shakespeare saga
> started with this prince kid, his moms, and his father.
> His pops got took for his props undercover by his brother man,
> Damn! Now his brother's king lover man:
> Acting real trite he took his brother's life
> for his green and to sex up his queen.
> But the prince, he ain't going for it, he's out for revenge.
> His pop's ghost comes and then,
> "Dammit, Hamlet, those are your ends.
> So just chill and cool for now,
> Play the fool 'til you take him out.
> Cause all eyes is on you, so one way or another,
> It's a kamikaze style, or do it undercover.
> But either way-eh, you gotta say-eh, so what the hey-eh.
> Strap on your black and get set for the payback."
> Ain't got no gat, but he's sporting a tool
> Straps on his sword for the Laertes duel.
> Cause he's trying to blame Hamlet for his sister's death.
> But she took her own last breathe, she ain't got shhhh left.
> Never heard yet a more absurd set of circumstances,
> Murder, and romances, so—
> Incest, we had to put it to rest.
> We had time to manifest, he stuck the dagger in the king's chest.
> To be or not to be, the double DMCs is letting it be.[18]

This rap, purportedly demonstrating the newfound love and under-standing of the play that the soldiers have by putting the plot into their own words creatively (one of the exercises from *Shakespeare Set Free!*) is translation, reduction, and reference simultaneously. The rap references the play and plot of *Hamlet*, some of its characters, and the occasional term and words of specific scenes ("revenge" and "incest," among others). It is reductive in that only the plot of Shakespeare's play is left, and even that is reduced down to the most basic components. The poetry, the original text, the subplots, the themes, and everything else is gone. Only two characters are mentioned by name: Hamlet and Laertes. Claudius is "Uncle," Gertrude becomes "queen" and "moms," and Ophelia is only Laertes's sister. The rap also translates the play from one medium to another (dramatic text to rap song), and from one language to another (Elizabethan English to African American vernacular English). Such summaries of plays by the RSC and in *Renaissance Man* are a "Bottom translation," as indicated in the introduction.

O.B. (Original Bard)—Shakespeare as Rapper

In opposition to theatre artists appropriating hip-hop in productions of Shakespeare, the hip-hop community appropriates Shakespeare and reinscribes both the man and the culture in the hip-hop world. In introducing his review of the 2nd Annual New York Hip-Hop Theatre Festival, Jeremy McCarter observes, "There were no rhyming Hamlets or beatboxing Jack Falstaffs at the 2nd New York City Hip-Hop Festival, the largest and highest-profile showcase of hip-hop theatre to date, but Shakespeare did make some appearances."[19] In the festival offering *The Revival*, the performers noted that Shakespeare used "Elizabonics." In *Rhyme Deferred*, one character raps Capulet's "But woo her, gentle Paris . . ." monologue, prompting McCarter to respond "On top of everything else, the Bard has got *flow*!"

Rennie Harris, the creator of *Rome and Jewels*, claims that, "Hip-hop is an almost exact twin of the way Shakespeare was perceived in his day"—it has broad appeal and is rooted in popular culture."[20] Professor Rickerby Hinds, the creator of *Keep Hedz Ringin'*, argues that "Shakespeare is now the elite, but his plays were loved by people who I would consider the hip-hop generation of England at the time. . . ."[21] In other words, Shakespeare was the original O.G. (Original Gangster), who engaged in word play and the hip-hop artists of today are his heirs more than the elitist theatre that actually performs Shakespeare's plays.

Hinds is not alone in constructing Shakespeare, his characters, and the Elizabethans as being more hip-hop than high culture. In *Black Studies: Rap and the Academy*, Houston A. Baker Jr. argues by example in favor of using rap to help students understand Shakespeare better. In teaching *Henry V* to General Certificate of Secondary Education students (GCSE) in London, Baker told them that "Shakespeare would incorporate rap if he were writing today," and that "Henry V was a rapper—a cold dissing, def con man, tougher-than-leather and smoother than ice, an artisan of words."[22] Adam Sexton uses Shakespearean comparisons to help those outside rap understand how hip-hop performance works: "[The human beatbox] is a little like a pre-Restoration performance of *As You Like It* in which a boy played a girl playing a boy."[23] Sexton sees beatboxing as a human reproducing mechanical sounds intended to punctuate human voices and uses a Shakespearean example to explain.

Hip-hop and rap have also been posited as means to educate youth to understand Shakespeare in terms of that which they already know. Teachers at high schools in Los Angeles have used hip-hop to teach poetry and to blend the worlds of contemporary Los Angeles and Shakespeare's plays. Alan Sitomer, who teaches at Lynwood High School, instructs his students that Hamlet is a "regular dude" who "wants things to be cool in his 'hood," but the conflicts of the older generation keeps the 'hood in a state of violence.[24] Later, a student tells a reporter from the *Los Angeles Times* that as a result of the class, his favorite book is "definitely *Hamlet*," and that Shakespeare is "definitely hip."[25]

Sitomer is also the coauthor of *Hip-Hop Poetry and the Classics*, an instructional guide for secondary school teachers that links the poetry of such writers as Tennyson, Shelley, Keats, Frost, Blake, Plath, and Dickinson to such rappers as Tupac Shakur, Ice Cube, Run DMC, Eminem, Mos Def, The Notorious B.I.G., and Public Enemy. Placing poems beside rap lyrics, the authors demonstrate the comparative use of alliteration, allusion, hyperbole, imagery, irony, metaphor, simile, mood, personification, onomatopoeia, and symbolism. The goal of doing so "is to make the academic study of poetry accessible, relevant, comprehensible and enjoyable," as well as to make students appreciate and embrace traditional poetry, even as educators appreciate and embrace hip-hop.[26] The authors then use Shakespeare's sonnet 18 ("Shall I compare thee to a summer's day?") as a model for writing Advanced Placement essays from a hip-hop perspective. In short, Shakespeare in the classroom is being presented as the Elizabethan equivalent of a hip-hop superstar, the urban voice in the Elizabethan text, as it were.

James Bulman informs us that "we reconfigure the Elizabethans as ourselves," and the hip-hop generation is no exception.[27] Yet

Shakespeare and all of his characters are now being posited as hip-hoppers and rappers. Whereas, argues Bulman, those who change Shakespeare's English "are called (at best) adapters or (at worst) butchers," the hip-hop theatre artists who approach Shakespeare do so from the viewpoint that he is one of their own.[28] They signify Shakespeare as they would another rapper (or, for that matter, any culture as signifyin(g) is rooted in free play of all ideas and referents). They see Shakespeare as doing the same thing: taking material from others and referencing it to tell a story and to demonstrate his own linguistic skill.

Rap music is inherently linguistically driven. Given the traditional lack of melody and even harmony in the typical hip-hop performance, it is the words, the rhythms, and the rhymes that shape the performance. Hip-hop relies upon the same elements that Shakespeare's verse does: alliteration, assonance, homonyms, synonyms, repetition, images, metaphors, etc. Compare Hamlet's "The play's the thing / wherein I'll catch the conscience of the king," with Ice T's "My brain is a hand grenade—catch / I'll hit you with an overload of bottomless thought / reversing all the shit you're taught / then throw words at you syl-la-ble at a time / your brain recites the rhyme."[29] Both rely on rhyme, rhythm, reference, metaphor, and word-created image.

Shakespeare Hip-Hop in Production

Hip-hop Shakespeare, linguistically driven, signifying, and referential as it is, creates what might be termed "double reception": it is aimed at two audiences, although the ideal audience is one that recognizes both sets of references. When a Shakespeare play is rewritten in the codes and language of hip-hop the new text refers to both the Shakespearean original, and to the hip-hop world, and, often, to other Shakespearean works or even the man himself. Double reception is most clearly seen in *The Bomb-itty of Errors*. For example, the courtesan's house at which Antipholus of Syracuse is entertained is here called OPP (hip-hop slang for "Other People's Pussy" as well as the name of a song by Naughty-by-Nature, a hip-hop group). The characters, however, explain that it refers to "Othello's Pleasure Palace." This one term thus creates a set of references operating on several levels of meaning, making reference to both hip-hop culture and the works of Shakespeare. Some audience members may only get one of the references. Some may get two. The performers hope that the audience will pick up on the lyrical cleverness, but no matter if they do not.

Hip-hop is first and foremost aimed at the initiated. In hip-hop Shakespeare, however, there are two sets of initiated.

One of the cocreators of *Bomb-itty*, Jason Catalano, observes, "We generally get two sets of audience members: Those that expect a play and those that expect a concert. We try to please both."[30] Likewise, fellow cocreator Jordan Allen-Dutton confides, "Secretly we're injecting the Shakespeare audience with hip-hop and hip-hop heads with classics."[31] Rennie Harris, the creator of *Rome and Jewels*, says of his audience, "You'll have the hip-hop cats figuring out the Shakespearean stuff" and the middle-class (read: white) theatre cats figuring out the hip-hop.[32] The audience, regardless of background, is challenged by the work.

Likewise, the performers must be aware of this double reception. In fact, they rely upon it. Tricia Rose states that "Black culture in the United States has always had elements that have been at least bifocal—speaking to both a black audience and a larger, predominantly white context."[33] Hip-hop Shakespeare is bifocal in that sense, filtering Shakespeare's work through hip-hop in a theatrical context to speak to hip-hop audiences and Shakespeare aficionados.

Hip-hop Shakespeare might be viewed on a continuum, from plays that retain Shakespeare's text almost entirely and use the music incidentally and has some actors rap the monologues to productions that blend original text and rewrites to plays that completely rewrite the text leaving almost nothing of Shakespeare. Many productions rely upon Shakespeare's narrative and characters ultimately to reflect upon issues very far removed from Renaissance England, or even the original themes of the play.

As You Like It as presented by the Washington Shakespeare Company and the African Continuum Theatre Company in Washington DC in April of 2000 demonstrates the most basic type of hip-hop Shakespeare. Shakespeare's original text remains more or less intact, the production simply used hip-hop music and had some of the speeches rapped. Set in New York's Central Park instead of the Forest of Arden, the mostly African American cast presented "a mixed bag of rap," in the words of *Washington Post* critic Nelson Pressley.[34] No attempt is made to change the Shakespearean text—the hip-hop is kept at the level of incidental music and occasional rhythms for speaking the original verse. Not so the other three productions considered here, all of which alter the text, in some cases unrecognizably, while keeping the characters and plot.

Rennie Harris, founder of the Puremovement Troupe, developed his hip-hop / dance piece *Rome and Jewels*, a hip-hop version of *Romeo and Juliet*. Mixing some of Shakespeare's original text with "Ebonics-style street lingo" and setting the struggle between rival street gangs, many reviews posit the play as the contemporary *West Side Story*.

Rome is a member of the Monster Qs, a b-boy gang (break dancers). Their rivals, the Caps, are a gang of hip-hop singers. Rome falls in love with Jewels and must fight the Caps to win her. Interestingly, Jewels is not present on the stage—there is no person playing the Juliet role. Instead, Jewels "is meant to be symbolic of the black male quest for material possession as a means to build esteem."[35] She is literally a "precious jewel" that Rome wishes to possess. Shakespeare's love story is turned into a tragedy, not about gang warfare, as *West Side Story* is, although that aspect is certainly present. Instead it is about the replacement of love with material possession and status symbols as a way to define one's identity. Rome does not die for love, as his Shakespearean predecessor did, he dies playing the hip-hop game, as did real life rappers and murder victims Tupac Shakur and Christopher "Notorious B.I.G." Wallace.

The play refers as much to this aspect of hip-hop culture—the real-life violence that often comes into play in the hip-hop world—as it does to Shakespeare. It signifies on Shakespeare, the urban experience, and the history of hip-hop culture. Gates argues that the discourse of the Signifyin(g) Monkey is "a meta-discourse, a discourse about itself."[36] Similarly, hip-hop theatre is often about hip-hop as much as any other cultural aspect that it signifies.[37]

This aspect is seen as clearly in *MacB*, a hip-hop version of *Macbeth* set in the hip-hop world. Created by San Francisco's African American Shakespeare Company in March of 2002, *MacB* tells of the rise of MacB, a young rapper, who is signed by ScotLand Records producer Duncan. As he rises in the hip-hop world, MacB must turn to murder in order to maintain his standing. The director of the production, Victoria Evans, cites the similarities between Shakespeare's play and the hip-hop world as the impetus for creating it: "Both the classical text and hip-hop music are edgy and jarring, Shakespeare's *Macbeth* has many similarities to the musical hip-hop industry in terms of the atmosphere, which is treasonous and distrustful."[38] Evans posits Shakespeare's play as being similar to the rap industry, not the other way around—the rap industry being similar to Shakespeare. This positioning partly asserts the hip-hop nature of Shakespeare, but also asserts the primacy of hip-hop culture over Shakespeare.

The African American Shakespeare Company "produces European classical works with an African American cultural perspective."[39] In

the case of *MacB* the work has been translated out of its original context and into a contemporary one. Shakespeare's narrative and many
of the characters have been preserved (MacB is Macbeth, Lady MacB
is Lady Macbeth, Duncan is Duncan, the three witches become a girl
trio that would rather be produced by MacB than Duncan, etc.) but
the original text is transformed and rewritten.

The Bomb-itty of Errors, on the other hand, it might be argued,
is true youth-culture Shakespeare. Unlike the professional productions
in Washington and San Francisco that utilized rap, *Bomb-itty* began
as a senior project at New York University's Tisch School of the Arts,
became an Off-Broadway hit for its creators, and has now been
presented with entirely new casts in Chicago, Florida, the U.S.
Comedy Arts Festival in Aspen, and the Edinburgh Fringe Festival and
is even being optioned as a film by MTV. The creators call it an "ad-
rap-tation" of *The Comedy of Errors*, setting it in an Ephesus very
much like contemporary New York. Four performers and a DJ, who
collectively created the show, tell the story of two sets of twins, four
brothers born to a rap star who was arrested for selling marijuana to
support his family. Raised separately, one Antipholus and one Dromio
each finally meet up with their twins after a series of, well, errors.

The plot remains very close to Shakespeare's, but the language is
anything but. While wooing Luciana, Antipholus informs her:

> I'll serenade you in Spanish, woo you in Swahili,
> Ask you in German, "Yo, vas is die dealy?"

The actors play themselves playing the characters. Each one even goes
by his given name and a street name in the program, to which is added
the character name. Erik Weiner, for example, is also called "Red
Dragon," in addition to being "Dromio" and a number of other roles,
just as Marshall Mathers is "Eminem" but also "Slim Shady."
Identities, and names, are fluid in the hip-hop world, as they are in
Shakespeare. Characters are dropped instantly in order to become
one's own character. After one of the Antipholi tells one of the
Dromios that another character's behavior is offensive, Dromio
responds, "You want offensive, man? Take a look at thy momma." An
argument ensues out of character about why the actor has to bring up
the other actor's mamma. It is a very telling moment in the show, in
which Shakespeare is dropped and the actors, now in character as themselves engage in "playing the dozens"—telling "yo mamma" jokes.

Bomb-itty was a popular success that has received mixed critical
reviews. Otto Luck, for example, considered it "one of the most original

outings to take place in the entertainment industry in years."[40] In a review in *Theatre Journal*, Sarah J. Rudolph gave a fairly positive review, focusing on "the sending up of various theatrical and musical styles," and finding the play to be "a clever collusion of images."[41]

On the other hand, the *New York Times*'s Bruce Weber stated that *Kiss Me Kate* "doesn't do half the damage to Shakespeare that *Bomb-itty* does," that the story "matters not at all" and referred to the actual lyrics as "persistent doggerel."[42] In a review that primarily argues that there is no Shakespeare present in *The Bomb-itty of Errors*, Weber admits to not liking or understanding hip-hop. He also notes, however, that "there is a generation gap at work here," as the young audience with whom he saw the show loved it, and that he had not seen an audience display that much enthusiasm for the theatre in a long time.[43]

It is interesting to note that Weber sees rap as "do[ing] damage to Shakespeare," especially considering that the production does not claim to be the Shakespearean original. If we regard *Bomb-itty* as a youth-oriented translation instead of an adaptation, is "damage" still done? Would Weber find the production "damaging" if it had been a Japanese, or French, or Russian translation, many of which would use more modern (read: accessible to a contemporary audience) language? There is not only a generation gap at work here, hip-hop, despite its acceptance into mainstream culture, is seen by the guardians of high culture as one of the largest threats on the cultural landscape. We should also note that the title of Weber's review, "Rap is to Shakespeare as Bomb is to Comedy," demonstrates not only Weber's pejorative attitude toward hip-hop and rap, but also the linguistic differences between the generations: To Weber, something that "bombed" is a failure, whereas to the current generation, to call something "da bomb" is to state that it is excellent and enjoyable.

Interestingly, it is the idea that hip-hop is generational, rather than ethnic, that the creators of *Bomb-itty* offer as a defense against charges that they are simply suburban white actors appropriating black culture. Isaac Guzman argues that the cast "preserves the spirit of Shakespearean comedy," but does not always preserve the spirit of hip-hop.[44] The preshow music consists entirely of African American artists, but no black actors were involved in the actual original production. The creators argued that hip-hop is generational, not ethnic. Erik Weiner offers that the cast "don't really feel like we've appropriated it" and that "it's definitely coming from a pure place within us," although this argument is not entirely supported by either history or the conditions of performance.[45] The performers might be seen as appropriating a popular cultural commodity from a culture other than their own, but one that has become highly commercial. Their answers to this charge are not entirely satisfactory.

The use of rap music by whites to reconfigure Shakespeare is further problematized by the history of actors of African descent performing Shakespeare on the stages of Europe and America. Errol Hill's definitive work on the subject, *Shakespeare in Sable*, celebrates the noted triumphs. Yet often in Renaissance drama itself, people of color are represented in negative ways.[46] Furthermore, nontraditional casting at the Royal Shakespeare Company has tended to put actors of color in roles centering on lust, lawlessness, and violence, such as Paris in *Troilus and Cressida* and Brachiano in *The White Devil*.[47] Even in the United States, institutions such as the New York Public Shakespeare Festival, known for Joseph Papp's commitment to nontraditional casting, cannot get around the fact that, as Celia R. Daileader points out, the casting may be color-blind but the audience is not, and race is always coded into the meaning of the play and the performance.[48]

What Set You Claimin'? Shakespeare, Rap, Youth, and America

Considering these four production, we might view hip-hop Shakespeare in terms of four different contexts.

First, as noted of rock Shakespeare in the previous chapter (chapter 3), rap and hip-hop centered productions can be viewed as adaptations of Shakespeare, just as Nahum Tate's reworking of *King Lear*, *Rosencrantz and Guildenstern Are Dead*, or Kurosawa's *Throne of Blood*. The texts are transformed and reworked to varying degrees, for a variety of purposes, but the use of hip-hop to create a new text is no different from Kurosawa Akira's transplanting *Macbeth* to medieval Japan or Tom Stoppard's focus on two marginal characters in the best known tragedy in the world.

Second, the plays can be contextualized as examples of the hip-hop theatre movement, still in its infancy. As hip-hop theatre grows, it will continue to develop, define, and redefine itself. In looking to move beyond monologues, one-person pieces, plays simply about hip-hop, the creators who appropriate Shakespeare are looking to use narratives that are already established and perhaps familiar to audiences in order to create new pieces as the new form develops. There is also the appeal of using Shakespeare's status to pump up one's own work.

Interestingly, rap Shakespeare is a controversy within the world of hip-hop theatre. In a recent manifesto in *American Theatre*, Danny Hoch "dissed" (heavily disrespected and criticized) *Bomb-itty of Errors*, arguing that it is not hip-hop. Hoch used the production to argue against any ad-rap-tations of Shakespeare:

> This play, for me and several of my peers, was painful to watch—not because it was poorly written, acted or directed. It was actually a genius adaptation of *Comedy of Errors* . . . The problem was that, as universal and timeless as Shakespeare is, performing his plays in rap does two very damaging things. First, it sends the message that the hip-hop generation has no important stories of its own, and that in order for hip-hop to qualify as theatre, it must attach itself to such certified texts as those of Shakespeare. Second, it devalues hip-hop as art by regulating rap to humorous accompaniment—the feeling that results is of watching a hip-hop minstrel show. Not only wasn't the play *about* the hip-hop generation, but the audience (and ticket prices) failed to reflect the generation as well. This was not a hip-hop theatre piece, but a Shakespeare adaptation that infused rap. Ouch.[49]

It is interesting that the producer of the Hip-Hop Theatre Festival used the exact same wording as the *New York Times* critic. Weber sees the production as "damaging" Shakespeare; Hoch sees it as "damaging" hip-hop. He fears that hip-hop will be seen as just another "style" in which to do Shakespeare, and that adaptations will undercut (and perhaps result in the underfunding of) "legitimate" hip-hop theatre productions.

Given the history of adaptations of Shakespeare in other forms, it is as likely that *Bomb-itty* will "send the message that the hip-hop generation has no stories of its own," as the *Kabuki Macbeth* sends the message that Japan has no stories of its own, or that *Kiss Me Kate* means musical theatre has no stories of its own, or that the Plautine original sends the message that Shakespeare has no stories of his own. The second charge, that the play relegates rap to "humorous accompaniment" would hold more weight if the rapping wasn't 90 percent of the performance. Almost all text was not spoken but "rapped," so the rapping was not accompaniment. As for the humorousness of the piece, one might argue that the rap world is rooted in humor, word play, parody, and caricature. Hoch does not dismiss such performers as Eminem, De Le Soul and Del the Funky Homo Sapien who rely on very broad humor in their work as well. One wonders if Hoch, who is also Euro-American, must judge fellow Euro-Americans more harshly in finding the black voice in a white text.

Third, the plays are emblematic of youth culture. Rap music is counter-hegemonic, offering an alternative view to official narrative of urban life and the African American experience, and yet it also reinforces contemporary cultural attitudes toward women ("bitches and hos"), homosexuals, and other ethnicities. Rap and hip-hop at times advocate maintaining a system of exploitation that allows the rapper to "get mine" at the expense of other people. Like hip-hop itself, hip-hop Shakespeare explores these conflicting impulses in youth culture—the desire to conform and the desire to rebel. Hip-hop Shakespeare is a way of taking parent culture and making it acceptable to youth.

Fourth, hip-hop Shakespeare might be read as an example of post-colonial theatre in postindustrial America. Tricia Rose states that hip-hop "replicates and reimagines the experiences of urban life" in postindustrial, post-civil rights America.[50] She also argues that "rap music is a contemporary stage for the theatre of the powerless."[51] Hip-hop theatre literalizes Rose's metaphor, making theatre out of the music that is the theatre of the powerless. Hip-hop theatre is thus a site of resistance to the dominant, mainstream culture and to what Cornell West calls "the brutal side of American capitalism" and its inherent racism and sexism.

Roberta Uno, after Augustin Lao Montes, argues that hip-hop music has been globalized on "two parallel yet permeable tracks": the first is "top-down globalization of the marketplace and global capital," that is, corporate appropriation of the form, and the second is "ground-up, grass roots" development, that is, individual artists using the form to engage their own context and community.[52] In this sense, both of these globalizing strategies are represented in the world of hip-hop Shakespeare, sometimes simultaneously, as in the case of *Bomb-itty of Errors* in which the creators began as students in New York City, rewriting Shakespeare in a familiar style and ended up with creative and performance contracts on MTV, the embodiment of corporate youth culture.

Shakespeare is therefore, a natural source for material for hip-hop theatre, not only because it uses Euro-culture to fight the supremacy of Euro-culture, but also gives ironic distance from which to narrate and deconstruct the urban experience of African Americans. As Dennis Salter says of postcolonial Shakespeare elsewhere in the world, "It is the insight that Shakespeare belongs not to 'us' but to 'them' that post-colonial actors find oddly liberating."[53] Similarly, it is because Shakespeare is not urban, African American, or American that makes his narratives useful for hip-hop theatre.

Similarly (and fifth), as noted about rock-based productions in the previous chapter (chapter 3), we might see hip-hop Shakespeare as "foreign Shakespeare," in Dennis Kennedy's sense, the plays of the bard presented in translation in the audience's indigenous language. John Russell Brown states that all Shakespeare outside of Renaissance England is "foreign" Shakespeare, especially American Shakespeare.[54] The archaic language that many scholars feel will be incomprehensible to the average audience member within half a century becomes in hip-hop adaptations playful street language, perhaps equally incomprehensible to audience members unfamiliar with the black vernacular, but they are not the target audience.

Shakespeare's world and language are "foreign" to contemporary America, in every sense of the word. When Shakespeare is translated into French, German, Japanese, Chinese, or Kiswahili, it sounds much more contemporary and vibrant to the audiences hearing it in their indigenous vernacular. The original poetry is lost in translation, but what is gained is comprehensibility. Hip-hop Shakespeare does the same for American youth—it translates Shakespeare into a language that can be understood.

Lastly, hip-hop/Shakespearean cross-expropriations might also be seen as a return to the American Shakespeare of a century before. As with rock and roll, hip-hop is popular music, and both serve Shakespeare in the same way. Both make Shakespeare accessible; both reduce, translate, and refer. As noted in the previous chapter (chapter 3), Lawrence Levine argues that Shakespeare was considered popular culture in America in the nineteenth century, only becoming high culture in the twentieth. The most popular forms were parodic reworkings that involved everything including a title change. The performance cited in the last chapter titled *Ye Comedie of Errours, a Glorious, Uproarious Burlesque, Not Indecorous nor Censorious, with Many a Chorus, Warranted Not to Bore Us, Now for the First Time Set Before Us* is an example of the popular Americanization of Shakespeare's plays. (One might note that one can rap that title.) *The Bomb-itty of Errors* more or less does the same thing a century later with the same exact play—playing on rhyme, rhythm, and popular culture to reshape the play for a contemporary audience. In other words, hip-hop Shakespeare is just the most recent manifestation of what Michael Bristol calls "America's Shakespeare."

Bruce Weber's and Danny Hoch's apocalyptic concerns notwithstanding, Shakespeare is becoming strongly linked to rap and serves as a point of comparison for the rap world. Amusingly, Eminem himself has been compared to a Shakespearean character. Chris Erskine, reviewing Eminem's autobiographical film *8 Mile*, claims that, "Like Shakespeare's Prince Hal, [Eminem] is royalty in mufti, wrestling with inner demons before feeling the confidence to declare himself the heir apparent, if not the king."[55] In addition to interpreting Shakespeare through rap music, one can also interpret rap music through Shakespeare.

In an article in the *Los Angeles Times* recently, Erika Hayasaki reports that high school teachers use rap to teach every subject. It is not unusual that Shakespeare would become part of the "educational rap" trend. One student quoted in the article stated, "We need to learn about Shakespeare, but hip-hop is history, too. As far as Shakespeare goes, we can't relate to that. We can relate to what's going on now."[56] At least the student recognizes the need to learn about Shakespeare, but also recognizes the very real cultural, historical, and linguistic distance between the bard's plays and contemporary (urban?) American life. Hip-hop and rap bridge that gap.

Students are also shown the similarities between Shakespeare as an artist and popular rappers. One teacher told students that Tupak Shakur "was not a paragon of virtue, but neither was William Shakespeare."[57] Furthermore, like Shakur, "Shakespeare [also] wrote about murder, rape, and suicide."[58] Such assertions serve two purposes. First, they equate the rapper with a man acknowledged as one of the greatest writers and artists of all time. By doing so, they answer to the criticism that rap has a negative influence on youth and culture, or is inferior to traditional, Western culture, or has no artistic merit or value. Shakur and Shakespeare are similar in terms of personal behavior and topics about which they write, therefore Shakur is as legitimate and valuable as Shakespeare.

Second, they equate Shakespeare with the popular rappers of contemporary America. Thus, Shakespeare is cool, cold-lounging, chillin' like a villain, and on the hip-hop tip. You like Shakur? Then peep Shakespeare. In other words, by linking the two in the classroom, Shakur gets academic respectability and Shakespeare gets street credibility. Shakur is a poet and Shakespeare is a rapper. Youth have their heroes validated in the eyes of the educational institution and mainstream culture and Shakespeare is made more accessible and interesting.

In conclusion, hip-hop expropriations of Shakespeare and Shakespearean expropriations of hip-hop represent an attempt to reinscribe Shakespeare on the hip-hop tip as not only our contemporary, but as a forerunner of hip-hop culture. They also represent an attempt to reinscribe hip-hop in a larger cultural sphere. Is it an industry of white boys stealing black culture or the product of a generation that is refiguring all elements of American culture (European Shakespeare, African-derived music, etc.) in a new cultural tradition? Perhaps it is American interculturalism at its best, or the capitalistic appropriation of other cultures for a profit. Most likely, as all good hip-hop fans will note, it is all of the above and then some. Or, in the words of the epigram to this chapter, it is whatever we want it to be.

Notes

1. "II Be or Not II Be," in *Round the Outside! Round the Outside!*, lyrics by Malcolm McLaren and Jason van Sugars, music by Malcolm McLaren, performed by MC Hamlet, Virgin 2–91599.
2. Henry Louis Gates, Jr., *The Signifying Monkey: A Theory of African-American Literary Criticism* (Oxford: Oxford University Press, 1988), p. xxiv.
3. Ibid., p. xxv.
4. James R. Andreas, Sr., "Signifyin' on *The Tempest* in *Mama Day*," in *Shakespeare and Appropriation*. Edited by Christy Desmet and Robert Sawyer (London: 1999), p. 114–115.
5. Armond White, "Who wants to see ten niggers play basketball?" in *Droppin' Science: Critical Essays on Rap Music and Hip-hop Culture*, edited by William Eric Perkins (Philadelphia: Temple University Press, 1996), p. 200.
6. Ibid., p. 201.
7. Quoted in Russell A. Potter, *Spectacular Vernacular: Hip-Hop and the Politics of Postmodernism* (Albany: State University of New York Press, 1995), p. 16.
8. Ibid., p. 20. The consumption of hip-hop by whites is in and of itself controversial, as music industry data indicates that whites purchase more rap than blacks. Some rap experts, however, argue that such data does not include bootlegs, shared copies, etc., and that blacks "own" far more rap works than sales records would indicate. The appeal of rap to whites is also a controversial topic, especially in regards to the cause. David Samuels argued that "rap's appeal to whites rested in its evocation of an age old image of blackness: a foreign, sexually charged and criminal underworld against which the norms of white society are defined" (quoted in Eric Bennett, "Rap," in *Africana*, edited by Kwame Anthony Appiah and Henry Louis Gates, Jr. [New York: Basic Civitas Books, 1999], p. 1590), a reductivist and possibly racist construction of rap's appeal which does not take into account any of the complex cultural negotiations of late-twentieth-century America that Tricia Rose and Russell A. Potter take into account in their studies of black/white interaction via hip-hop.
9. Potter, *Spectacular Vernacular*, p. 36. In the interests of complete disclosure, it should be noted that the author of this essay is a white, middle-class academic who maintains a proximity to rap fan culture. Following Adam Krims, however, I am forced to note that my own identity "exacerbates the tangle of objective situational impossibility," writing about a culture that is not mine, and in danger

of increasing the distance "of commodified forms from the underprivileged creators of those forms" (*Rap Music and the Poetics of Identity* [Cambridge: Cambridge University Press, 2000], p. 6). Like Krims, "any claim I could make to hip-hop authenticity would be preposterous. So I do not make it" (p. 7). Instead, I am forced to approach hip-hop Shakespeare as an inside outsider.

10. Andre Lefevere, "Why Waste Our Time on Rewrites? The Trouble with Interpretation and the Role of Rewriting in an Alternative Paradigm," in *The Manipulation of Literature: Studies in Literary Translation*, edited by Theo Hermans, (New York: St. Martin's, 1983), p. 234.

11. Errol Hill, *Shakespeare in Sable: A History of Black Shakespearean Actors* (Amherst: University of Massachusetts Press, 1984); Lawrence Levine, *Highbrow/Lowbrow: The Emergence of Cultural Hierarchy in America* (Cambridge: Harvard University Press, 1988).

12. The Troubadours have made a practice of expropriating the music of the 1970s for Shakespearean adaptation since their founding in 1994. Other shows include *Twelfth Dog Night* (a blend of *Twelfth Night* and the music of Three Dog Night and *Midsummer Night's Fever Dream* (a disco version of Shakespeare's *Dream* featuring the music of the BeeGees). While popular with younger audiences and generally well received by Los Angeles critics, the execution of such conceptual productions is sometimes good, as in *All's Kool* when "Cherish" is played ironically at the wedding of Bertram and Helena and the singing of "Ladies Night" as Bertram and the Young Lords prepare to enjoy the house of the widow of Florence, but sometimes nonsensical and arbitrary as when "Jungle Boogie" is performed for curing the King of his illness.

13. The Reduced Shakespeare Company, *Complete Works of William Shakespeare (Abridged)* (New York: Applause Theatre Books 1994), p. 33. This text became available for performance by other groups in 1996, and proved very popular on college campuses, summer stock theaters, and regional theaters. The lines quoted become problematic when African American actors are cast in the play. Copyright laws notwithstanding, each company must create its own solution that leads to "Rap Othello."

14. Reduced Shakespeare Company, *Complete Works*, p. 34.

15. Ibid., p. 33.

16. Potter, *Spectacular Vernacular*, pp. 16–17.

17. Reduced Shakespeare Company, *Complete Works*, p. 33.

18. *Renaissance Man*, dir. Penny Marshall, writ. Jim Burnstein, 1994. What is written here is neither the full rap (there are extended pieces at the beginning and end, mostly revolving around the phrase "to be or not to be"), nor does it capture the fullness of the performance, with overlapping lines, varying rhythms, additional sounds and beats, and how the rapper's personalities shape the lines.

19. Jeremy McCarter, "Why Hip Hop Could Revitalize the Theatre—If It Wanted To," *The New Republic Online* (July 18, 2001) <http://www.tnr.com/online/mccarter071801.html> Accessed May 29, 2002.

20. Quoted in Anne Midgette, "Fall Preview/Dance," *Los Angeles Times*, September 17, 2000, p. Calendar 7.

21. Eisa Davis, "hip-hop theatre: the new underground," *The Source*, March 2000, p. 173.
22. Houston A. Baker, Jr., *Black Studies: Rap and the Academy* (Chicago: University of Chicago Press, 1995), pp. 98–99.
23. Adam Sexton, "Don't Believe the Hype: Why Isn't Hip Hop Criticism Better," in *Rap on Rap: Straight Up Talk on Hip-Hop Culture*, edited by Adam Sexton (New York: Delta 1995), p. 7.
24. Quoted in Mitchell Landsberg, "Hip-Hop Unlocks the Meaning of Literary Classics," *Los Angeles Times* (June 19, 2005), p. B2.
25. Quoted in Landsberg, "Hip-Hop Unlocks," p. B2.
26. Alan Sitomer and Michael Cirelli, *Hip-Hop Poetry and the Classics* (Beverly Hills: Milk Mug Publishing, 2004), p. 2.
27. James C. Bulman, "Introduction: Shakespeare and Performance Theory," in *Shakespeare, Theory and Performance*, edited by James C. Bulman (London: Routledge, 1996), p. 5.
28. Ibid., p. 8.
29. Ice T, "Mind Over Matter," *OG Original Gangster*, Sire 9–26492–4.
30. Quoted in Jesse McKinley, "On Stage and Off," *New York Times*, December 24, 1999, p. E2.
31. Quoted in Kevin Conley, "Fresh Bard," *The New Yorker*, March 27, 2000, p. 130.
32. Quoted in Sarah Rodman, "Bard to the Bone," *Boston Herald*, 29 November, 2000, p. 51.
33. Tricia Rose, *Black Noise* (Hanover: Wesleyan University Press, 1994), p. 5.
34. Nelson Pressley, "As You Sort of Like It: Shakespeare's Mildly Hip-Hop Romp," *Washington Post*, April 6, 2000, p. C2.
35. Rodman, "Bard to the Bone," p. 51.
36. Gates, *Signifying Monkey*, p. xxi.
37. Articles have been appearing noting that hip-hop theatre needs to move beyond the narcissism of dealing primarily with hip-hop. Danny Hoch, among others has called for playwrights and rapper to create works that utilize hip-hop but are not primarily about hip-hop. The form must move into new content.
38. Quoted in a press release by the African American Shakespeare Company dated June 2, 2002.
39. From the company's Web site <http://www.troubie.com> Accessed August 10, 2003.
40. Otto Luck, "*The Bomb-itty of Errors*: A Masterpiece by Any Other Name," *NYRock*, 2000. <http://www.nyrock.com/reviews/2000/bomb.htm> Accessed March 28, 2002.
41. Sarah J. Rudolph, "Performance Review: *The Bomb-itty of Errors*," *Theatre Journal*, 54, no. 2 (2002), p. 309.
42. Bruce Weber, "Rap is to Shakespeare as Bomb is to Comedy," *New York Times*, December 21, 1999, p. E3.
43. Ibid., p. E3.
44. Isaac Guzman, "Boppin' with the Bard," *Newsday*, January 27, 2000, p. C1.
45. Quoted in Guzman, "Boppin'," p. C1.

46. See Anthony Girard Barthelemy, *Black Face, Maligned Race: The Representation of Blacks in English Drama from Shakespeare to Southerne,* (Baton Rouge: Louisiana State University Press, 1987).

47. Celia R. Daileader, "Casting Black Actors: Beyond Othellophilia," in *Shakespeare and Race,* edited by Catherine M.S. Alexander and Stanley Wells (Cambridge: Cambridge University Press, 2000), p. 185.

48. Ibid., p. 183.

49. Danny Hoch, "here we go, yo," *American Theatre* 21, no. 10 (December 2004), p. 70.

50. Rose, *Black Noise,* p. 22.

51. Rose, *Black Noise,* p. 101.

52. Roberta Uno, "The 5th Element," *American Theatre* 21, no. 4 (April 2004), p. 27.

53. Denis Salter, "Acting Shakespeare in postcolonial Space," in *Shakespeare, Theory, Performance,* edited by James C. Bulman (London: Routledge, 1996), p. 115.

54. John Russell Brown, "Foreign Shakespeare and English-speaking Audiences" in *Foreign Shakespeare,* edited by Dennis Kennedy (Cambridge: Cambridge University Press, 1993), p. 25.

55. Chris Erskine, " 'Yo, dog': Positively Shakespearean Rap," *Los Angeles Times,* November 13, 2002, p. E8.

56. Quoted in Erika Hayasaki, "Reading, 'Riting, and Rap," *Los Angeles Times,* January 14, 2003, p. A16.

57. Quoted in Hayasaki, "Reading . . .," p. A16.

58. Quoted in Hayasaki, "Reading . . .," p. A16.

5

"The Amazing Adventures of Superbard": Shakespeare in Comics and Graphic Novels

Kevin J. Wetmore, Jr.

In his essay "Shakespeare and the Media of Film, Radio, and Television," written in 1987, Anthony Davis remarks that, "only comparatively recently has it become respectable to concentrate serious discussion on the media of cinema, radio and more especially television" in the realm of Shakespeare studies.[1] Writing 15 years later, I suspect the comic book, or graphic novel to use the "serious" name for the medium, must now fill the category of newly respectable and recently serious subject of study by Shakespeareans, especially given the attention paid by critics such as Michael Bristol, Richard Burt, and Douglas Lanier, among others, to Neil Gaiman's graphic novel *Sandman*, which ran for 75 issues, several of which incorporated Shakespeare as a character and the writing of his plays as a subject, although Puck, Titania, and Oberon appeared in their own right as characters in other issues.[2] It would seem the scholarly community has finally recognized the significance of comics and especially Shakespeare in the comics, a presence that has been maintained steadily since the 1950s, in ways other than negative, dismissive, or condescending.

Two great periods of comic Shakespeare have emerged: the immediate postwar period into the 1950s and the late 1980s and early 1990s. Interestingly, these periods saw a shift in the age range at which comic books were aimed. During the postwar period, comics were aimed at children: 90 percent of children in grades four, five, and six read an average of ten comics a month.[3] By the late 1980s, however, the age of the average reader had increased to the late teens, with many comics indicated as being "For Mature Audiences Only," not because they were pornographic but because they were the equivalent to an R-rated movie, featuring adult themes and content and containing frank and graphic depictions of sex and violence, and the target market was young male adults with some gender and age crossover as well.[4] This shift in age and content is also indicated in the approach to Shakespeare in the comics. In the 1950s, the main presence of Shakespeare in comics was through adaptation in the form of *Classics Illustrated*, explored later, which sparked a debate about who was influencing whom: did the presence of Shakespeare elevate the form, or did the form debase Shakespeare? In the late 1980s and early 1990s there was a reemergence of adaptation of the plays aimed more at the target audience of young adult males and appropriation of the plays and man into the ongoing narratives of such graphic novels as *The Sandman*.

One of the biggest challenges to the academic study of graphic novels is that scholars have treated comics as text with pictures instead of a media in its own right. Comics have their own aesthetic and their own methods of narrative that, like theatre, combines word with image. To ignore the image is to ignore half (or sometimes more than half) of the "text." In fact, many involved in graphic novel production (as the very name suggests, the medium is a novel in visual form) assert the similarities between theatre and comic books. Will Eisner, creator of *The Spirit* and longtime comic book theorist, argues that like theatre, comic books begin as a "script," often written by a single writer, which then undergoes a collaborative process of visual storytelling.[5]

Also, like the theatre, the artists creating a graphic novel, when adapting a classical, well-known narrative, must make the same choices as the design team of a theatre company. They can place plays in new visual contexts. Like in the theatre, the graphic novel version of *Hamlet* can be period, can be modernized, can be generic, nonspecific, or specific history, for example, seeing the play in Elizabethan England or the period in which the play is set. Connected to this is the notion of "casting" in comics: how does one draw the character and represent him or her. For the original *Classics Illustrated Hamlet*, it seems quite clear visually that the play is set in medieval Denmark and that Hamlet is a Viking of some sort. In short, the same choices that are faced in the theatrical production of Shakespeare (and, for that matter, in filmed productions of Shakespeare) are faced in the graphic production of Shakespeare.

This design element is significant because, like in the theatre, the image determines much of the meaning. Will Eisner refers to comics as "sequential art," although Scott McCloud prefers the extend definition of "spatially juxtaposed pictorial and other images in deliberate sequence," often, but not always for the purpose of narrative.[6] McCloud also sees the origin of graphic storytelling in Egyptian tomb painting, the Bayeux Tapestry, the pre-Columbian painted screen of 8-Deer Ocelot Claw, and medieval illustrated manuscripts, citing specifically *The Tortures of Saint Erasmus* (1460) as an example of the blend of image and text in which the whole is greater than the sum of the parts.[7]

Eisner also argues that graphic novels rely upon "visual literacy" upon the part of the reader. One must not only recognize the image, but also recall if it has been used elsewhere or in connection with a different set of words.[8] Likewise, the reader is an active, not passive, participant: "The reader is forced to participate by supplying unspoken dialogue."[9] The reader is required to not only link the pictures sequentially and link the pictures to the text; one must fill in the missing part of the pictures. Also, as David Carrier observes, Alfred A. Knopf's post-text note on typeface not withstanding, only in graphic novels does the literal appearance of the words themselves generate meaning: "the physical way in which a text is presented—the typeface, color of paper and binding—does not usually constitute an aesthetically relevant feature of the novel," whereas in comics much of the determined meaning is from these features.[10] So, in a sense, a comic book version of Shakespeare's plays blends the elements of both textual adaptation and visual representation that in many ways comes remarkably close to theatrical production, missing only the liveness—the presence of artist and audience in the same space as the text is presented temporally. What theatre does in time, comic books do in space: juxtapose text and image to tell a story.

As a side note, others see in addition to the influence of theatre on graphic novels a rising influence of graphic novels on theatre, not just as subject matter, such as in *Superman the Musical*, but in terms of shaping notions of visual culture. For example, in Japan the *manga* (comic book) and *anime* (animated cartoons) cultures have influenced Japanese theatre artists who came of age in the 1980s and 1990s, resulting in what Yoshiko Fukushima has called "*manga* discourse": plays that engage in intertexts with graphic novel culture.[11] Both forms, argues Fukushima, are image oriented and seemingly infantile, although capable of great depth. This discourse is beginning to be felt in the West as well, particularly with the rise in popularity of *manga* and *anime* among young people in the United States and Europe.

The comic is a form associated with youth, inherently American, and is also an inherently reductive form, not least of which because of the limit on the number of pages allowed for each book. When attempting to represent *Hamlet* in graphic form, one must cut a good deal of text. How is this any different, however, from a stage production that, in order to have the audience out by 11:00 p.m., cuts the Fortinbras plot and some of the longer scenes? Partly the concern is over substitution: the comic book is seen as a substitute for the text for young people in a manner that the production is not. But partly the concern is rooted in a critical judgment: when theatre cuts (even for practical reasons) it is artistic interpretation; when comic books cut (even for practical reasons), it is because they are a juvenile form. When Samuel Beckett recycles Shakespeare text, it is interpreted as profound. When *Superman* or *Sandman* recycles Shakespeare, it is seen as crass and an attempt to link popular forms to higher culture to gain some sort of intellectual respectability. We will see later how Shakespeare has been translated into the medium of comics, how comics have sought to echo stage production in the representation of Shakespeare, the inherent intertextuality of comic book Shakespeare, and the debate about whether Shakespeare elevates comics or if comics debase Shakespeare.

Shakespeare and the Comics Code: *Classics Illustrated*

In 1941 the Gilberton Publishing Company began a unique experiment, publishing an adaptation of Alexander Dumas's *The Three Musketeers* as a comic book, following it rapidly with *Ivanhoe* and *The Count of Monte Cristo*.[12] Unlike other comics of the time, which relied on continuing characters and continuing storylines, *Classic Comics* as it was first known used the continuity of adapting works of literature to attract readers. It had no advertisements, and as such the cover price was higher than other comics. As Milla Bongo observes, *Classics Illustrated* "were generally more expensive and not as popular as the regular comics."[13] Yet there was clearly a market for the comic book versions of classical works of literature. In fact, they were drafted for use in the classroom. *Classic Comics* and *Classics Illustrated* were the only comics allowed in many school systems. They were sold on newsstands, but some schools also distributed them. They were perceived as having an educational value that regular comics did not.[14] This case is an instance of youth culture being used in an educational venue to encourage students to embrace the texts, much like contemporary teachers use the DVD of *Romeo + Juliet* or "*O*" to teach the text.

On March 9, 1950, Albert Kanter, the president of Gilberton publicly announced that *Classics Illustrated* would expand and "would include, for the first time anywhere, illustrated adaptations of Shakespeare's plays."[15] To ensure the quality, accuracy, and value of the adaptation, in addition to the artist actually doing the adapting, Gilberton promised "an editorial staff of twenty literary researchers" hired to "insur[e] that the comic book adaptation would adhere rigorously to the author's language and plot."[16] Gilberton, in fact, refused to join the Comics Code because it "maintained that its adaptations of literary classics were not comic books" per se, but literature in graphic form.[17]

The first Shakespeare play to be adapted was *Julius Caesar* in February 1950. It was the sixty-eighth title in the series overall. Over the next decade four more followed: number 87, *A Midsummer Night's Dream* (September 1951), number 99, *Hamlet* (September 1952), number 128, *Macbeth* (September 1955), and number 134, *Romeo and Juliet* (September 1956). Only one other work of dramatic literature was included, Rostand's *Cyrano de Bergerac* (number 79). These comics paradoxically used the comic medium to adapt the works of Shakespeare, but simultaneously attempted to deny the form by including educational aspects as well. As noted above, there were no advertisements. Each issue contained a biography of the author. Each Shakespeare comic included essays to contextualize the plays. For example, *Romeo and Juliet* had a description of Elizabethan playhouses at the end.[18] *Macbeth* included a brief biography of James I. Gilberton and went out of its way to distance its product from regular comic books and show them to be educational. Shakespeare was a part of that plan. Albert Kanter believed that the publication of Shakespeare's plays "offered incontrovertible evidence . . . of the seriousness of his publication's purpose."[19] That purpose was to encourage youth to read the classics.

Each issue of *Classics Illustrated* had on the last page a call to read the original: "Now that you have read the *Classics Illustrated* edition, don't miss the enjoyment of the original, obtainable at your school or public library." Interestingly, the text refers to the adaptation as an "edition." The encouragement also assumes that someone who purchased a comic would not want to buy the original as well, but one could borrow a free copy from a lending institution. Although Kanter genuinely hoped the comic would guide the reader to the original, the opposite effect was often true: one would read the comic instead of the original. *Classics Illustrated* offered a substitute for Shakespeare.

Despite Gilberton's assertions, the narratives were adapted rather fully into the milieu of comics. For the "To be or not to be" soliloquy, the panel take up the entire page. Hamlet stands center panel and the speech forms a series of word balloons around him. In the distance, behind him, the King and Polonius rather visibly hide to observe while Ophelia waits for him at the bottom of the panel. The entire panel sets up a series of events from the play in a single image in order to incorporate the entire soliloquy text. Although William B. Jones, Jr. asserts that, "Shakespeare's language may have been abridged, but it was never rewritten," text was added to as part of the comic form.[20] At the top of the same page with the above soliloquy is a linking word bubble noting, "The following day, Polonius sets the stage for his scheme."[21] Oftentimes the illustrators would use this standard comic book device to set a scene, connect the narrative, or explain what a character was doing.

Jones also praises Alex A. Blum, who was the artist on *A Midsummer Night's Dream* and *Hamlet* for adapting the plays to the form so well. Blum, he notes "broke down short exchanges of dialogue into naturally flowing smaller panels, incorporating dramatic theatrical gestures in larger panels, and kept longer speeches, such as Hamlet's two soliloquies, intact in large balloons."[22] In other words, Blum utilized the elements of comic illustration to create pace, flow, and to attempt to render a dynamic theatre text into a two dimensional form. The physical representation of the text reflected both Shakespeare's text and a sense of theatricality.

The theatre also profoundly influences Shakespeare as offered by *Classics Illustrated*. Hubert H. Crawford notes that, "The characters and setting were drawn in such a way that the reader might sense he was viewing an artistic rendering of an actual performance of *Hamlet* on stage."[23] Not only was the attempt made to make the comic seem theatrical, it used an already familiar *Hamlet* to do so: Claudius, Gertrude, and Polonius's appearances were modeled on the actors in the 1948 Laurence Olivier film.[24] As with the Toy Theatre, popular versions of the play shaped the comic version. One might also note a linkage between the different pop forms that Shakespeare manifests in: the movie, inspired by the play, shapes the comic that is adapted from the same play.

Henry Carl Keifer, himself a former amateur actor, adapted *Julius Caesar* following the model of Victorian theatre: "The characters' dramatic attitudes recall Victorian stage poses, particularly in Mark Anthony's funeral oration, delivered in Henry Irving style," observes Jones.[25] Although one might ask how a comic can deliver an oration in any style, the influence of images of Victorian performances of *Caesar* in general and Henry Irving's in particular are undeniable. Although *Classics Illustrated* was ostensibly about adapting literature to comic form, the theatricality of Shakespeare's plays was not only taken into account, it became a significant part in how the text was represented, and served to connect the comic version to the theatrical and filmic traditions. Shakespeare was used as a defense for comic books in the 1950s. During the height of the comic books scare, Leslie Fielder wrote in *Encounter* magazine that comic books were not inherently evil, as even "the plays of Shakespeare were created for illiterates," linking the non-literate people in Shakespeare's audience with those contemporaries who would rather read the comic version than the original text.[26] Likewise, Delmore Schwartz, writing in the same period, noted that the plays themselves were really for children: "Shakespeare's play was intended for an audience which was very much like the juvenile readers of *Classics Illustrated*, and *A Midsummer Night's Dream* is one of the most playful and child-like of plays."[27] Clearly, these critics already see Shakespeare as a kind of youth culture, aimed at the lowest common denominator and youngest in society.

It is both the use of the comic medium and the linkage to the theatrical tradition that did not keep *Classics Illustrated* safe during the comic book scare of the 1950s. Although Gilberton argued that the use of Shakespeare elevated comics, others argued that the comic form debased even Shakespeare. Schwartz objected to the unpoetic representation of the text and the deleterious effects it may have on youth:

> This failure to make it clear that the speeches are often poetry and not prose may seem not as serious, at first glance, as in actuality it is. For the speeches are bound to be read incorrectly; and worse still, when the juvenile reader does at some later date encounter poetry printed as poetry he is likely to be annoyed, if not irritated to the point where he refuses to read whatever is printed as poetry at all.[28]

Schwartz fears that the comic book tendency to represent even poetry as prose through the use of word bubbles will not only ruin the Shakespeare play, it will put the youth off reading poetry forever.

Whereas Kanter and Gilberton believed the comic would lead the reader back to the play, Schwartz feared that it would not only lead the reader away from the play, it would lead the reader away from all plays and poetry. Once the youth read it in comic form, he wouldn't be coming back. Others shared this fear for other reasons.

Gershon Legman, who believed that violence in culture was a response to sexual Puritanism, condemned all *Classics Illustrated*: "all the most violent children's books of the last two centuries are condensed into forty-eight-page picture-sequences, omitting every literary element . . . and squeezing together every violent scene that can be found in the original."[29] Although one glance at *Hamlet* shows him wrong (indeed, the Fortinbras subplot, requesting permission to invade Poland and make war there is cut, and an entire page is given over to each of the soliloquies, placing focus on the text and not the violence), the seeds had been planted to read comic book Shakespeare not as adaptations to a different medium, influenced by theatre and possibly popular with youth, but as incitements to violence, danger, and juvenile delinquency. Enter Fredric Wertham.

Wertham became famous as a self-proclaimed expert on the danger of comic books, cumulating in his book *Seduction of the Innocent*, which argued that reading comics, even *Classics Illustrated* causes reading disorders, mental illness, racism, illiteracy, juvenile delinquency, "sex mania," and even murder. *Macbeth* serves as his key example that even Shakespeare in comic form is detrimental.

> *Macbeth* in comic book form is an example. On the first page the statement is made: "Amazing as the tale may seem, the author gathered it from true accounts," the typical crime comic book formula of course. The first balloon has the words spoken by a young woman (Lady Macbeth: "Smear the sleeping servants with BLOOD!"
>
> To the child who looks at the first page "to see what's in it," this gives the strongest suggestion. And it gives the whole comic book the general appearance of a crime comic book. As for the content of this *Macbeth*, John Mason Brown, the well-known critic expressed in the *Saturday Review of Literature*: "To rob a supreme dramatist of the form at which he excelled is mayhem plus murder in the first degree . . . although the tale is murderous and gory, it never rises above cheap horror . . . what is left is not a tragedy. It is trashcan stuff".[30]

For Wertham, the use of comic form and the elements of visual storytelling reduce Shakespeare beyond the usual depths of the media. *Macbeth* is reduced to a crime comic, based on a true story and designed to titillate. "Children," he asserts, "know a crime comic when they see one, whatever the disguise."[31] He argues the same thing that I do here: that comic book artists translate Shakespeare into comic book form using the elements of the medium, but Wertham perceives this as dangerous to the reader and destructive to Shakespeare.

Wertham sees an intertextuality behind comic book Shakespeare. Not only does the form mimic popular comics, but also the illustrations are designed not to remind one of Shakespeare, but of other comics. Citing David Dempsey writing in the *New York Times*, Wertham argues that the *Classics Illustrated Julius Caesar* has "a Brutus that looks astonishingly like Superman."[32] Everything about comic book Shakespeare is done in order to drive the child away from actual Shakespeare. Children read the comic, instead of the original, which "cuts the children off from this source of pleasure, entertainment and education."[33] The end result is that, "Shakespeare and the child are corrupted at the same time."[34]

Wertham sees neither the possibility of legitimate pleasure, entertainment, and education from comic book Shakespeare nor the possibility espoused by Gilberton, that the comic would lead the reader to the original. Shakespeare is inevitably debased when translated into the medium of comic books. Wertham, however, also is using Shakespeare as the extreme example to prove his point that comic books are evil. If even Shakespeare can be corrupted, what must *Batman* or *True Crime Stories* do to young minds?

Given that other than adding narrative bubbles *Classics Illustrated* did not change a single word of Shakespeare (other than cuts), Wertham's argument that comics (and television) would result in the loss of the original seems a bit disingenuous. He writes:

> "Scholars will be interested in this new version of Shakespeare's *Hamlet*:
> The Death Scene (Hamlet Speaking):
> Fear not queen mother!
> It was Laertes
> And he shall die at my hands!
> . . . Alas! I have been poisoned
> And now I, too, go
> To join my deceased father!
> I, too,—I—AGGGRRRAA! [*sic*][35]

But it was not Shakespeare's language that was changed. As Schwartz objects, poetry was presented as prose, but it was Shakespeare's poetry/prose. This sort of transformation when adapting Shakespeare occurred much more in the theatre and on film.

Ironically, comic book Shakespeare is arguably one of the most faithful media, cutting lines, as argued above in this manner of a theatrical production, but little else is changed. Instead, a visual media is also employed. One might ask how this is different from theatre or film. Bradford Wright, writing in 2001, argues that in the 1950s, comic books offer "a crude, exaggerated, and absurd caricature of the American experience tailored for young tastes."[36] Although in the late 1930s and early 1940s comic books had relevance to the larger adult world, by the postwar period "social commentary," such as Superman as metaphor for the immigrant (and specifically Jewish immigrant) experience was deemphasized in favor of "juvenile fantasy."[37] *Classics Illustrated* Shakespeare walked the line, providing adaptations of works of literature as faithfully as the medium could allow, influenced by theatre and film versions of the same story, in the guise of juvenile fantasy. In another sense, Wertham was right that comic book Shakespeare echoes and forms an intertext with the medium and other comics, but he was wrong in that this fact did not cause children to murder, go mad, or attempt to become the Thane of Cawdor. Gilberton was right in that the comics theoretically could point the way to the original, but as often as not served as a substitute for the original. Yet they were still used in the educational system to introduce Shakespeare. The comic book versions of the plays were both riding the youth-culture market to make a profit for the publisher and educational tools. As we will see below, *Classics Illustrated* Shakespeare would be introduced again 40 years later for the same exact reasons.

Shakespeare's Comic Collaborators

Shakespeare was not only present in the comics through adaptation of the plays. The other aspects of youth-culture Shakespeare, especially reference, were present as well. Shakespeare served as inspiration. The role of his plays within society could be explored and examined or quotations from the plays employed to either elevate the comic, or for other purposes. Comics have even entered the authorship debate: according to *Superman* 44, a time-traveling Clark Kent helped Shakespeare write *Macbeth*.[38] Another coauthor was suggested in *Flaming Carrot* comics, as will be explored later. In addition to arguing for who inspired Shakespeare, the comics have been inspired by Shakespeare beyond mere appropriation of the plays or the man. For example, The Human

Torch, who made his first appearance in *Marvel Comics* 1, November 1939, was created by Carl Burgos, who was inspired by Casca's strange journey during the storm from *Julius Caesar*.[39]

> A common slave—you know him well by sight—
> Held up his left hand, which did flame and burn
> Like twenty torches join'd, and yet his hand,
> Not sensible of fire, remained unscorch'd.
> Besides—I ha' not since put up my sword—
> Against the capitol I met I lion,
> Who glaz'd upon me, and went surly by
> Without annoying me. And there were drawn
> Upon a heap a hundred ghastly women,
> Transformed with their fear, who swore they saw
> Men, all in fire, walk up and down the streets.
> (1.3.14–25)

The image of a flaming hand that does not burn or hurt the owner, and of men "all in fire" walking around the city inspired Burgos to create The Human Torch, initially an escaped science experiment that was a man-like being of fire, but evolved into a normal man who could cover some or all of his body in fire and "walk up and down the streets," not to mention fly over them.

It was the image from Shakespeare that inspired the piece, although nothing of Shakespeare doth remain in it. His presence, though inspirational, remains unfelt and unappropriated. While no one would consider The Human Torch an example of a Shakespearean appropriation, it does show the influence of Shakespeare on the early comic book artists and writers, even if the use is not direct.

Similar inspiration would help acclaimed author Alan Moore develop *V for Vendetta* in the 1980s for *Warrior Magazine*. Depicting a future totalitarian England, Moore created an antihero who fights the government from behind a Guy Fawkes mask. Moore writes that he wanted to use a Shakespeare quotation to open the book, presumably as Shakespeare is synonymous with England, English cultural authority, and tradition. He opened a copy of the complete works at random and scanned the page, finding a passage that "seemed to fit, exactly, line for line, with the sequence of actions that I planned for V in his first skirmish."[40] The passage was *Macbeth* 1.2.11–21 and the first skirmish occurs when V, planning to blow up the Houses of Parliament as Fawkes failed to do, rescues a young girl about to be raped and murdered by a group of policemen.

As the police prepare to harm the girl, V appears (the first time we see him in action), stating, "The multiplying villainies of nature do swarm upon him. And Fortune, on his damned quarrel smiling showed like a rebel's whore" (1.2.11–12, 14–15). A policeman surmises that he is "some kinda retard," but V pushes through the policemen, grabs the girl, and leaves them with a grenade that explodes, killing three, and all the while he says, "But all's too weak; For brave Macbeth (well he deserves that name), Distaining Fortune, with his brandished steel, Which smok'd with bloody execution, Like Valor's minion carv'd out his passage Till he faced the slave; Which nev'r shook hands, nor bade farewell to him" (1.2.15–21)[41] The passage, of course, is the Sergeant's report from the battlefield, of Macbeth fighting the traitor Macdonwald, although one might note that the editing transforms the meaning. V refers to the police as "the multiplying villainies of nature," but in the original the line refers to Macdonwald, not Macbeth. The lines are cut and taken out of context to mean what Moore wants them to mean, not necessarily their actual, original meaning.

On the other hand, the rest of the line is contextually appropriate. The sergeant's speech refers to an intranational fight: in Shakespeare's play it's Scot versus Scot for control of the nation; Moore's graphic novel features English police fighting an English terrorist for control of the nation. One might argue that the quotation employed makes V Macbeth, not exactly a role model, but both characters are someone who sees his ultimate goal as toppling the government. If Shakespeare is a symbol of England, and all that is good in England, it makes sense to have your hero seize control of that symbol, even if through a destabilizing quotation that calls into question how heroic in the traditional sense the hero is. If, as Alan Sinfield has argued, that in education Shakespeare "has been made to speak for the right," then *V for Vendetta* marks an attempt to make Shakespeare speak for the left, or at least for those opposed to the right.[42] The words may be ironic about Macbeth, considering how he rebels against his king and kills him, but when they are spoken the lines are of someone defending the nation against those who would do it harm. In *V*, the anarchist speaks Shakespeare, therefore assuring that Shakespeare does not speak for the right, but for what is best for the nation. Given the time period when the comic was written, it may mark Alan Moore's attempt during the Reagan and Thatcher years to move the culture away from the right.

Other Shakespearean appropriations in the comics are referential to the plays qua plays and engage the role of theatre as fantasy. In Mike Baron's *Badger*, knowledge of the canon is not only its own reward, it is the only way to save the world (or at least Wisconsin) from demonic invasion. Badger is a Vietnam veteran with multiple-personality disorder, one of whom is a crime-fighting superhero. He lives in Wisconsin with a "Weather Wizard" named Ham and is oftentimes called upon to use his multiple-personality disorder to fight supernatural beings. In "The Actor," Larry Oliver, a telephone company repairman who played Richard III in high school and always wanted to be an actor, picks up a hitchhiking Badger on Christmas Eve, fleeing from a demon horde under the command of Lord Weterlackus. The demons are concerned that they have not invaded Madison, Wisconsin, but Cruikshank, a ghost dimension "inhabited by Shakespeare-spouting bozos."[43] Demons, Badger explains, love Shakespeare, but on Cruikshank "they know their Shakespeare too damn well"![44] Demons will thus flee any location they believe to be Cruikshank.

Badger and Larry hole up at a local hotel and enlist the hotel guests to trick the demons into believing that they are actually on Cruikshank, and the only way to do that is to quote Shakespeare correctly. "Do you know Marc Anthony's funeral oration?" he asks the innkeeper.[45] Badger attempts to fight the demons, but is defeated. Larry, emerging from the closet in which he was hiding begins to recite the opening of *Richard III*: "Now is the winter of our discontent, made glorious summer by this sun of York; and all the clouds that lour'd upon our house in the deep bosom of ocean buried. Now are our brows bound with victorious wreaths . . ." (1.1.1–5).[46] As with *Classics Illustrated*, the verse is reduced to prose. The demons interrupt the recitation with jeers and criticism of his performance. Larry continues: "Unmanner'd dog! Stand thou, when I command: Advance thy halberd higher than my breast, or, by St. Paul, I'll strike thee to my foot, and spurn upon the beggar, for thy boldness!" (1.2.39–42).[47] By doing so, he transforms the dynamic. He is no longer Richard addressing an audience that can criticize him; he is now Richard addressing the guards of Henry's corpse, making them an active part of the scene. When Weterlackus commands him torn apart for such a poor performance, he continues: "But soft! Here come my executioners. How now my hardy stout resolved mates! Are you now going to dispatch this deed?" A demon immediately steps into the role of first murderer and states "We are, my lord; and come to have the warrant." "Well thought upon," Larry replies, handing him a phone bill, "I have it here about me" (1.3.338–341).[48] He transforms them yet again into a subordinate role, this time as his allies who will help him murder his brother. It is not just the quotation of Shakespeare that matters. Larry (and presumably Baron) quotes very specific sections of the play designed to move the demons into subordinate position to Larry and against Weterlackus. Given that the issue is titled "The Actor," one might argue that Larry does what actors are intended to do: move from storyteller to embodiment of a real person. Larry stops being Larry and becomes Richard. The willingness of the demons to accept this and play along is a metaphor for what all audience members must also do.

There is also something in here of the heroic fantasy, in which an ordinary person has the ability to save the world, which is standard comic book material, combined with the widespread belief that anyone can act. Larry played Richard in high school (many years before) and wonders if he could have been an actor. Popular culture thrives on the construction of actors as silly, often stupid, pretentious, self-important artistes who are actors because they look good and because they can't do much else. Likewise, when one spends weeks rehearsing Shakespeare, giving hours, days, weeks to the development of character, the creation of the world, discussion of the play, learning the fights, dances and songs, and then performing the entire thing eight times a week for several weeks, the first question one is inevitably asked is, "How do you remember all those lines?," as if acting were mere memorization. Larry remembers his lines and can shift gears into the *Tempest*, even though there is no indication that he has performed in that play. He wonders at the beginning of the comic if he could have been a professional actor, by the end of the comic he knows that he could have. But this construction is also a pop fantasy.

Weterlackus then accuses the demon of conspiring against him. Speaking to Larry, the demon says, "How does thy honor? Let me lick thy shoe. I'll not serve him, he is not a valiant" (3.2.23–24).[49] As Larry made the demon into the murderer by addressing him as such, the demon now makes Larry into Stephano, the drunken butler that Caliban perceives as a god-king. With this line, the demon is not only quoting Shakespeare and continuing the game of who knows the texts better, but he is also cementing the relationship that Larry has proposed. He assumes the subservient role and asks for Larry's protection and leadership. The two then continue this scene from *The Tempest*. When Weterlackus threatens the demon again, Larry tells him, "Trinculo, keep a good tongue in your head: If you prove a mutineer, the next tree! The poor monster is my subject, and he shall not suffer indignity" (3.2.35–37).[50] Weterlackus declares that there are no monsters in *Richard III*, which inspires both a demonic mutiny because "he does not know his Bard" and he did not recognize *The Tempest* and a retreat from the battle, for fear that they are on Cruikshank.

The lines indicated the shift from Weterlackus's leadership to Larry's, as Larry used Shakespeare to set himself as a dominant leader to demons that "are crazy for Shakespeare." His performance also allows Larry to be recognized by the other people at the inn as the "great actor Larry Oliver."[51] It is both parody of theatre aficionados gushing over Sir Laurence's own performances and fulfillment of the actor fantasy. He wonders if he could have been an actor and his performance has saved the world. Anyone who knows Shakespeare by heart could have done it. In this sense, Baron shows the Shakespearean aficionado as superhero; rather than unnatural strength or super powers, it is knowledge of lines beyond the mere catchphrases ("to be or not to be" "wherefore art thou, Romeo") that is Larry's superpower. *Badger* is unique in that it privileges the amateur who loves Shakespeare and he is the one to save the world. Not scholars, not actors, but an ordinary telephone repairman with dreams of acting is the one who really knows his Shakespeare. Baron gives the reader a working-class Shakespeare with practical value, in contrast to the Shakespeare-quoting V, or the Shakespeare of *The Sandman*, discussed later. Shakespeare is everybody's favorite author in the universe in *Badger*.

The comics have even entered the authorship debate, the Shakespearean version of Intelligent Design. As Douglas Lanier put it, " 'Shakespeare' outgrew Shakespeare," and the middle-class glover's son was too small to contain the mythic writer.[52] The aristocracy provided the candidates for those who believe someone else must have written the plays, whether Edward de Vere, Sir Francis Bacon, or even Queen Elizabeth. Even Marlowe at least had degrees from Cambridge University. Shakespeare, however, with his little Latin and less Greek, is not particularly elite.

Entering into the fray of the authorship debate is *Flaming Carrot Comics* 31 from October 1994. Entitled "Herbie in *Alas, Poor Carrot*," the comic book mocks the authorship debate while also positing Shakespeare firmly into the middle and working class as *Badger* does. Herbie the Fat Fury, an annoying, rotund man, travels back through time with the eponymous Carrot (actually a man with a giant, featureless carrot for a head, in a parody of mainstream superheroes) to the year 1607. They discover that Shakespeare, who goes by the name "Billy Bob" is a bit of a hayseed. In addition to writing plays he is also an inventor along the lines of Da Vinci or Ben Franklin.

Herbie and the Carrot discover Shakespeare's great secret: that Buddy Hackett was Shakespeare's collaborator. Hackett traveled through time because his first love was the high arts and the public had forced him to be a lowbrow comedian. He feared that if his audiences learned he preferred classical theatre to film and stand up his career would be over. Also, he argues, that if a work has not passed the test of time audiences don't respect it. Therefore he traveled back in time to help Shakespeare write his plays. Thus, his temporal journey served two purposes: concealment of his own true nature and the credibility that would come from inserting his work into history 400 years before he was born.[53] The comic demonstrates what Lanier terms "the fantasy of some participation in Shakespeare's authorship," that one can help write the plays, but there are also other substantial parodies and satires present in the comic as well.[54]

Flaming Carrot, like many alternative comics is rooted in irony, satire, and parody. Mainstream comics are quite often the first subject of parody, and given the attention paid to the use of Shakespeare in *Sandman* and the advent of new *Classics Illustrated*, it is quite possible that idea of Shakespeare in the comics becomes a target for satire here. The comic also represents a parody of the authorship debate. Buddy Hackett is not only a ludicrous choice for the "real" author of the canon, he is an impossible one. Also targeted is the notion of high culture: Shakespeare is a rural hack at best (one of the objections to him from the anti-Strafordians), but the person who really wrote the plays is known for broad, low comedy. The author replacing Shakespeare has all the same faults ostensibly attributed to Shakespeare by those who disbelieve in his authorship. Even the idea of authorship is mocked, as the silliness of it all indicates a certain contempt for those who place importance on the authorship debate. In a metaphoric sense, and in a supreme gesture of youth culture, the comic bites its thumb at the book. It should be noted that the Shakespeare issue is the most popular of *Flaming Carrot*, sold a great deal more than the others and is, in fact, "sold out." This popularity may be attributed to the value added by Shakespeare, whose presence may also be seen as self-serving, as his presence usually results in higher sales of a particular comic, or the ability to claim higher culture status that comes with familiarity with Shakespeare. Although they approach it in different ways, *V for Vendetta*, *Badger*, and *Flaming Carrot* all reference Shakespeare in order to be taken seriously by intelligent fans and also hold him at an ironic, hip-critical distance for their own purposes.

In that Sleep What Dreams May Come: *The Sandman*

Shakespeare's plays are full of dreams: Posthumous's dream in *Cymbeline*, Richard's nightmare before Bosworth, Caesar's wife dreams of his death, and even Mercutio's *Queen Mab* speech is dream inspired. Obviously, *A Midsummer Night's Dream* is all about dreaming. It is not unusual that the last play also links dreams with theatre. Marvin Carlson reports that dream therapists see "distinct similarities" between the "private experience" of dreaming and the "public experience of theatre."[55] The theatre is temporally phantasmagorical, playing out fantasies (often at night) and things that never were and then ending, much like dreams. Shakespeare himself refers to theatre as dreams in the epilogue of *A Midsummer Night's Dream* ("...you have but slumb'red here / While these visions did appear. / And this weak and idle theme, / No more yielding but a dream" (5.1.425–428)) and in Prospero's speech to Ferdinand and Miranda ("We are such stuff / As dreams are made on . . ." [4.1.156]). It is not surprising then that these two plays are appropriated by Neil Gaiman and his collaborators for the graphic novel *The Sandman*.[56]

The Sandman, which ran from 1988 to 1996 in 75 issues, a monthly special, and various smaller excerpts in other DC and Vertigo comic books, is ultimately an intertextual story of stories. It is also one of the most written about graphic novels in the world, not just by Shakespeare scholars but in its own right as well.[57] The protagonist, Morpheus, also called Dream of the Endless, the Lord Shaper, Oneiros, and uncounted other names, is the personification of the abstract idea of dreams. He is their master as well as their servant. He is also, therefore, the lord of stories, which, as Lanier points out, allows the graphic novel to engage Shakespeare as an emblematic author not only of theatre but of fantasy.[58]

Shakespeare is therefore appropriate as a character for the graphic novel, as Shakespeare's works not only embrace fantasy and dreaming, but also the power of stories as well, from Desdemona, weeping and falling in love with Othello for his tale ("She thank'd me, / And bade me, if I had a friend that lov'd her, / I should but teach him how to tell my story, / And that would woo her." (1.3.163–166)), to Egeus, who begins the *Comedy of Errors* with his narrative ("Thus have you heard me sever'd from my bliss, / That by my misfortunes was my life prolong'd, / To tell sad stories of my own mishaps" (1.1.118–120)), to Hamlet, who not only sends Horatio a letter telling the story of his escape by pirate kidnapping, but also insists that Horatio remain alive, "And in this harsh world draw thy breath in pain / To tell my story" (5.2.348–349), Shakespeare is full of animating tales, stories that move the audience and move the action. Storytelling and dreams are important in Shakespeare.

Shakespeare was incorporated into *The Sandman* in several ways. Although critics have focused on the use of the man juxtaposed with his texts, especially in the two issues "A Midsummer Night's Dream," and "The Tempest," both of which feature Shakespeare as a main character and form intertexts with the plays of the same names, Gaiman also incorporated the characters of Puck, Auberon, and Titania into his larger narrative. They appear on their own several times without Shakespeare present. Lines from the plays are quoted, often without acknowledgement of the source, and Morpheus even watches a Central European production of *A Midsummer Night's Dream* once: "He was mildly disappointed by the translation. He was, however, extraordinarily amused by the performance of the actor playing Bottom."[59] So beyond biography, the larger graphic novel interacts with Shakespeare, his plays and his characters on several levels. Because of its use of both the plays and biography, *The Sandman* has received more critical attention than any other comic book Shakespeare.

Michael D. Bristol's *Big-Time Shakespeare* begins its fifth chapter with an analysis of "Men of Good Fortune," the thirteenth issue of *The Sandman*.[60] Bristol cites Morpheus's statements about stories as if the character were a real scholar, making observations. Tellingly, Neil Gaiman, the creator and author of Morpheus does not appear in Bristol's index, although "Morpheus, Lord of Dreams" does. Bristol also notes in the acknowledgements that, "Lord Morpheus showed me how to bring this project to and end."[61] Lanier focuses on Shakespeare as kin to Gaiman, noting that when *Sandman* employs Shakespeare, it is to "reflect on the nature and costs of fantasy authorship," and that the use of *Tempest* and *Dream* are "self-reflexive" for both Shakespeare and Gaiman.[62] I do not dispute either of these contentions. It is, however, easy to anatomize the conflation of Morpheus, Shakespeare, and Gaiman when one considers these three issues in a vacuum. The larger context of the narrative, however, reveals a different agenda. "Men of Good Fortune" appears in a graphic novel called *The Doll House* (no relation to Ibsen). "A Midsummer Night's Dream" is in *Dream Country*, and "The Tempest" appears in *The Wake*. The other stories in the volume provide a larger context for reading the Shakespeare segments, and the entire cycle provides an even larger reading of the nature of Shakespeare, drama, dreaming, and stories.

In *The Wake*, for example, Morpheus is dead. Daniel, a human child conceived and brought to term in a dream is transformed into the new Dream of the Endless. The Endless are personifications of abstracts: Death, Dream, Destruction, Desire, Destiny, Despair, and Delirium (who was once Delight). Daniel, who was kidnapped by Puck and the Norse god Loki as revenge against Morpheus is a changeling child. Just as Puck works in Shakespeare's play to wrest a changeling from Titania, Gaiman's Puck wrests a changeling from its mother to begin its transformation into a king. "The Tempest" is the last story in *The Wake* and the last story in the *Sandman* series, although chronologically it is set at the end of Shakespeare's life and 400 years before the narrative begun in the first issue begins.

Shakespeare, in his (and our) last meeting with Morpheus, tells him that, "Prospero and Miranda, Caliban and Gonzalo, aethereal Ariel and silent Antonio, all of **them** are more real to me than silly, wise Ben Jonson; Susanna and Judith; the good citizens of Stratford . . ."[63] Just as Bristol speaks of Morpheus as if he were real, so much of Shakespearean criticism speaks of the characters as if they were real, and in a sense, to most Shakespeareans, the characters are more real than other people in one's life and certainly than people one has never met. Gaiman, speaking here through Shakespeare, says something about the power of creation. Sometimes the creation is bigger and more real than the creator. Hamlet, Romeo and Juliet, and Prospero and Puck are more real than Shakespeare even, because they live in individual imaginations in a manner that Shakespeare, as an historic personage rooted in "facts," is not able to.

In *The Sandman*, stories are larger and have greater power than their creators. In this sense, *Sandman* is the ultimate postmodern fiction. The author does not control the text; the text has power over the author. Puck as a character influences events, not only at the first performance of *Midsummer Night's Dream*, but in the early 1990s, when he kidnaps Daniel. When finally his mischief is discovered, he introduces himself via Yeats: "I am the Puck, called Robin Goodfellow. I am a trickster, an antic prankster, a will o' the wisp. 'Things fall apart, the centre cannot hold, mere anarchy is loose upon the world.' That's me."[64] Puck cites Yeats's "The Second Coming" as being about him.

Puck was first introduced in "A Midsummer Night's Dream," in which as part of his bargain with Morpheus Shakespeare has written the titular play, which is performed initially in front of the fairies about which it concerns. Titania and Oberon (here called Auberon), Puck and Peaseblossom, and all the fairies come to see the play on the downs of Sussex where the Lord Chamberlain's Men are on tour. Eventually, Puck knocks out the actor playing Puck, telling him, "You played me well, mortal. But I have played me for time out of mind, and I do Robin Goodfellow better than anyone."[65] This speech is another expression of the one in "The Tempest," that Puck is a more real than any actor playing Puck. Gaiman seems to suggest that the idea of Shakespeare's characters is bigger and more real than any performer in the role.

By solely focusing on the three issues that feature Shakespeare as a character, critics such as Lanier and Burt miss the issues with Puck, Auberon and Titania, who appear several times in the series and clearly are seen as having an existence beyond that envisioned by their creator. Also missing from such criticism is the dialogue that *Sandman* has within itself, and references, both textual and visual, to other moments from the graphic novel. For example, in Gaiman's *A Midsummer Night's Dream*, not only is Puck echoing the Shakespeare play when he says "Lord, what fools these mortals be!" he is also echoing Morpheus quoting the same line in the very first issue. Morpheus spent 70 years trapped in a glass box in England, held captive by a magician. When he is released, he condemns the magician's son for continuing to hold him after the magician died, noting, "You had no thought for the harm you must have brought to your world. Lord what fools these mortals be."[66] When Puck issues the same line 20 issues later, he is not only quoting Shakespeare, canny readers know that Morpheus has also uttered these sentiments, and since Morpheus inspired the play, the line has been his all along.

Gaiman's Puck is not Shakespeare's, but he is rooted in the tradition that gave birth to him. In the twenty-first century, *Dream* has become safe, fun, popular, and considered family friendly. Schools and community groups that would not touch *Titus Andronicus* perform *Dream*. But Gaiman reinscribes the play within its Celtic context. In "A Midsummer Night's Dream," when the actor playing the stage Puck says, "I am that merry wanderer of the night," (2.1.43), Peaseblossom comments, "I am that giggling-dangerous-totally-bloody-psychotic-menace-to-life-and-limb, more like it," to which another fairy responds, "Shush, Peaseblossom. The Puck might hear you."[67] This exchange returns the fairies to the pre-Christian context, when they were dangerous, but it also once again returns the reader to comic book Shakespeare. The villains must be dangerous. This Puck is the equivalent of *Batman*'s Joker: lethally funny.

Shakespeare is clearly out of his league. He tries to control the company and keep his end of the bargain, but he is unnerved by the reality of the world he created. This Shakespeare is not playwright as magician in Alvin Kernan's sense; it is, instead, playwright as sorcerer's apprentice: unable to control or manipulate the powers he has summoned.[68]

Shakespeare's son Hamnet is one of the apprentices, preparing to play girl's roles. His father ignores him. He even tells another boy, "Judith—she's my twin sister—she once joked that if I died, he'd just write a play about it. 'Hamnet.' "[69] Later the audience is shown Hamnet talking with Titania, and we learn later that she asked him if he wanted to go live in a magical land forever. The story ends with a textual note that "Hamnet Shakespeare died in 1596, aged eleven."[70] Shakespeare's son has become the changeling child of the play. Once again, the story has shaped and reflected the reality.

In creating the Shakespeare stories for Sandman, Gaiman and Charles Vess used Anthony Burgess's *Shakespeare* as a reference. Vess cites the reason:

> We both had a bunch of different biographies, most of them from academic viewpoints that had no idea what the creative impulse could possibly be. And they were making assumptions about why Shakespeare would have done something. They just didn't know what happened. Burgess is a writer and he's creative, so he did. It was really a nice biography, very interesting.[71]

The differing viewpoints, between Lainer and Vess as to who truly understands Shakespeare and who is self-involved and limited is actually what is very interesting. In this case, scholars and artists, who, by definition need each other, still conflict over who owns Shakespeare. *The Sandman* itself, however, presents the idea that Shakespeare is ultimately owned by the characters and the ideas within the plays, but anyone is free to play with them.

Ultimately behind every story in *The Sandman*, especially the Shakespearean ones, is the exploration of the interaction between reality and fantasy, and how stories are used to control both, but stories can end up also blurring lines or even taking control of reality. As Puck himself remarks upon seeing himself onstage in Gaiman's version, "This is magnificent—and it is **true**! It never happened; yet it is still true. What magic art is this?"[72] The answer, of course, is theatre, which makes the unreal real. But it could also refer to graphic novels and comic books, which depict events that never happened but which the reader knows in his or her heart are somehow true. The truth of false stories might be the ultimate theme of Gaiman and Shakespeare, and explain the appeal of both to youth of all ages.

A New Generation of *Classics Illustrated*

Comic book Shakespeare has come full circle since the 1950s. In 1990, First Comics reached an agreement with the owners of the copyright to *Classics Illustrated* and began producing new versions for contemporary graphic novel enthusiasts. Like the original, it was more expensive and less popular than other comic books of its time. Unlike the original, which used many of the same artists to adapt the classics, First used the most popular artists of the period, asking each one to adapt one. For First, the selling point was not the classical work of literature, but to see how, for example, Bill Sienkiewicz drew *Moby Dick* or Jill Thompson would draw *The Scarlet Letter*, much like an aficionado of Cheek by Jowl or Robert Lapage or Robert Wilson would seek out their respective adaptations of classical works for the stage.

As with the original *Classics Illustrated*, the reader is informed of the relationship of comic to original text. The inside front cover contains a similar acknowledgement of the adapted and abridged nature of the project.

> *Classics Illustrated* are adaptations of the world's greatest works of literature, produced by some of the world's most talented writers and artists. Each lavishly illustrated volume is an accurate representation of the original work—distinctive, fresh and innovative, yet faithful to the book and true to the intentions of the author . . .
>
> While they stand on their own merits, *Classics Illustrated* are not substitutes for the originals. Rather they are artistic interpretations, perfect introductions to an exciting world of remarkable ideas and unlimited possibilities . . .[73]

This boilerplate for every issue contains contradictory assertions of accuracy and innovation, of being true "to the intentions of the author," while representing the work of the adaptors. So much for Barthes's "death of the author." But, unlike the original *Classics Illustrated*, this one approaches the classics as a theatre company would. Instead of arguing that the comic exists to encourage youth to go and read the original, they identify themselves as "artistic interpretations," just as a stage performance is not the original play, but an artistic interpretation of it.

The only Shakespearean offering in this series was an adaptation of *Hamlet* by Steven Grant and Tom Mandrake. As with the original comic adaptation, the verse is gone; all is prose. Fortinbras and his sub-plot are gone as well. There are also numerous other reductions and cuts to the text. In 1.5, for example, only Horatio accompanies Hamlet to see the ghost, who only asks him once to "swear." The arrival of the players is reduced to a four panel scene in which Hamlet greets them: "You are welcome, Masters, welcome all" (2.2.421), and immediately leaps to "We'll hear a play tomorrow. Can you play 'The Murder of Gonzago'?"(2.2.535–537)[74] The "O, what a rogue and peasant slave am I" (2.2.550–605) soliloquy follows, taking up an entire page. The four panels of the next page consist of a truncated version of the beginning of 3.1, in which Claudius and Polonius set Ophelia upon Hamlet. The entire next page is taken up with the "To be or not to be soliloquy" (3.1.55–89). Two pages in a 48 page book are given over to soliloquies. A third full page is given over to the ghost's narration. The full page, single picture approach to the larger speeches actually makes the least use of the comic aesthetic discussed earlier.

As in theatre, all three moments are given over not to reenactments, but focused on the words the character speaks. While the ghost tells his tale, the adaptors could have shown images from it to accompany the text, as they do later when Ophelia tells of Hamlet coming to her chamber and a series of black and white images accompany her description of the event. Instead, the focus is on the text on each of these pages, not the image. They are distinctly un-comic moments that are perhaps reflective of the importance given to the words of the solil-oquy, just as what happens in theatrical production.

This adaptation is easily read as indicative of the graphic novel tradition of the late 1980s and early 1990s: beautifully painted (not penciled, inked, and then colored, as ordinary comics are) by an artist known for his achievements in other comics,[75] approaching the form as serious literature, focusing on the dark, adult elements and firmly rooting the narrative in the reality of the world. One of the great advances of graphic novels in the mid-1980s was the abandonment of juvenile fantasy and the embracing of "realism" in comics in such titles as Alan Moore's *Swamp Thing* and *Watchmen* and Frank Miller's *The Dark Knight Returns*. Such books approached the superhero genre asking what the world would be like if such people really existed and what such people would be like if they really existed. *Watchmen* does not even use the term "superhero," preferring instead to refer to the characters as "costumed vigilantes" and focus on their quasi-legal status as crime-fighters.[76] Grant and Mandrake's adaptation of *Hamlet* emerges from this milieu.

Yet nostalgia would also result in the re-emergence of the original as well. In 1997, Acclaim Comics reprinted digest-size versions of *Classics Illustrated* adaptations of Shakespeare: *Julius Caesar, A Midsummer Night's Dream, Hamlet, Macbeth,* and *Romeo and Juliet,* and one entirely new one: *Henry IV, Part 1.* They were marketed under the motto, "Your doorway to the classics," and were re-titled *Classics Illustrated Study Guides.* While one might perceive these reissues as attempting to profit from the recent boom in comics and the success of Shakespeare-affiliated graphic novels, the re-title leads one to see in them an attempt to profit from the growth in translating and reducing Shakespeare as represented by the growth industry of Shakespeare substitutes such as *No Fear Shakespeare* and *Shakespeare Made Easy.* No longer comic book size, by being published in digest size they are similar in size and shape to these other books and fit easily in a backpack. The comic book is no longer a comic book. It is now a study guide, an acceptable means to engage youth in Shakespeare; no longer *Seduction of the Innocent,* but valuable educational tool. Gilberton insisted all along that its comic books were educational and literature. Acclaim has made it so.

Most recently, *Picture This! Shakespeare,* was issued by Barron's, the publisher of standardized test preparation guides, the *Simply Shakespeare* series, and the *Shakespeare Made Easy* series. On the cover of each *Picture This! Shakespeare* is loudly proclaimed, "Shakespeare's immortal comedy / tragedy ***Illustrated in the style of a graphic novel*** with extensive excerpts from the play's original dialogue." Like the other publications by Barron's, it is marketed as a study aid. Including a list of literary terms, a glossary, and dramatis personae that includes pictures of the corresponding characters, the publications in the series alternate between several pages of black and white comic book adaptation and the original text in verse with boxed notes. The illustrations are used to indicate action and make clear the events of the narrative. Unlike *Classics Illustrated* there is very little editing, although the text is still an abridgement.

The art is not particularly good or inspiring. Unlike First's line of illustrated classics, which many purchased not because of the work being adapted but because of the artist doing the adaptation, the focus in *Picture This! Shakespeare* is not beautiful artwork, translating Shakespeare into the medium of graphic novels, or linking the plays to a theatrical or filmic context. Instead, the plays are reduced to what Wertham and others accused the original *Classics Illustrated*: simplistic, unartistic reductions of Shakespeare to the lowest common denominator for the purpose of translating the play for those who find reading the original difficult. *Picture This! Shakespeare* is Cliffs Notes in graphic form, but with no real aesthetic content. Like the *No Fear Shakespeare* series, it represents an attempt to translate Shakespeare that will be acceptable in the classroom, because at least one is getting the full text (or close to it). It is an educational tool far more than a true graphic novel. The comic book Shakespeare no longer even needs to be a good comic book. Now it just needs pictures and text.

The comic industry is no longer in the shape that it was in during the late 1980s and early 1990s. Profits and output are a fraction of what they were 15 years ago. Despite this, however, the continued popularity of the form (especially now as source material for movies) indicates the form will continue to exist for the foreseeable future. Shakespeare is less of a presence now, but as the occasional emergences in the past half century have proven, it would not be unusual for new Shakespeare-influenced and inspired graphic novels to appear in the future.

Notes

1. Anthony Davies, "Shakespeare and the Media of Film, Radio and Television," *Shakespeare Survey* 39 (1987), p. 1.
2. Michael D. Bristol, *Big-Time Shakespeare* (London: Routledge, 1996); Richard Burt, *Unspeakable Shaxxxspeares: Queer Theory and American Kiddie Culture* (New York: St. Martin's, 1998); Douglas Lanier, *Shakespeare and Modern Popular Culture* (Oxford: Oxford University Press, 2002).
3. Amy Kiste Nyberg, *Seal of Approval: The History of the Comics Code* (Jackson: University Press of Mississippi, 1998), p. 1.
4. Ibid., p. 1; Will Eisner, *Graphic Storytelling* (Tamarac: Poorhouse Press, 1996), p. 5.
5. Eisner, *Graphic Storytelling*, p. 113.
6. Will Eisner, *Comics and Sequential Art* (Tamarac: Poorhouse Press, 1985), p. 1; Scott McCloud, *Understanding Comics* (New York: Harper Perennial, 1993), p. 9.
7. McCloud, *Understanding Comics*, pp. 14, 12, 10, 16.
8. Eisner, *Graphic Storytelling*, p. 3.
9. Eisner, *Graphic Storytelling*, p. 58.

10. David Carrier, *The Aesthetics of Comics* (University Park: Pennsylvania State University Press, 2000), p. 30.
11. Yoshiko Fukushima, *Manga Discourse in Japanese Theatre* (London: Keegan Paul, 2003).
12. Hubert H. Crawford, *Crawford's Encyclopedia of Comic Books* (Middle Village, NY: Jonathan David Publishers, 1978), p. 205.
13. Milla Bongo, *Reading Comics: Language, Culture, and the Concept of the Superhero in Comic Books* (New York: Garland Publishing, 2000), p. 8.
14. Crawford, *Encyclopedia*, p. 205.
15. Quoted in Crawford, *Encyclopedia*, p. 212.
16. Quoted in Crawford, p. 212.
17. Nyberg, *Seal of Approval*, p. 117.
18. William B. Jones, Jr., *Classics Illustrated: A Cultural History with Illustrations* (Jefferson: McFarland and Company, 2002), p. 4.
19. Ibid., p. 89.
20. Ibid., pp. 4–5.
21. William Shakespeare, *Hamlet*, adapted by Alex A. Blum, *Classics Illustrated* 87 (New York: Gilbertian September 1951).
22. Jones, *Classics Illustrated*, p. 66.
23. Crawford, *Encyclopedia*, p. 212.
24. Jones, *Classics Illustrated*, p. 66.
25. Ibid., p. 51.
26. Reproduced as Leslie Fiedler, "The Middle Against Both Ends," in *Arguing Comics: Literary Masters on a Popular Medium*, edited by Jeet Heer and Kent Worcester (Jackson: University Press of Mississippi, 2004), p. 125.
27. Delmore Schwartz, "Masterpieces as Cartoons," in *Arguing Comics: Literary Masters on a Popular Medium*, edited by Jeet Heer and Kent Worcester (Jackson: University Press of Mississippi, 2004), p. 54.
28. Ibid., p. 55.
29. Gershon Legman, *Love and Death: A Study in Censorship* (New York: Hacker Art, 1948), p. 50.
30. Fredric Wertham, *Seduction of the Innocent* (New York: Rinehart and Company, 1954), p. 22.
31. Ibid., p. 22.
32. Ibid., p. 36.
33. Ibid., p. 142.
34. Ibid., p. 143.
35. Ibid., p. 388.
36. Bradford M. Wright, *Comic Book Nation* (Baltimore: Johns Hopkins University Press, 2001), p. xiv.
37. Ibid., p. 59.
38. See Lanier's analysis of the issue, *Shakespeare*, pp. 136–137.
39. James Steranko, *The Steranko History of Comics Volume* I (Reading, PA: Supergraphics, 1970), p. 57.
40. Alan Moore, "Behind the Painted Smile," in *V for Vendetta* (New York: DC Comics, 1990), p. 273.

41. Alan Moore and David Lloyd, *V for Vendetta* (New York: DC Comics, 1990), pp. 11–12.

42. Alan Sinfield, "Give an Account of Shakespeare and Education, Showing Why You Think They Are Effective and What You Have Appreciated about Them; Support Your Comments with Precise References," in *Political Shakespeare: New Essays in Cultural Materialism*, edited by Jonathan Dollimore and Alan Sinfield (Manchester: Manchester University Press, 1985), pp. 134–135.

43. Mike Baron, *Badger* 46, First Comics (April 1989), First Publishing, p. 5.

44. Ibid.

45. Ibid., p. 10.

46. Ibid., pp. 17–18.

47. Ibid., p. 21.

48. Ibid., p. 21.

49. Ibid., p. 22.

50. Ibid., p. 22.

51. Ibid., p. 26.

52. Lanier, *Shakespeare*, p. 134.

53. Bob Burden, "Herbie in *Alas, Poor Carrot*," *Flaming Carrot Comics* 31 (1994 October). Dark Horse Comics, I am in debt to Hy Bender for his insights into this comic.

54. Lanier, *Shakespeare*, p. 118.

55. Marvin Carlson, *The Haunted Stage* (Ann Arbor: University of Michigan Press, 2001), p. 3.

56. They appear, respectively, as "A Midsummer Nights Dream" in *The Sandman: Dream Country* (New York: DC Comics, 1991) and "The Tempest" in *The Sandman: The Wake* (New York: DC Comics, 1997).

57. See Hy Bender, *The Sandman Companion* (New York: DC Comics, 1999); Alisa Kwitney, *The Sandman: King of Dreams* (San Francisco: Chronicle Books, 2003); and Joseph McCabe, *Hanging out with the Dream King: Conversations with Neil Gaiman and His Collaborators* (Seattle, Fantagraphics, 2004) in addition to the earlier scholarly works mentioned.

58. Lanier, *Shakespeare*, p. 120.

59. Neil Gaiman, *The Sandman: The Kindly Ones* (New York: DC Comics, 1996), n.p.

60. Reproduced in the collection *The Sandman: The Doll's House* by Neil Gaiman, which collected issues nine through sixteen (New York: DC Comics, 1995).

61. Michael D. Bristol, *Big-Time Shakespeare* (London: Routledge, 1996), pp. 121–124, 126, 138, 231.

62. Lanier, *Shakespeare*, p. 120, 121.

63. Gaiman, *The Wake*, p. 180.

64. Gaiman, *The Kindly Ones*, n.p.

65. Gaiman, *Dream Country*, n.p.

66. Neil Gaiman, *The Sandman: Preludes and Nocturnes* (New York: DC Comics, 1991), p. 36.

67. Gaiman, *Dream Country*, n.p.

68. Alvin Kernan, *The Playwright as Magician* (New Haven: Yale University Press, 1979).
69. Gaiman, *Dream Country*, n.p.
70. Ibid.
71. Quoted McCabe, *Hanging Out*, p. 101.
72. Gaiman, *Dream Country*, n.p.
73. Taken from the inside front cover of *Hamlet*, in *Classics Illustrated 5*, adapted by Steven Grant and Tom Mandrake (New York: First Publishing, 1990), but on the inside front cover of all issues in the series.
74. Ibid., p. 21.
75. Tom Mandrake, the artist, is also known for his work on *Batman*, *Captain Marvel*, *Swamp Thing*, and *Grimjack*, among others.
76. Alan Moore and David Gibbons, *Watchmen* (New York: DC Comics, 1987).

6

"Adolescence, Thy Name is Ophelia!": The Ophelia-ization of the Contemporary Teenage Girl

Jennifer Hulbert

Recently I was shopping on Melrose Avenue in Hollywood, the virtual aorta of American trend. While en route from one trendy boutique to another, a poster in the window of an ultra-hip record store exposed my inner Shakespeare-geek. It was an advertisement for a performance of Ophelia Rising, a band of four young women dressed defiantly in rocker makeup and slashed black mesh and leather. They looked a little miffed at the world, and the word "Rising" in their title suggests that they are not willing to suffer a pounding of injustices from the patriarch that raised them. My retro Pumas stopped dead in their tracks. I put down my latte and reached into my handbag for a pen and paper. On the back of a Starbucks receipt I wrote: "OPHELIA RISING: zombie hipster or bad metaphor?" I wondered what Shakespeare's hopeless mad-girl and these hard-core chicks actually had common; why was it suddenly cool to be Ophelia?

According to their Web site, Ophelia Rising's name originates with the lead singer, who calls herself Ophelia.[1] In their late teens and twenties, the women in this Boston-based, hard-rock band are part of the generation of blooming girls and young women that were the first to collectively be dubbed Ophelia. This association of late twentieth- century adolescent girls with the most famous of Shakespeare's victimized women invaded psychological pop culture with the publication of Mary Pipher's best-selling social inquiry, *Reviving Ophelia*.[2] The seminal book exposed the rarely discussed aspects of the troubled teenage self and became a bible for anyone confronting female adolescence: mothers, fathers, teachers, preteens, and teenaged girls. The book was atop the *New York Times* Best-seller list for 27 weeks and remained on the list for an additional 127 weeks. Of course, with such popularity, came an obligatory parade of reactionary works that employed the term Ophelia to refer to the teenage self. With *Ophelia Speaks*, a volume of self-reflexive prose written by adolescent girls and edited by the teenaged Sara Shandler, young women agreed with Pipher that Ophelia would be their spokeswoman.[3] *Ophelia's Mom* edited by Sara's mother, Nina Shandler, followed two years later.[4] This venture addressing the experiences of teenage girls' mothers is ironically titled considering Shakespeare's Ophelia was motherless. More works followed, including Cheryl Dellasega's *Surviving Ophelia* and the drama *Are We Reviving Ophelia?* by Greg West, Jackie Boyland, and the students of Masconomet High School in Massachusetts.[5] If the literary outpouring were not enough, there has even been the development of a nonprofit organization designed to aid and mentor teenage girls in our dilapidatingly commercial society aptly named Project Ophelia.[6] With all these cultural links between Ophelia and the adolescent girl, Mary Pipher created a new prevailing metaphor for the experience of the American teenage girl; Ophelia inadvertently became the Shakespearean spokeswoman for a generation.

I was a contemporary teenage Ophelia myself in 1994, when the book first enlightened our parents, our teachers, our society, and ourselves to the unique and often unspoken problems of our generation of girls. At a time when my mother and I did not discuss anything more profound than whether or not the dishes in the dishwasher were clean, I came home from school to find that she had subtly placed the book on my bed. She had already read it, earmarking the pages that reminded her of me. I thumbed through it, like many of my peers, and recognized pieces of my friends and myself in the case studies it disclosed. Of course, I just read the juicy parts—the ones fit for Oprah or Rikki Lake—but I could not help but feel at ease in the comfort of solidarity that it provided. I realized that not only was I not alone in my loneliness, rejection, and hatred of my body, but it could be worse. I could be pregnant, parentless, or addicted to huffing paint.

In all honesty, I probably would not have opened the book had it not been for its intriguing title. I was 14 and would rather have been watching Nirvana on MTV. But I was attracted to *Reviving Ophelia*, to the beauty of its words and the image I attached to them. At the time, I had technically never read William Shakespeare's *Hamlet*. It

was a part of the Senior English curriculum, and I wasn't even a sophomore. But I had seen the Mel Gibson film, and found the seductively
pale, doomed image of Helena Bonham-Carter's Ophelia romantically
melancholic like the sounds of Smashing Pumpkins. She had satin skin
and stunning dark curls, wore gorgeous dresses, and made out with
the ruggedly bearded Mel Gibson; I lingered in the association.
Bonham-Carter's Ophelia was meekly powerless and sad, but alluring
and chilling in her madness, the way I saw myself in my depressed funk
and lines of adolescent poetry. Girls younger than I was had their own
subsequent cinematic Ophelias to emulate. In 1996 a fair Kate Winslet
brought youthful rosy cheeks to a very sexual Ophelia in Kenneth
Branagh's epic film of the play. And four years later, the new
Shakespearean "it" girl, Julia Stiles, brought a New York hip edge to the
name in Michael Almereyda's film, which so modernized the play that
the proverbial "To be" speech was spoken in a Blockbuster Video store.[7]

These cinematic images of Ophelia have morphed with her mainstream assignment as a synecdoche for all teenage girls. The result is a
clear and decisive understanding of the character that is engendered
without a word from Shakespeare himself. My perception of Ophelia
as a beautiful but troubled young woman just like me preceded my
introduction to and study of Shakespeare's text and undoubtedly
shaped my conception of it. In a more educated and well-read retro-
spect, I am sure that my 16-year-old insight of Mel Gibson could not
have comprehended the layers of significance in which Pipher's
metaphor positioned my peers and the accuracy of such a comparison.
In fact, I question whether these layers have been explored by many of
the parents, publishers, and young women who have used the character
of Ophelia to name a generation four centuries removed. Is the general
awkward melancholy and self-destructive angst experienced by the
average American teenager as parallel to the suffering of Ophelia as
Pipher and others imply? Or is the Ophelia-ization of the teenage girl
just an arbitrarily and romantic metaphor gone too far?

Of course, the selection of Ophelia is not entirely random. William
Shakespeare's canon is so prevalent in Western civilization that his
characters are some of the most prominent in our culture; the mere
mention of their names evoke Shakespeare's allegedly universal
themes. His characters are arguably as powerful in allusion as those of
the Bible and Greek mythology, and invoked as often, if not more so,
in popular culture. The beautiful Ophelia is one such character. Of
course her youth, suffering, and madness are not unique among
Shakespeare's women, but her name holds more beauty and popularity

in relation to others in the canon. A title such as *Reviving Lavinia* is more likely to be mistaken for a book about a dangerous new sexually transmitted disease than to provoke the relatively obscure image of Titus Andronicus's ill-fated teenage daughter. This lack of prowess in notoriety is the same for the disowned Cordelia, the publicly humiliated Hero, the ostracized and banished Rosalind, and finally, the island-bound Miranda, whose name is more likely to be connected by today's generation with her friends Carrie, Samantha, and Charlotte on *Sex and the City* than with Prospero's daughter.

Even if the names are familiar, their plights are not. Though more popular than most of her afflicted Shakespearean peers, Ophelia is by no means the playwright's most famous teenage girl. Juliet, as one half of Western drama's most glamorous couple, wins that title hands down. Unfortunately for Pipher's purpose, she is not pathetic enough. Her life is not all sadness; she is in love with the sane Romeo, and despite her climactic death, she is not alone when it occurs. Above all, Juliet is a key inciter of the play's action. Her downfall is largely the result of her own choices. She willfully defies her parents by refusing their choice of husband in Paris and choosing her own husband in Romeo. Unlike Ophelia, Juliet is not mad when she ends her own life—she again makes a conscious decision, first, to fake her own death through the friar's potion and then to stab herself with Romeo's dagger, which is a much more masculine form of death.[8] Because of the control she maintains over her own life, Juliet is too strong a force in her play and too well adjusted to be an apt depiction of a contemporary teenage girl in the manner that those who would construct such girls as suffering from being too much put upon.[9] *Romeo and Juliet* is doused in her; her voice is loud and cannot be overlooked. She is too bold a character to speak for the girls in Pipher's book, a book with the intention of bringing to the forefront the psyche of a population that has traditionally been silent and ignored.

By providing this microphone and stage for the quelled teenage girl, Mary Pipher and her literary disciples have made leaps in feminist assertion with their focus on Ophelia, both the character and the teenage girl she represents. One reason why Ophelia serves as an apt representative of the silent sufferings of adolescent girls is because she is a subservient and marginalized character in the world of the play, unlike Juliet. Her character is defined in terms that include the men around her: she is Polonius's daughter, Laertes's sister, and Hamlet's lover. Her decisions, motivations, actions, and downfall, stem from the men of the play, without whose influence she does not make a decision.

She lives in full obedience of her father, even when his wishes compromise the trust she shares with her love, Hamlet. When circumstances cause Hamlet to withdraw his love and affections for Ophelia and subsequently take her father's life, the poor girl is left alone without guidance and takes her leave of the play. Of course her personal story and will are overlooked in the text, because the play belongs to the sources of the action: Claudius, Polonius, and Hamlet. She has no long soliloquies like Hamlet or monologues laden with "Neither a borrower nor a lender be," adages like Polonius. She does not sweep in at the end, eulogizing Hamlet and taking control of the state, as does Fortinbras. She simply disappears into the action and finally into the river. It would take a troupe of feminists (or at least one psychologist/ anthropologist) to fish her out.

Pipher's demarginalization of the teenage girl is resonate of a practice in feminist dramatic criticism dubbed "New Poetics" by Sue-Ellen Case in her book *Feminism in Theatre*. According to Case, the natural movement of postfeminist criticism is away from the traditionally passive critique, which simply interprets and comments on the patriarchal structures within the text. Academics focus on the role of women in the play, their subservience and inferiority within the patriarchal confines of the world of the play and the world that spawned it. After 30 years of this approach to the Shakespearean canon, it has been tapped dry, with few avenues left unmapped. Case proposes a budding mode of feminist criticism based on Aristotle's "Poetics." She writes:

> New Feminist theory would abandon the traditional patriarchal values embedded in prior notions and form, practice and audience response in order to construct new critical models and methodologies for drama that would accommodate the presence of women in the art, support their liberation from the cultural fictions of the female gender and deconstruct the valorism of the male gender . . . This "new poetics" would deconstruct the traditional systems of representation and perception of women and *posit women in the position of the subject*. [Emphasis added][10]

One such model and methodology can be found in the work of Mary Pipher, Sarah Sanders, and others. By handing the title of their works to Ophelia rather than Hamlet, they are unearthing her from deep within the play and positioning her at the center of the action. At last, Ophelia is the core of discussion and concern and Hamlet is only addressed in his relation to her, if at all.

Subsequently, the teenage girl Ophelia represents is brought into the forefront with her. By "reviving" Ophelia, these authors are giving her a voice independent of her family and male peers and acknowledging that this voice has something to say. In fact, with *Ophelia Speaks*, Sara Shandler and other contemporary "Ophelias" are granted a microphone and a stage all their own. This is the very act of positioning women as the subject that Sue-Ellen Case prescribes. The problems of Hamlet and the King—or male teenagers and parents—have gone by the wayside and been replaced at the center, both in Shakespeare and in society, by a traditionally marginalized voice.

It is worth noting that in this demarginalization both Pipher and Shandler address the Self of the teenage girl in the subtitles of their books. The full title of Pipher's book is *Reviving Ophelia: Saving the Selves of Adolescent Girls*. Subsequently, Shandler labels her book *Ophelia Speaks: Adolescent Girls Write about Their Search for Self*. This concept of "Self" is more than who one is; it is proclamation of one's importance and centrality in the grand scheme of things. In *Comic Women, Tragic Men*, Linda Bamber asserts that in Shakespeare's tragedies, the male characters—Hamlet, Othello, Lear, Titus, the Richards, and the Henrys—are the Self on whom the play focuses. Accordingly, the women become the "Other" of their plays: characters defined in their relation to and role in the life of the male Self.[11] For example, Shakespeare's Hamlet chronicle's the title character's search for and justification of Self. The audience sees the play through his eyes and hears his inner thoughts in soliloquies. Ophelia is simply his girlfriend, a passenger along for the tumultuous ride of Hamlet's experiment with the Self.

Bamber notes that the female characters in the tragedies are the victims of a misogyny she labels "sex nausea," and "of all Shakespeare's tragedies, *Hamlet* is the one in which the sex nausea is most pervasive."[12] As Hamlet's world and sense of Self deteriorates, he begins to direct his anger and blame toward the Other.[13] "Frailty, thy name is woman!" he declares as his newly widowed mother marries his uncle (1.2.146). Later he coldly tells Ophelia that he never loved her, describing her and all women thusly:

> God has given you one face, and you make yourselves another. You jig, you amble, and you lisp, and nick-name God's creatures, and make your wantonness your ignorance. Go, to, I'll no more on't; it hath made me mad. (3.1.143–147)

Pipher and her followers save Ophelia from woman-despising perspective, and depict her separate from Hamlet and his anger.

By removing Ophelia from the misogynistic world of *Hamlet* and declaring her and the girls she represents as the Self, these young women become people in their own right, no longer part of the definition of someone else.

Though Pipher's intention was not one of dramatic criticism, thanks to her work and those that followed, Ophelia has never been given so much press. After having read *Reviving Ophelia* (well, the juicy parts at least), my high school introduction to *Hamlet* was with a peaked concentration on the parts with Ophelia and the romantically tragic character I thought her to be. In fact, at the time I didn't even read Act V; Ophelia was dead and I'd already seen the movie. Because I was told that I was just like her, I identified with her more than with Hamlet, and for me, she became Juliet to Hamlet's Romeo. With Ophelia now in the spotlight, the question is what is the image of Ophelia that has taken center stage? If teenage girls are meant to identify with Ophelia, who, precisely is it with whom they are identifying?

Because Pipher's book marks the beginning of the linkage between Ophelia and contemporary teenage girls, her conception and translation of the character is a central source of pop culture's definition of Ophelia. Her book is not meant to provide dramatic analysis of Shakespeare's play. Rather, as a result of Pipher linking her theories about the place and construction of teenage girlhood in modern American society to Shakespeare's character, any theorizations about the original character are consequential to modern teens' understanding of the play. Pipher only addresses her choice of Shakespearean spokeswomen once in the book with a paragraph in the introduction:

> The story of Ophelia, from Shakespeare's *Hamlet*, shows the destructive forces that affect young women. As a girl, Ophelia is happy and free, but with adolescence she loses herself. When she falls in love with Hamlet, she lives only for his approval. She has no inner direction; rather she struggles to meet the demands of Hamlet and her father. Her value is determined utterly by their approval. Ophelia is torn apart by her efforts to please. When Hamlet spurns her because she is an obedient daughter, she goes mad with grief. Dressed in elegant clothes that weigh her down, she drowns in a stream filled with flowers.[14]

This reference to the Shakespearean original is actually one of only a handful in the entire book. Thus, with this brief reading of Ophelia, Pipher goes on to create a movement that defines the teenage girl. She maintains that the girls she encounters in her practice suffer a similar shift as they enter their teen years. She describes her subjects as girls who are suffering to find themselves amid the contradictions and uncertainty that accompany adolescence. They grow from independent and optimistic little girls into young women who are faced with mountainous expectations from family, friends, and society. They "stop thinking, 'Who am I? What do I want?' and start thinking, 'What must I do to please others?' "

While Shakespeare does not depict this shift from childhood to womanhood in Ophelia, it is undeniable that her identity is built upon her desire to please others, most notably her father and Hamlet, and her fate is dependent on the rift in the contradictions of these men's expectations of her. Inspired by Pipher's book, Sara Shandler would later dub this shared torture of being drowned by others expectations as the "Ophelia Syndrome."[15]

Pipher cites the work of other psychologists and anthropologists in noting that this is the period in life when a young woman denies her true self, the one that could play in the candor of childhood, and adopts a false self based on the demands of those around her. She describes these girls as "saplings in a hurricane" and outlines three factors that make young women so sapling-like.[16] One is the hormone factor: the sprouting of curves and zits, the anxiety over one's place in the world, and the pendulum of mood swings. These constant changes and the confusion and insecurity they bring make it even more difficult to weather the pressures heaved upon the young. Pipher's second factor is the burden of American culture, which begins in early adolescence with a bombardment of "girl-hurting 'isms,' such as sexism, capitalism, and lookism, which is the evaluation of a person solely on the basis of appearance." These cultural constructions create an ideal that is advertised as obtainable with the right body or pair of jeans but is ultimately impossible to achieve. Finally, the third factor in the teenage girl's susceptibility to the pressures of society is American culture's demand that teen girls distance themselves from their parents emotionally and turn to their peers for guidance and support.[17] At this age, girls push their parents away. They are private, moody, and sullen. Everything their parents do is embarrassing and detrimental to the false self they create for their peers. The result is a chasm in a once close relationship between parents and daughter, and the teenage girl is left to frantically tread water in a culture designed to drown who she truly is.

These three factors create the tide in which Pipher's Ophelia finds herself drowning, but does Shakespeare's Ophelia suffer from the same restrictive predicament? The first factor of the inevitable hormonal storm and identity crisis of the teen years is undeniable. All ensuing tragedy aside, Ophelia is in a period of life when she is unsure of her place: she is torn between a child that wants to honor her father and a woman who wants to be loyal to her lover. Nevertheless, it is important to note that Ophelia is in her middle to late teens, old enough to have been courted by Hamlet for a while, before he left to study at Wittenburg. This age range may seem insignificant, but in terms of adolescence, it means the difference between a perplexed mess of a 16-year-old girl in the thick of her teen angst and a recovering, well-adjusted woman of 19 who has pulled herself through with only a few scrapes and bruises remaining.

Pipher herself maintains that by the late teen years, the young American woman is stronger. She has survived the blitzkrieg and is healing though she may carry the scars of her injuries into adult-hood.[18] The case studies she relays in her book are mostly of girls in the early to middle teens, some as early as twelve. Her oldest subjects are 18, and there are only three of them. Likewise, the average age of the girls who voice their stories in *Ophelia Speaks* is 16. There are only a few stories from young women as old as 18 and none from 19 year olds. If Shakespeare's Ophelia is indeed in her later teens, it cannot be assumed that her problems are born from any hormonal upheaval. She is not the only household Shakespeare heroine to go mad; there are Lady Macbeth and Queen Margaret, among others. And she is not the only one to meet an untimely death despite her attempt to live up to the expectations of others; there is Desdemona. However, she is the only well known Shakespearean teenager to suffer in this manner, a fact that may be merely incidental.

It is in the romances that Shakespeare deals with the problems of teenage girls at more length, and it is in the romances that the only other teenage girl to go mad appears. Miranda, Imogen, Marina, and Perdita all suffer a variety of problems, both personal and social, shared by Ophelia, including rejection by former lovers (Imogen), living without a mother (all four), the presence of an overbearing father (Miranda, Imogen, and Perdita), and the threat of sexual assault (all four). The only other teenage girl in Shakespeare to go mad occurs in a play cowritten with John Fletcher, *The Two Noble Kinsmen*.

In this play, the teenage daughter of the jailer falls in love with Palamon, helping him escape from prison. Just as Hamlet uses Ophelia, performing his madness to her, knowing that Polonius and Claudius are watching, so, too, does Palamon use the jailer's daughter's love for him to benefit himself at cost to her. She goes mad when her love for him is not requited. The doctor suggests that she might be cured by being seduced by her former suitor. Such a character, despite her similarities to Ophelia would never serve as well in Pipher's schema.[19]

Along with the hormonal factor, the element of parental distance is common between Shakespeare's Ophelia and the Ophelias of today. Like Pipher's subjects, the Elizabethan Ophelia is freed from her parental bonds in the course of her teenage years. After all, her mother was never in the picture (a fact that is overlooked for the sake of convenience in the Ophelia metaphor), her older brother goes off to France, and her father dies.[20] Nevertheless, there is one marked difference between Ophelia and her present-day peers. Her estrangement from her parents is not voluntary, as Juliet's is. She shows no sign of pushing her father away; in fact she holds no secrets from him, showing him Hamlet's love letter to her upon request. She risks the love of her boyfriend to maintain the trust, respect, and closeness of her father. The loss of her father is physical, unnatural, and premature. This lack of foundation drives her mad. Upon learning of his death, she sings nonsensical songs of mourning and laments: "I cannot choose but weep, to think they should lay him i' the cold ground" (4.5.69–70). This simple statement is one of the last coherent things she utters. The shock and pain of this detachment of family, at the hands of her lover no less, is so unbearable for Ophelia that it is the impetus that drowns her. This situation is certainly a one that the average contemporary teenage girl, rife as she may be with the constant humiliation that is her mother picking her up from school in the wood-paneled station wagon, does not face.

The remaining factor that Pipher assigns to the plight of the contemporary Ophelia is the most problematic to the accuracy of the metaphor. The unbearable demands of American culture that are so responsible for the teenage loss of self are obviously not applicable to the Ophelia of Shakespeare's play. Like any character, Ophelia is influenced by her culture. Though the play is set in Denmark, she is clearly the product of Elizabethan England—the world of her author. Under the demands of Elizabethan society, she relinquishes her autonomy to her father and the man she assumes will someday be her husband. Nevertheless, the problems Pipher's Ophelia endures go beyond those that are tied to a patriarchal culture. The troubles of the contemporary Ophelia were not prominent 300 years ago because they are born from a capitalist, commercial, advanced technological society. They are deeply American problems. Pipher's Ophelias are the children of divorce, single mothers, or two working parents. These were rare familial situations for aristocrats in Shakespeare's England. In fact, divorce, in the modern sense, was unheard of in Elizabethan times. A generation before, the king had to separate himself, his country, and his people from the Catholic Church in order to secure a divorce from his wife. For those men and women without the temerity and where-withal to start new churches, divorce was simply not an option. Now, it is a custom all its own, spanning races and classes. It eats over half of the marriages in our society and extensive stepfamilies and single-parent homes abound. This contemporary American restructure of family disrupts these girls' foundation when they need it most and leaves them questioning everything they once thought was sound.

In these broken homes with absent parents live latch-key children, raised by the television that poisons them. They have been nurtured by the demands of late capitalism, which had just begun to rise when Shakespeare wrote his play. Pipher's subjects suffer in a society that advertises an image of perfection that leads them to eating disorders to be beautiful, premature sexuality to fit in, and substance abuse when they do not measure up. They are the survivors of a culture that has experienced a Feminist Revolution and produced a vague and often contradictive ideal of womanhood. On the one hand, they are told that they should be independent women; on the other, anyone over a size six is ridiculed for being "overweight" and Hillary Rodham Clinton is labeled "bitch" for speaking her mind.[21] All the while, the constant swarm of media—television, magazines, radio, MTV, movies, billboards—remind them from one second to the next how women should look and act: smokin' hot and submissive. While Elizabethan Ophelia had a perfect lady paradigm dictated to her by society as well, it was not as complex or layered. She was to obey men, marry, and produce heirs. There were no contradictions: either marry or "get thee to a nunnery" (3.1.120). Ophelia would never have been told that she deserved anything else or anything more.

Pipher maintains that the teenage girl is kept in submission to the American culture by the ever-present eye of her peers. In fact, much of the struggle that the contemporary Ophelia faces is due to peer pres-sure and its enforcement of an arbitrarily prescribed way of looking, dressing, and acting. The expectations of other teens inspire the eating disorders, drug addiction, alcoholism, and premature sexuality that are key symptoms of "Ophelia Syndrome." All of the Ophelia books discuss the dangers that accompany this need to fit in with the crowd and the toxic way teens treat those who break the mold or jeopardize their place it. In fact, the Ophelia Project, a group designed to save teenage girls from the clutches of society, first entered the public eye when it announced that its goal was to address and allay the aggressive ways in which teen girls treat each other. In the spring of 2002, stories about the program and its stand against "Relational Aggression" ran in the *New York Times, Chicago Tribune*, and on *Dateline NBC*.

Project Ophelia defines Relational Aggression as "behaviors that harm others by damaging (or threatening to damage) or manipulating one's relationships with his/her peers, or by injuring one's feelings of social acceptance."[22] This form of aggression is more prevalent in girls than the physical violence practiced by males and is difficult to see due to its mental rather than physical manifestations. Contemporary Ophelias love games such as spreading hurtful rumors and giving others the silent treatment. They berate girls who do not fit the mold that they themselves find impossible to achieve. The irony is that Shakespeare's Ophelia is wholeheartedly passive; there doesn't seem to be an aggressive or bitchy bone in her waterlogged body.

Peer involvement in a young woman's life is not all cat fights and back stabbing. A teenage girl's friends are her new family. Pipher notes that at a time when "girls pull away from parents, peers are everything"; they are who they turn to for support and validation.[23] Without her friends, a girl has no way of knowing that what she is experiencing is okay, is normal. Sara Shandler agrees, maintaining that an adult editor could not have solicited the honesty that she as a 17 year old girl could. In her introduction she notes, "There is a capacity of openness among adolescents; adults are rarely trusted with our emotional reality."[24] This bittersweet bond between teenage girls is so important that Shandler dedicates one of the four sections of her book to it, aptly titling it "The Best and Worst of Friends."[25]

This element of peer influence belongs only to the contemporary Ophelia. Shakespeare's Ophelia is alone in her adolescent anguish. There is never any talk of her having female friends or classmates. She does not attend schools where fellow girls judge her, manipulate her, or measure themselves against her. At the same time, she does not have girlfriends who share her experiences and provide support. Unlike Shakespeare's other heroines, Ophelia has no confidante: no Nurse, no Emilia, no Celia, and no Beatrice. She has no female companionship, not even a mother. In fact, Ophelia has no social circle outside of her small nuclear family. She defines herself entirely by her father, brother, and lover. In contrast, the contemporary Ophelia would most certainly include the opinion of her peers in the definition of herself, probably as the central factor.

The magnitude of what others think is a staple of America's highly commercial culture. Maintaining an image of perfection is responsible for most of the modern Ophelia's struggle. During a time in life when she is in complete shock and disarray on the inside, the teenage girl must look like an Abercrombie and Fitch model on the outside. This of course is difficult when one's body is sprouting breasts, curves, and zits and one's only solace can be food or booze. Thus enters the mandatory eating disorders chapter in the contemporary-Ophelia book. Anorexia and bulimia in the land of plenty is a troubling juxta-position, one that was not at all prevalent (or, perhaps, even present) in Elizabethan times. Girth was a sign of wealth, not ugliness and lazi-ness. Of course, Shakespeare's Ophelia was not under the influence of the body-image poison found in teen magazines, commercials, and the ever-thinning cast of *Friends*. Besides, the obsession of looking good in a pair of low-rise jeans tends to fall by the wayside when your boyfriend goes mad and kills your dad (as the introduction observed, nobody outcrazies Ophelia!). Nonetheless, Ophelia did have an ideal to live up to, as does any woman in a patriarchal culture. This need to be the proper, obedient, aristocratic woman does not go unnoticed by Contemporary Ophelia-ites. They take a single passage detailing Ophelia death and run with it. In the play, Gertrude reports the image as one where the mad Ophelia found herself in the waters, singing:

> [S]natches of old lauds;
> as one incapable of her own distress . . .
> But long it could not be
> Till that her garments, heavy with their drink,
> Pull'd the poor wretch from her melodious lay
> To a muddy death.
> (4.7.177–178, 180–183)

This image remains the dominant one in the modern mind's eye. In her description of Ophelia's relevance to today's teenage girl, Pipher notes, "Dressed in elegant clothes that weigh her down, she drowns in a stream filled with flowers."[26] In following, Sara Shandler describes her Elizabethan peer in these terms: "Trying to be good and righteous, she loses her father's love, her lover's respect, and her own dignity. Ophelia is drowned by the weight of her clothes."[27] These women do not portray Ophelia as having committed suicide or drowned in her madness; rather, it is her dress that pulls her down into her death. She could have been saved, had she been wearing boxers and a tee shirt (or the Elizabethan equivalent). They imply that it was her need to maintain appearances that killed her. While recent events certainly made it difficult to live up to the Elizabethan ideal of womanhood, wasn't it the loss of her father at the hands of a man she once thought loved her as she did him that sent her spiraling into madness? And wasn't it said madness that put her in the river, intentionally or not, in the first place? Besides, Gertrude describes Ophelia's clothes simply as "garments." This does not necessarily mean they are elegant, expensive, or beautiful. Then again, Gertrude's blaming of Ophelia's death on the clothes she was wearing rather than the turmoil that was sparked by Hamlet's reaction to her marriage to Claudius is its own method of maintaining appearances.

The obsession with appearance is a theme that is prominent in the most recent film adaptation of *Hamlet*. The Michael Almereyda's film, released as late as 2000, relays the play's plot and themes, but removes it entirely from its Elizabethan context. Julia Stiles's Ophelia is the Ophelia of Pipher's book speaking an edited for length and content rendering of Shakespeare's words. Living in Manhattan, she dresses in punk chic, is an aspiring photographer, and dates the equally hip and bohemian artist Hamlet. Her face looks young because it actually belongs to a teenager, a rare occurrence in Hollywood. She could just have easily been a fellow classmate, living with the same confines and expectations. A product of the 1990s American culture, she is an upper-middle-class, average American girl searching for her place in a world obsessed with images.

In this adaptation, the contemporary power of image is woven throughout the once-familiar narrative. It begins with Claudius giving a media-slathered press conference and ends with a nightly newscaster relaying the events that had unfolded. All through the film, Hamlet carries a handheld camera and we see the images he records, some of which are sexy recordings of Stiles' Ophelia. This version is so imbued with the importance of images, that the famous "To be" speech is spoken in the Hollywood distribution machine of a Blockbuster Video, and Ophelia's famous crazy scene is marked by her tossing pictures of the flowers she rants about rather than the flowers themselves. In fact, in this mad scene, Stiles wears a designer form-fitting black coat with a daring feather collar—the outrageousness of which is most likely meant to reinforce her lunacy. Her hair is in a sophisticated up-do of several individual braids intricately wrapped together. This is the most put-together she has looked in the course of the film. Ironic, but as a teenager, I would never have felt like fixing my hair when I have a cold, let alone when I am driven mad by the misery of my boyfriend killing my father. In a commercial world where appearances are equated with happiness, the mad Ophelia gives up her shabby chic that has defined her for another crafted image, which takes even longer to create, all to "prove" that she is mad.

It is important to highlight the power of this and other films when it comes to the first-time reader's understanding of Shakespeare. Though Cliffs Notes, Spark Notes, study guides, online summaries, and films like Almereyda's are designed as an accompaniment to the text, in the high schools and colleges of the United States they are often substitutes for it. As a high school student as recently as the mid-1990s, I can attest that even in AP English classes, exams on Shakespeare's plays are mostly concerned with plot points and the most obvious themes; both of which can be found in any of the several summaries available and often free of charge on cable or DVD, at the school library, in a loitering-friendly Barnes and Noble, or on the Internet. Assumed to be antiquated to the point of incoherence, the text itself is traded for an Americanized translation.[28] It is much faster and easier to skim a Cliffs Note's summary than swallow the metaphorical images and iambic pentameter of Shakespeare's words. So the present-day high school student gets her or his Shakespeare primarily from places other than the man himself. Some, like me, create their perceptions of Ophelia from books about teenage girls, while others rely on the obligatory filmed adaptation, presented on video over the course of several class periods that accompanies every play read in class. In a culture so packed with technology that cable television and the Internet are more accessible than a stage production or physical copy of Shakespeare's work, the ease factor of a movie or a hip-talking summary are bound to dominate a young student's studies of the bard. The rudimentary understanding of the work that is thus created is even more susceptible to the hype that Ophelia is just like the modern day teenage girl.

Furthermore, a Shakespeare-novice's reading of *Hamlet* cannot help but be influenced by the coolness factor of Ophelia that resulted from Pipher's work. There is no proof that the hard-rock divas of *Ophelia Rising* were so inspired by Pipher's book that they adopted her metaphor for the title of their band. Nonetheless, Pipher's best-selling book set Ophelia free into the pop-culture vernacular, and ever since there seems to have been something Ophelia in the air. The ladies of Ophelia Rising are not the only female musicians with Ophelia on their mind. The very Goth band Rasputina wrote a song about the drowned waif and singer/songwriter Natalie Merchant titled an entire album Ophelia. *Swamp Ophelia* is the title of a popular Indigo Girls album. As observed in chapter 2, Ophelia is arguably the most popular pop music reference after Romeo and Juliet.

Of course, this artistic glamour and attention is nothing new for the Shakespearean character. Ophelia has long been the subject of artists' works. She found her heyday in the late nineteenth century with famous paintings from Eugene Delacroix, John Waterhouse, and John Everett Millais. On an interdisciplinary Web site discussing art's link to Ophelia, Melissa Ide and Leslie Merriman note that at the time, psychiatrists were studying hysteria, a mental incapacity thought to be unique to women. Ophelia and her madness became representative of hysterical women everywhere.[29] In fact, "when photography came into vogue, young women often posed as Ophelia in photographic portraits."[30] The most popular denotation of Ophelia was flowers in the hair. Even then, there was something celebratory, romantic, and aesthetically beautiful about being linked to Ophelia. It was just as cool as it is today. Gregory Crewdson's 2001 photograph, *Untitled: Ophelia*,[31] echoes those of the late nineteenth century that took the plight of Shakespeare's heroine as their subject. Crewdson, known for the spectacle of his shots, depicts a beautiful and pale Ophelia floating dead in a flooded suburban living room. While Ophelia photographer's highlighted the madness of Ophelia, in this photograph, Crewdson highlights the suffocation she endures at the hands of her culture, specifically middle-class suburbia. It is a poignant and melancholy photo of Pipher's Ophelia. It seems that even today, Ophelia's artists' follow the lead and trends posed by psychiatry.

Like her eighteenth-century colleagues, Mary Piper has used Shakespeare's Ophelia as a metaphor for the psychological state of women. She is not the first, and most likely not the last, academic to hold Ophelia as the epitome of what it means to be a woman in Western society. She has simply followed the lead of those in her profession, alluding to Western myths to better understand a psychological human truth. The most famous example, of course, is that of Sigmund Freud's Oedipal Complex. In previous centuries, Ophelia was synonymous with crazy, fostering a very shallow understanding of the character. In Pipher's allusion, it is not the character's madness that has become her defining feature; it is her age. The tragedy experienced by Pipher's Ophelia is one that is inherent in modern adolescence. She is happy and willful as a little girl and corrupted by the demands of becoming a woman.[32] However, there is no mention in Shakespeare's text that the real Ophelia was happy as a little girl and that the onset of her misery is due to the onset of adolescence. In fact, it is assumed that all were happy in the state of Denmark before the King's murder and Claudius's seizure of the throne, even Ophelia. She was loved by and in love with Hamlet. She had a very close relationship with her father and showed no signs of purposely distancing herself from him like Pipher's subjects. Her future was a bright one; perhaps it held the title of Queen of Denmark. Everything that happens to Ophelia is core-shakingly traumatic. Her happy life is corrupted by a succession of actions and events that send her spiraling into madness in a matter of days. Her misery is particular to her circumstances, not her age or station in life.

Likewise, it is not her culture that has driven her to suffer. Pipher declares that unlike previous books on the subject of female adolescent angst, *Reviving Ophelia* is about how pressure these girls face to be someone that they are not "comes not from parents but from the culture."[33] It is the American culture that bombards young women with high expectations and the parents are left powerless in the attack. On the contrary, the burden of Shakespeare's Ophelia is thrown on her by her father and brother—her immediate family. She caves to the demands of her father, so much so that upon her father's request she turns on her lover and suffers the resulting scorn. She shares his personal love letter and is party to setting him up to reveal his madness. She heeds her father and brother's advice to stay away from Hamlet. When she loses the guidance of her father as well as the love and trust of Hamlet, she loses her senses and will to live. Other than the patriarch it enforces, the culture has little hand in Ophelia's downfall.

Nineteenth-century psychologists may have had more reason to link Shakespeare's Ophelia to their mad women than Pipher to the present-day teen. Their culture had not yet seen a feminist revolution that deconstructed and exposed a patriarchy that spanned Western civilization. Their women still wore the long gowns and constraining corsets that Elizabethan women wore. With constricted lungs and layers of heavy skirts, they actually could "drown by the weight of their clothes."[34] The mothers of today's Ophelia burned their bras so that their daughters could live life with fewer restrictions. This is a very different young woman from the entirely subverted Ophelia of the past. Though she still faces the pressures of a "girl-poisoning culture,"[35] she is afforded the opportunities of education and freedom of expression.

Her culture's expectations of her go beyond marriage and family and allow for career. Hers is the generation that must reconcile postfeminism prospects with the remnants of a patriarchy that still expects girls to look pretty and be sexy. This is a paradox that an Elizabethan or even a nineteenth-century Ophelia never had to marshal the guts to tackle.

To be fair, this dichotomy between Elizabethan and Contemporary societies has not gone unnoticed by the Pipher club. In the 1998 theatrical experiment, *Are We Reviving Ophelia*, teacher Greg West lead his Masconomet Regional High School students in the writing and performance of a piece founded on the suggestions of Pipher's book. Starting in 1997, he recruited students from freshmen to seniors to read *Reviving Ophelia*, embark on an open discussion, and put their own spin on the topic in a series of organic vignettes focused on the themes of body image, over sexualization, and sexual violence. The play begins with a teacher discussing Shakespeare's *Hamlet* with her English class. "In William Shakespeare's classic tragedy Hamlet, Ophelia is a young girl driven to suicide. Those of you who read last night should have known that. (*She aims that statement to the Comedian. The class giggles, the Comedian shrugs.*) Ophelia is the classic teenage girl."[36] The comedian whom the teacher accuses of slacking serves as the voice of opposition to the cross-era comparison between Elizabethan Ophelia and his teenage classmates. As the teacher relays how Ophelia serves as a model of the adolescent girl, the comedian mocks the character's story and the idea that it could fit into contemporary culture.

> *Teacher:* She falls in love with someone and goes crazy, longing for him. When her father orders her to not see the love of her life, she becomes enraged.[37]
> *Comedian:* "Today on Rikki Lake . . ."
> *Teacher:* She convinces herself that she is so in love with Hamlet that she can't stand to be without him. This unsatisfied infatuation drives her to insanity.
> *Comedian:* That and her crack habit.
> *Teacher:* Does anyone know what happens next in the story?
> *Comedian:* Does she binge on a five pound bag of M&Ms and then go shoe shopping?[38]

Though the comedian's observations are intended to appear superficial and sophomoric—he is after all the most unreliable, uneducated source—there is some significance in the most jarring disparities between Ophelia's story and the reality of a contemporary teenage girl. Of course, the teacher is quick to censure him. As the erudite voice of Pipher, she cuts down any claims that Ophelia is not quite the American teenager by likening them to the babble of an ignorant teenage boy who probably smoked a bowl in the parking lot before class.

> *Teacher:*   We're so funny today! Perhaps you can explain to the class why Ophelia is a classic teenage girl. (*Comedian makes a fart sound. Males all laugh, females are insulted.*) You just earned yourself three detentions. The reason Ophelia is the classic representation of today's teenage girl is because she puts herself aside to please others. She cannot please her father or her love and she fails to see how perilous it is to lose her self [*sic*]. This is what destroys her.[39]

Here I concede that Pipher and her followers make an accurate comparison. Ophelia and her modern-day sisters both buckle under the pressures of pleasing others and compromise their own happiness in a struggle to satisfy contradicting expectations from those around them. Yet, just like the book that inspired it, this play fails to acknowledge that the "others" that Shakespeare's Ophelia sacrifices herself to please are not society in general. They are family and a lover, not images on television, boys in high school hallways, or girls hanging out in malls. This difference is easy to overlook when the name "Ophelia" becomes a trade mark detached from its origin and creator.

Like in most of the Pipher-related books, this is the last time that Ophelia is mentioned in this play. Instead a series of adolescent monologues ensue. Young women talk about the influence of Barbie, the unwanted catcalls of men, the humiliation of sexual encounters over the Internet, and the degradation of pornography. These aren't really Elizabethan predicaments, but nonetheless, the students who created these monologues associate them with the name Ophelia. Because this play is written and performed by the teenage girls at the center of this discussion, it is evidence that the Ophelia that has become vernacular for adolescent woman is the Ophelia of Pipher's book, not the Ophelia of Shakespeare's play. And in turn, the Ophelia that these young women see in their understanding of *Hamlet* is an Ophelia saturated in the context of their own contemporary lives. She is subject to a culture that sends her into a state of confusion and unrest—a teenage angst that manifests itself in sex, drugs, and diet pills. Perhaps, this is what Ophelia could have been had she had the chance to survive, had she had the chance to become the subject of the play. Maybe we would have learned that Ophelia had been raped, feared pregnancy, was addicted to the opium, or thought she was ugly compared to the beauty of the women in Renaissance paintings.

However, the result of this "what-if?" Ophelia is the subversion of the Elizabethan Ophelia, one who is pre-American Revolution let alone pre-Feminist Revolution. This noble-class, European white girl from 400 years ago did not face half the "isms" that teenage girls face today. Teaching teenage girls that they are one in the same with her distorts their understanding of the literary Ophelia. While it certainly speaks of the procrustean nature of Shakespeare, it makes Ophelia's age the most important aspect of her character. In point of fact, Ophelia's young age was most likely by default, really the only choice that would make the character believable. In Shakespeare's time, teens were of marrying age. To seriously be courted by Hamlet while having her virginity constantly questioned and her beauty at its peak, Ophelia had to be of marrying age. With a shorter life expectancy, and the human social lifecycle ahead several years compared to today's standards, Ophelia was more than a teenager; she was a woman. To truly examine her in the spirit of Sue-Ellen Case's New Poetics, perhaps we have to drop this notion that Ophelia is just another teenage girl in need of saving from her friends, her culture, and herself. Pipher's Ophelia is not Shakespeare's, and it is inaccurate, dangerous, and severely limiting to define contemporary teenage girls as Ophelias. Perhaps the romances need to be taught in high school: Imogen, Perdita, Miranda, and Marina never had to be revived.

Notes

1. www.opheliarising.net
2. Mary Pipher, *Reviving Ophelia* (New York: Putnam, 1994).
3. Sara Shandler, *Ophelia Speaks* (New York: Harper Collins, 1999).
4. Nina Shandler, *Ophelia's Mom* (New York: Crown, 2001).
5. Cheryl Dellasega, *Surviving Ophelia: Mothers Share Their Wisdom in Navigating the Tumultuous Teenage Years* (Cambridge, MA: Random House, 2001); Greg West et al., *Are We Reviving Ophelia?* (Boston: Baker's Plays, 1998).
6. This name is copyrighted. I find it noteworthy that a Shakespearean name has been copyrighted. In an economically driven youth culture, Ophelia is no longer a timeless character of Western drama, but a commercially viable entity. See the group's Web site at <http://www.projectophelia.org>
7. See chapter 2 for more about this film and the other Shakespearean films of Julia Stiles.
8. Compare *Romeo and Juliet* with Shakespeare's Roman plays. The male characters kill themselves by falling on their swords, while the women, such as Cleopatra,

poison themselves. In this case, however, the man poisons himself and the woman, it can be argued, falls on her sword.

9. Aside from the romance and the (hot) male actors who often play Romeo in film versions, the popularity of Juliet among teenage girls might also be ascribed, at least in part, to this positive reading of her character. Juliet is a strong teenage girl who lives in a society that seeks to bend her to its conventions. She, however, defies both convention and her parents, unlike Ophelia.

10. Sue-Ellen Case, *Feminism in Theatre* (New York: Macmillan, 1988), pp. 114–115.

11. Linda Bamber, *Comic Women, Tragic Men: A Study of Gender and Genre in Shakespeare* (Stanford: Stanford University Press, 1982), pp. 4–6.

12. Ibid., pp. 71.

13. Ibid., pp. 72.

14. Pipher, *Reviving Ophelia*, p. 20.

15. Sara Shandler, *Ophelia Speaks*, p. xii.

16. Pipher, *Reviving Ophelia*, p. 22.

17. Ibid., pp. 22–23.

18. Ibid., pp. 24–25.

19. In his introduction to *The Two Noble Kinsmen* in *The Riverside Shakespeare*, Hallett Smith observes that "[r]eminiscences of Ophelia are numerous and striking," but he also ascribes the development of the character to Fletcher, rather than Shakespeare (p. 1640). The general lack of public awareness of the play, combined with Fletcher's coauthorship, indicates that the character is no real threat to the centrality of Ophelia. Yet the Jailer's daughter, it might be argued, is even more put upon than Ophelia, as she does not even have a name. She is indicated in the text solely as "Daughter," her role in relation to her father, who is named by his job: jailer. Besides, *Reviving the Jailer's Daughter* just does not have quite the same ring or sales potential, and sounds more like bad melodrama or a cheap Western.

20. Ironically, there are two entire books dedicated to voicing the concerns of the modern-day Ophelia's mother: Nina Shandler's *Ophelia's Mom* and Cheryl Dellasega's *Surviving Ophelia*, subtitled *Mothers Share Their Wisdom in Navigating the Tumultuous Teenage Years*. Nina is Sara Shandler's (*Ophelia Speaks*) mother. In addition, almost all of the Ophelia books, including Pipher's, devote chapters to the relationships between teenage girls and their mothers. The contemporary mother struggling with a daughter who is pushing her away is an entity that has no corresponding symbol in the Shakespearean Ophelia metaphor, as Ophelia has no mother figure. Gertrude arguably holds this position, but there is no sign that she had a hand in raising Ophelia. Rare in Shakespeare is the mother of a teenage girl: Hero and Miranda's mothers are dead, Imogen's mother is dead and she has only a wicked stepmother (literally), Perdita and Marina are separated from their mothers at birth and are raised by others, reunited with their mother only at the conclusion of their respective plays. When the mother of a teenage girl is present, such as Queen Elizabeth in *Richard III*, then the girl herself, in this case Elizabeth of York, is absent: mentioned by other characters, but not present herself. You cannot get more marginal than not there at all.

21. Pipher, *Reviving Ophelia*, p. 39.
22. www.projectophelia.org
23. Pipher, *Reviving Ophelia*, p. 67.
24. Sara Shandler, *Ophelia Speaks*, p. xvi.
25. Ibid., p. 135.
26. Pipher, *Reviving Ophelia*, p. 20.
27. Sara Shandler, *Ophelia Speaks*, p. xii.
28. See the introduction to this volume for an extended analysis of the mediation of Shakespeare through these other forms.
29. Melissa Ide and Leslie Merriman, *Interdisciplinary Shakespeare* <www.uaf. edu/english/faculty/reilly/NCHCproject/psychology.htm>
30. Georgiana Ziegler, *Shakespeare's Unruly Women* (Washington, DC: Folger Shakespeare Library, 1997), p. 71.
31. This photograph graces the cover of Crewdson's 2002 book of photography. See Gregory Crewdson and Rick Moody, *Twilight: Photographs by Gregory Crewdson* (New York: Harry N. Abrams, 2002).
32. Pipher, *Reviving Ophelia*, p. 18.
33. Ibid., p. 22.
34. Sara Shandler, *Ophelia Speaks*, p. xii.
35. Pipher, *Reviving Ophelia*, p. 12.
36. West, et al., *Are We Reviving Ophelia?*, p. 9.
37. Here the teacher's explanation reduces Ophelia's story to one of lust and rebellion when in fact it is more complex than this. Of course, to a high school audience—as with most American audiences—sex sells. What really leads Ophelia to madness is the madness around her—the hatred and disgust borne of the dubious sanity of her lover and the murder of her father at her beloved's hands.
38. West, et al., *Are We Reviving Ophelia?*, p. 9.
39. West, et al., pp. 9–10.

This Bard's for You(th), or "Get over Yourself, Ophelia!"

A Conclusion that Leaves Things Open for a Sequel

If Jan Kott is right and Shakespeare is our "contemporary," why can't we speak to him in our own tone of voice, in our own rhythms, about our own concerns? Must we forever be receiving Shakespeare? Why can't Shakespeare receive us? [Emphasis in original.]

—*Charles Marowitz*, Prospero's Staff[1]

It will impress them more, when such a fuckup like me turns good.

—*Gus van Sant*, My Own Private Idaho,
A "translation" of Henry IV, Part 1, 1.2.208–215

Alvin Kernan in *The Death of Literature* argues that universities are now forced to consider both classic literature, as represented by the canon of so-called dead white males, and "the literature of the present," defined by both its contemporariness and its multicultural nature, despite the fact that the more recent titles have not proven their endurance.[2] Youth culture-mediated Shakespeare seeks to move Shakespeare from Kernan's former category into his latter.

Kernan was part of the vanguard of those concerned about the death of Shakespeare on college campuses and in institutions of higher learning. Allan Bloom, Katha Pollitt, Maureen Dowd, and many others decried the loss of Shakespeare in American education.[3] Yet others have argued that this outcry was inaccurate at best and dishonest at worst. John Wilson, in "Come Not to Bury Shakespeare," observes that the "Shakespeare Scare" as he terms it has been dominated by anecdote and paranoia rather than facts and intellectual debate. Ninety-seven percent of universities offer at least one course solely devoted to Shakespeare and two thirds of the schools Wilson sampled require English majors to take at least one course on the bard. In the MLA's online bibliography, he notes, Shakespeare has 36 times as many entries as Toni Morrison. Yet others like cultural conservative Jonathan Yardley argue that Shakespeare is increasingly "marginalized," and that colleges are "academic whorehouses," and that even the above ratio of Toni Morrison to Shakespeare is "sheer vulgarity."[4] Cultural conservatives argue that unless Shakespeare is studied in the original textual form to the exclusion of an expanded canon, then he is vanishing from the canon and the campus. "Shakespeare's good name," Wilson concludes, must be rescued from those who use it to malign higher education and American youth. He believes, and we agree, that Shakespeare is alive and well in the classroom and in the minds of students.[5] Often, he and his work are present in other forms as well.

In this volume, we have considered Shakespeare's presence in toys, teen cinema, popular music, graphic novels, and pop psychology. This is to have but scratched the surface of youth mediation of Shakespeare that translates and reduces and references the man and his work, but in doing so keeps both present in our culture. Like so much else of youth culture, Shakespeare's presence in it remains paradoxical.

The final aspect of youth culture, not yet covered in this book and yet as true in Shakespeare's day as it is now, is that success for an artistic commodity breeds a sequel. Not only does the sequel answer the question, "what happens next?" it represents an opportunity to reuse a successful formula in the hopes of securing another success. Whether *Henry VI, Part III* or *Friday the 13th, Part 10: Jason X*, sequels provide an easy formula and a guaranteed return. The horror genre, more than any other, seems to lend itself to sequels, especially as the formula in teen horror is remarkably simple: gather a group of teens together and kill most of them in interesting ways. *Friday the 13th*, *Nightmare on Elm Street*, *Halloween*, *Jaws*, and other, lesser series: *Children of the Corn*, *The Substitute*, and *Puppet Master* have all had at least three sequels, some of which are only tangentially related to the original film. Following the theory of Marvin Carlson, however, we must note that the sequel is "haunted": the "ghost" of the original film "haunts" the newer version. The actors in these films are also "ghosted" by their earlier performances in the same role, or, in some cases, by the memory of another in the role.[6]

Now Shakespeare has his version of direct-to-video sequels via Youth culture: the "Bard's Blood Series": *Hamlet II: Ophelia's*

Revenge and *A Midsummer Night's Scream*, both by David Bergantino, aimed at a youth market, with the promise of more books to come. These books are haunted, both in terms of their narratives of teen horror, and in Carlson's sense of reading them while being haunted by the memory of the Shakespearean original and other mediations of it.

Hamlet II begins with the statement that, "Something was rotten in the state of Ohio."[7] Cameron Dean, Jr., quarterback of the football team at Globe University in Stratford, Ohio, has lost his father, Cameron, Sr. Though he wins the football game against the Fortinbras College Generals that opens the novel, his teammates Marc and Bernie (Marcellus and Bernardo) tell him they have seen the ghost of his father, the recently deceased former president of Globe University in the end zone. Cameron Sr.'s ghost then appears to his son, explaining that he was killed by his sister Claudia, a noted herpetologist who used the poison of a Mexican Beaded Lizard in the mouth of a pet turtle to kill her brother, when it bit him. Claudia has now become the president of Globe University and the lesbian lover of Geri, Cameron's mother.

Meanwhile, Cameron is dating Sofia, daughter of Dr. Paul Paulson, a guidance counselor at the university, who ignores his mildly retarded son Larry. Other supporting characters include the closeted but homoerotic freshman football players Rosenberg and Gyllenhal,[8] and Cam's (Cameron's) best friend Harry (Horatio). Unexpectedly, Cam inherits Ellsinore Castle in Denmark and a fortune. He flies his family and the football team there. Their presence awakens Ophelia, long dead, but now literally revived. She possesses Marc's girlfriend, Carla, and kills him through her.

As in Jennifer Hulbert's chapter on modern Ophelias, this Ophelia is not Shakespeares, but much closer to Lisa Simpson's Ophelia discussed in the introduction. She is an active avenger, able to possess other teenage girls and commit acts of violence through them. Ophelia has not only been revived, she is now out to revenge herself with a will that Hamlet never had. In making Ophelia a revenging, murdering ghost, however, Bergantino has strayed from Renaissance tradition and into the teen horror film genre. In English Renaissance plays, ghosts are either messengers, spectators (such as Don Andrea in *The Spanish Tragedy*), or accusing revenants (such as Banquo or Old Hamlet). Never are they actual agents of revenge. Never do they possess, never do they kill. This Ophelia is a riot grrrl and no oppressed teen who needs to be revived, as per Mary Pipher.

The reader is privy to this ghostly Ophelia's thoughts, and she is now thoroughly modernized.

> No, things would be different, and Hamlet would bear witness to her transformation. When they were together again, there would be no more of this 'Get thee to a nunnery' crap. He was going to find out who wore the leggings in the family.[9]

What is unique about this thought is that it places the narrative of *Hamlet* in the real world's Denmark and treats the play as history, not tragedy or construct. Shakespeare is also present in this world, although his plays are now treated as being all histories. According to one of Cameron's friends, "Some guy named Shakespeare chronicled the history of the castle."[10] The other unique aspect is Ophelia's postmodern, feminist attitude toward her former betrothed, which is certainly not found in the original. This Ophelia does not need to be revived. She has revived herself and is now seeking revenge.

Ophelia possesses Sofia and attacks first Cameron, then her father. She pushes Dr. Paulson out a window, and then doesn't remember it. Cameron and Harry hide the body, as Hamlet did to Polonius, so she won't learn the truth. Ophelia discovers she likes killing, and decides to reveal herself at Cameron's birthday party that night. "Tonight we're gonna party like its 1349," she decides, echoing the promotional line for the Troubadour's version of *Hamlet* from chapter 3.[11] Not only is this misquotation a reference to the pop song by Prince, it further places the events of Shakespeare's play into specific times and places within the real world of the novel and "ghosts" the Ophelia of this novel with the character from the play, the other "Ophelias" of filmed and stage versions, the "Ophelia" of pop psychology, and the rock musician Prince.

Continuing the postmodern teen deconstruction of the original play, paralleling its narrative even as the characters are aware of it, Cameron hires a local speed metal band called "The Playaz" to perform at his party, but, like his Shakespearean forbear, he asks them to play a song he was written, designed to reveal Claudia's guilt.

> I had a daddy
> My mommy was his wife
> He also had a sister
> Who took his life.
> Daddy's dead
> I got two mommies

Daddy's dead
I got two mommies

She's in my daddy's house
She's in my daddy's clothes
She's even in my mommy
Like the two of them are hos.

No one knows she killed him
No one knows but me
I know 'cuz daddy told me
His ghost appeared to me.[12]

"The Murther of Gonzago" it ain't, but it does the job for Cameron—Claudia blanches and flees the party, just as Claudius did.

Two boys are then attacked by a girl possessed by Ophelia. When Harry and Cameron stumble upon what they believe are their corpses, Cameron solemnly intones, "Rosenberg and Gyllenhal are dead," again "ghosting" not only *Hamlet*, but the Tom Stoppard play for the knowing reader[13] Claudia arranges for Larry, who has learned that his father is dead, to fight Cameron and kill him in front of Geri and Sofia. Sofia becomes possessed by Ophilia again, while Geri accidentally kills Larry with the shears she is using to free herself. Claudia snaps Geri's neck, killing her. Cameron then kills Claudia while Sofia fights the ghost of Ophelia within her.

Sofia defeats Ophelia by telling her to "move on."

In short, Ophelia my love, get over him. You've had more time than most to get over this guy. And while you're at it, get over yourself! . . . I'm sorry about the way things went with Hamlet. If I'd been around as your friend, you could have cried on my shoulder, and then we would have gone to a club, had a few beers, danced, found a few hot guys and gotten ya laid. Believe me, a much better situation than ending up at the bottom of a swamp.[14]

This statement, which in many ways epitomizes the book, is a clear embodiment of Charles Marowitz's idea expressed in the epigram of this conclusion that we must make Shakespeare receive us, rather than us always receiving him. The play and, in this case, Ophelia's character are evaluated by a young woman who rejects them and what they stand for. Ophelia's problems are not the problems of today's youth. Today's youth have problems of which Ophelia never would have dreamed. Conversely, they have solutions to Ophelia's problems that would never have been available to her. If the original play deals with characters that constantly "lose the name of action," the novel presents youths who are about nothing but action. Get over yourself, indeed.

The novel is also haunted by the concern we discussed in the introduction: the anxiety of relevance. By telling Ophelia to "get over herself," Sofia also gives voice to the typical youth response to Shakespeare: transcend your time and context and situation and make yourself relevant to now or don't waste our time. This response to Ophelia is a response to those who hold up Shakespeare as the pinnacle of culture and, in Lisa Simpson's words, the author of "the greatest thing ever written." Meet us on our terms, because your terms neither interest us nor have anything to do with our lives in the present moment. It is a limited point of view, but it is an accurate reflection of many youth toward unmediated Shakespeare.

The book ends with everyone dead except for Rosenberg and Gyllenhal and Harry. Globe University inherits the castle and Ophelia "moves on." In the inside of the back cover, however, is written "Read how the horrors at Ellsinore Castle began: Hamlet by William Shakespeare."[15] If you enjoyed the sequel, go back and see the original, much like in the Classics Illustrated comics. In doing so, the author has equated his own work with Shakespeare's while simultaneously acknowledging the existence of an original off of which this sequel (or, in the case of Classics Illustrated, this adaptation), has been built. Bergantino has given us a postfeminist Hamlet for a generation raised on horror films, sequels, and grrrl power. Ophelia is now the active revenger, while the Hamlet figure remains paralyzed. The story now serves as backdrop for a slasher flick. The sequel is the same story, just for a new generation.

Bergantino has written a second book in the "Bard's Blood" series, A Midsummer Night's Scream, also set at Globe University in Ohio, during a summer session psychology course, in which students are set up (some against their will) with a "spouse" and a five pound bag of flour "child" as an experiment in maintaining a household. When a carnival arrives, which is actually a front for Shakespeare's fairies, chaos is come again. As with the earlier volume, the book concludes with an encouragement to read the Elizabethan original: "Learn how this sinister magic began: A Midsummer Night's Dream by William Shakespeare."[16]

Despite the concerns of cultural purists, these novels indicate that Shakespeare is alive and well and in more places than ever. As this book has proven, he is a screenwriter, a rock star, a rapper, a graphic novel writer, and a teen psychologist. He is in our schools, our movie theatres, our video stores, our televisions, our shops, our libraries, and our books. Shakespeare is encountered everywhere in a young person's life.

The plays are in the theatres and bring each generation in, sometimes of their own free will. Both *"Naked" Hamlet* and *The Bomb-itty of Errors* were decried by the reviewers at the *New York Times* in the 1960s and the 1990s, respectively, yet both were among the most popular plays of their seasons, consistently selling out and inspiring the kind of devotion ordinarily only seen in audiences of large musicals.

The plays inspire new texts that function best when one knows and recognizes the original text. These texts take a variety of forms: graphic novels and comic books, which translate the plays into a new medium also based on image and word, David Bergantino's teen novels translate the plays into yet another media, and, of course the "translations" such as the *Simply Shakespeare* and *No Fear* Shakespeare series can be seen as an attempt to engage young readers with the works of Shakespeare. And, despite warning calls that he is in danger of vanishing from the cultural landscape, Shakespeare is still read in the vast majorities of high school and college English classrooms.

As Robert York observed, Shakespeare also remains a source for new popular culture appropriations and adaptations. MGM, as of this writing, has *'Lil Romeo and 'Lil Juliet* in development, setting Shakespeare's play yet again in "the hood," and featuring young African American rappers in the lead roles.[17] One might wonder about the effect that such productions have on the original, but they still draw young audiences into the sphere of Shakespeare.

The youth culture-mediated Shakespeare of today that causes concern among scholars and cultural critics becomes the canonical source of tomorrow. Zefferelli's *Romeo and Juliet* was quickly absorbed into the classroom experience in the 1970s, 1980s, and 1990s, until it was replaced by Baz Luhrmann's version. Even *Tromeo and Juliet* has now served as source material for over a dozen books, articles, and essays on Shakespearean adaptation. Dick Hebdige observes that, "Youth cultural styles may begin by issuing symbolic challenges, but they must end by establishing new sets of conventions; by creating new commodities, new industries, or rejuvenating old ones."[18] Each new youth-culture appropriation is quickly reappropriated by the educational or scholarly industries. Ultimately, youth-culture Shakespeare does not threaten Shakespeare or the Shakespeare industry, nor does it challenge it in any real way.

Shakespeare has gotten over himself and is alive and well in youth culture. And in forcing him to receive us, as Marlowe would have it, we have come to understand something of his world and art. Yes, youth Shakespeare is a mediated Shakespeare, but when has he not been mediated in one form or another? In a scene in the motion picture *Clueless* (itself a youth culture version of Jane Austin's *Emma*), Cher, the young high school heroine argues with her stepbrother's college girlfriend. To prove her point, the girlfriend cites Shakespeare:

> *Girl:*   It's like Hamlet said—'To thine own self be true.' "
> *Cher:*   No, Hamlet didn't say that.
> *Girl:*   I think I remember my *Hamlet* accurately.
> *Cher:*   Well, I remember Mel Gibson accurately and he didn't say that—that Polonius guy did.

Whereas some critics see in this exchange the privileging of the celebrity (and attractiveness) of Mel Gibson over the text of *Hamlet*, one might also note that the second character mentioned, Polonius, is not identified with the actor who played him. Also, Cher remembered the line itself and who said it. One wonders if she would as well with lines from *Mad Max*, *Braveheart*, or *Lethal Weapon*. It is the text of Shakespeare that has haunted her, that has stayed in her memory. Richard Burt sees this as the "dumbing down" of Shakespeare.[19] We see it as an example of Shakespeare receiving us in Marowitz's sense.

Cher demonstrates an example of what Steven Johnson calls "collateral learning," the "formation of enduring attitudes" that "goes far beyond the explicit contents of experience."[20] Johnson argues that "the culture is getting more intellectually demanding, not less," and that it is a fallacy to think that we only engage Shakespeare on his own terms, in his texts.[21] Today's student is constantly acquiring information from a variety of sources, comparing the data, and learning in a variety of manners not possible even a generation ago. In particular, a film like *Clueless*, a play like *Hamlet, The Artist Formerly Known as Prince of Denmark*, or a song like Tom Wait's "Romeo is Bleeding," relies upon the layering of references to a wide variety of sources, what Johnson terms, "devices that reward further scrutiny."[22] In other words, the youth who knows more not only "gets" the reference, but also is able to perceive himself or herself as part of a unique group that can do so.

Johnson concludes that the late twentieth century blurred youth and adult culture so that the boundary between the two is not easily distinguishable.[23] Many grown-ups read the Harry Potter books, even as *Shakespeare's Animated Tales* presented tragedy for the *Sesame Street* crowd. Films such as *Toy Story, Shrek, Monsters, Inc.,* or *The Incredibles* are clearly aimed at multiple markets. They, too, rely upon the layers of reference and parody that reward adult viewers with the knowledge that they are seeing a different film than the children. *Star Wars* and *The Lord of the Rings* are also aimed at multiple audiences. Theme parks, rock concerts, and even Las Vegas are both "family friendly," yet also maintain aspects that are adults only. Youth culture is mainstream culture, and everyone and anyone can be a youth in contemporary American culture. What is Disney if not the myth and promise of eternal childhood?

In the twenty-first century, then, we are not losing Shakespeare, we are transforming him into another celebrity, receiving a mediated version of him, drawing connections between his work and the latest remake at the multiplex, or watching a television show with the knowledge of the play the characters are discussing. We are translating, reducing, and referencing him for today—which means that Shakespeare is not only relevant to today's youth, he's also pretty cool. Dude, where's my Bard? Answer: He's right here, just chillin'.

Notes

1. Charles Marowitz, *Prospero's Staff: Acting and Directing in the Contemporary Theatre* (Bloomington: Indiana University Press, 1986), pp. 116–117.
2. Alvin Kernan, *The Death of Literature* (New Haven: Yale University Press, 1990), p. 32.
3. Allan Bloom, *The Closing of the American Mind* (New York: Simon and Schuster, 1987); Katha Pollitt, "Sweet Swan of Avon!" *The Nation*, 262, no. 9 (March 4, 1996), p. 9; and Maureen Dowd, "A Winter's Tale," *New York Times*, December 28, 1995, p. A21.
4. Jonathan Yardley, "The Immortal Bard is Dying on College Campuses," *Pittsburgh Post Gazette*, January 5, 1997, p. E4.
5. John Wilson, "Come Not to Bury Shakespeare," *Chronicle of Higher Education* 43, no. 23 (February 14, 1997), p. B6.
6. Marvin Carlson, *The Haunted Stage: Theatre as Memory Machine* (Ann Arbor: University of Michigan Press, 2001).
7. David Bergantino, *Hamlet II: Ophelia's Revenge* (New York: Pocket Books, 2003), p. 1.
8. Not only is this name a play on "Guildenstern," it would also be seen by any teenager as a reference to the family of actors, most likely Jake Gyllenhal, as he is the male, though his sister Maggie also has a very high Q rating. By naming the character thus, Bergantino connects the character with a brooding, but dreamy, actor known for roles in *Donnie Darko* and *The Good Girl*, among others. As always, youth Shakespeare refers not only to Shakespeare, but to a variety of other referents, giving multiple layers of meaning.
9. Bergantino, *Hamlet II*, pp. 109–110.
10. Ibid., p. 94.
11. Ibid., p. 101.

12. Bergantino, *Hamlet II*, pp. 174–175.
13. Ibid., p. 204.
14. Ibid., pp. 236–237.
15. Ibid., inside back cover.
16. David Bergantino, *A Midsummer Night's Scream* (New York: Pocket Books, 2003).
17. John Horn, " 'Chicago' Has Hollywood Saying 'Hey, Kids, Let's Put on a Show'," *Los Angeles Times*, February 12, 2003, pp. A1, A24.
18. Dick Hebdige, *Subculture: The Meaning of Style* (London: Methuen, 1979), p. 96.
19. Richard Burt, *Unspeakable Shaxxxspeares: Queer Theory and American Kiddie Culture* (New York: St. Martin's, 1998), p. xiii.
20. Steven Johnson, *Everything Bad Is Good for You* (New York: Riverhead, 2005), p. 40.
21. Ibid., p. 9.
22. Ibid., p. 87.
23. Ibid., p. 195.

Works Cited

Bibliography

Adams, Richard, ed. *Teaching Shakespeare: Essays on Approaches to Shakespeare in Schools and Colleges.* London: Robert Royce, 1985.

Anderegg, Michael. *Orson Welles, Shakespeare, and Popular Culture.* New York: Columbia University Press, 1999.

Andreas, Sr., James R. "Signifying' on *The Tempest* in *Mama Day,*" in *Shakespeare and Appropriation,* edited by Christy Desmet and Robert Sawyer. London: Routledge, 1999.

Bacalzo, Dan. "Tiny Ninja Theatre," *Theatremania.com* (April 9, 2003) <http://www.theatermania.com/content/news.cfm/story/3362> Accessed August 1, 2005.

Baker, Bob. "The Real First Family," *Los Angeles Times,* February 16, 2003, E1, E34.

Baker, Jr. Houston A. *Black Studies: Rap and the Academy.* Chicago: University of Chicago Press, 1995.

Bamber, Linda. *Comic Women, Tragic Men: A Study of Gender and Genre in Shakespeare.* Stanford: Stanford University Press, 1982.

Barlow, Melinda. "Size Matters." *American Theatre* 22, no. 2 (February 2005): 60–64.

Baron, Mike. *Badger* 46. First Comics, April 1989.

Barson, Michael and Steven Heller. *Teenage Confidential: An Illustrated History of the American Teen.* San Francisco: Chronicle Books, 1998.

Barthelemay, Anthony Girard. *Black Face, Maligned Race: The Representation of Blacks in English Drama from Shakespeare to Southerne.* Baton Rouge: Louisiana State University Press, 1987.

Bate, Jonathan. *Shakespearean Constitutions: Politics, Theatre, Criticism 1730–1830.* Oxford: Oxford University Press, 1989.

Baudrillard, Jean. *Simulacra and Simulation,* translated by Shelia Faria Glaser. Ann Arbor: University of Michigan Press, 1994.

Bauer, Erik. "Re-revealing Shakespeare: An Interview with Baz Luhrmann." *Creative Screenwriting* 5, no. 2 (1998): 32–35.

Beers, Joel. "And Now for Something Completely Different." *Orange County Weekly.* July 16, 1999, 29.

———. "Romeo Hall and Juliet Oates." *Orange County Weekly.* July 6, 2001, 29.

Bender, Hy. *The Sandman Companion.* New York: DC Comics, 1999.

Bennett, Eric. "Rap," in *Africana*, edited by Kwame Anthony Appiah and Henry Louis Gates, Jr. New York: Basic Civitas Books, 1999.

Bergantino, David. *Hamlet II: Ophelia's Revenge*. New York: Pocket Books, 2003.

———. *A Midsummer Night's Scream*. New York: Pocket Books, 2003.

Bloom, Allan. *The Closing of the American Mind*. New York: Simon and Schuster, 1987.

Bongo, Milla. *Reading Comics: Language, Culture and the Concept of the Superhero in Comic Books*. New York: Garland Publishing, 2000.

Boose, Lynda E., and Richard Burt. "Introduction: Shakespeare, the Film." In *Shakespeare, the Movie: Popularizing the Plays on Film, TV, and Video*, edited by Lynda E. Boose and Richard Burt. New York: Routledge, 1997, 1–7.

———. "Totally *Clueless*? Shakespeare Goes Hollywood in the 1990s." In *Shakespeare: The Movie*, edited by Lynda E. Boose and Richard Burt. New York: Routledge, 1997.

Borgeson, Jess, Adam Long, and Daniel Singer. *Complete Works of William Shakespeare (Abridged)*. New York: Applause Books, 1994.

Boucher, Geoff. "Gone to the Dark Side." *Los Angeles Times*, May 10, 2005, E1, E10.

Bristol, Michael D. *Big-Time Shakespeare*. London: Routledge, 1996.

Brode, Douglas. *Shakespeare in the Movies: From the Silent Era to Shakespeare in Love*. New York: Oxford University Press, 2000.

Brown, John Russell. "Foreign Shakespeare and English-speaking Audiences," In *Foreign Shakespeare*, edited by Dennis Kennedy. Cambridge: Cambridge University Press, 1996.

Buhler, Stephen M. "Reviving Juliet, Repackaging Romeo: Transformations of Character in Pop and Post-pop Music," in *Shakespeare After Mass Media*, edited by Richard Burt. New York: Palgrave, 2002.

Bulman, James C. "Introduction: Shakespeare and Performance Theory," in *Shakespeare, Theory and Performance*, edited by James C. Bulman. London: Routledge, 1996.

Burden, Bob. *Flaming Carrot Comics* 31 Dark Horse Comics, October 1994.

Burt, Richard. *Unspeakable Shaxxxspeares: Queer Theory and American Kiddie Culture*. New York: St. Martin's, 1998.

Carleton, Bob. *Return to the Forbidden Planet*. London: Methuen, 1985.

Carlson, Marvin. *The Haunted Stage: Theatre as Memory Machine*. Ann Arbor: University of Michigan Press, 2001.

Carrier, David. *The Aesthetics of Comics*. University Park: Pennsylvania State University Press, 2000.

Case, Sue-Ellen. *Feminism in Theatre*. New York: Macmillan, 1988.

Chanko, Kenneth M. "Dangerous Fun: Fishburne as Othello," *Boston Globe*, December 24, 1995, 31, 33.

Cohn, Ruby. *Modern Shakespeare Offshoots*. Princeton: Princeton University Press, 1976.

Conley, Kevin. "Fresh Bard," *The New Yorker*. March 27, 2000, 130.

Cooper, B. Lee and Wayne S. Haney. *Rock Music in American Popular Culture: Rock 'n' Roll Resources*. New York: Haworth Press, 1995.

Crawford, Hubert H. *Crawford's Encyclopedia of Comic Books*. Middle Village, NY: Jonathan David Publications, 1978.

Crewdson, Gregory and Rick Moody. *Twilight: Photographs by Gregory Crewdson*. New York: Harry N. Abrams, 2002.

Criniti, Steve. "Othello: A Hawk among Birds." *Literature/Film Quarterly* 32, no. 2 (2004): 115–121. <http//80proquest.umi.com.allstate.libproxy.ivytech.edu/pqdweb?index=0&did=653729321&SrchMode=1&sid=1&Fmt=4&VInst=PROD&VType=PQD&RQT=309&VName=PQD&TS=1124691219&clientId=54498> Accessed July 7, 2004.

Crowdus, Gary. "Words, Words, Words: Recent Shakespearean Films." *Cineaste* 24, no. 4 (1998): 13–19.

Crowl, Samuel. "Introduction: Where the Wild Things Are: Shakespeare in the American Landscape," in *Teaching Shakespeare Today: Practical Approaches and Productive Strategies*, edited by James E. Davis and Ronald E. Salomome. Urbana: National Council of Teachers of English, 1993.

Crowther, John, ed. *No Fear Shakespeare: Hamlet*. New York: Spark Publishing, 2003.

———. *No Fear Shakespeare: Macbeth*. New York: Spark Publishing, 2003.

———. *No Fear Shakespeare: A Midsummer Night's Dream*. New York: Spark Publishing, 2003.

———. *No Fear Shakespeare: Othello*. New York, Spark Publishing, 2003.

———. *No Fear Shakespeare: Romeo and Juliet*. New York: Spark Publishing, 2003.

Daileader, Celia R. "Casting Black Actors: Beyond Othellophilia," in *Shakespeare and Race*, edited by Catherine M.S. Alexander and Stanley Wells. Cambridge: Cambridge University Press, 2000.

Davies, Anthony. "Filming *Othello*," in *Shakespeare and the Moving Image: The Plays on Film and Television*, edited by Anthony Davies and Stanley Wells, 196–210. Cambridge: Cambridge University Press, 1994.

———. "Shakespeare and the Media of Film, Radio and Television." *Shakespeare Survey* 39 (1987): 1–22.

Davis, Eisa. "Hip-hop theatre: the new underground" *The Source*, March 2000, 172–176.

Davis, James E. and Ronald E. Salomome, eds. *Teaching Shakespeare Today: Practical Approaches and Productive Strategies*. Urbana: National Council of Teachers of English, 1993.

Dellasega, Cheryl. *Surviving Ophelia: Mothers Share Their Wisdom in Navigating the Tumultuous Teenage Years*. Cambridge, MA: Random House, 2001.

Desmet, Christy. "Introduction," in *Shakespeare and Appropriation*, edited by Christy Desmet and Robert Sawyer. London: Routledge, 1999.

Dixon, Wheeler Winston, ed. *Film Genre 2000*. Albany: State University of New York Press, 2000.

Dowd, Maureen. "A Winter's Tale," *New York Times*, December 28, 1995, A21.

Doyle, John and Ray Lischner. *Shakespeare for Dummies*. New York: Wiley Publishing, 1999.

Durband, Alan, ed. *Shakespeare Made Easy: Hamlet*. Hauppage: Barron's, 1986.

———. *Shakespeare Made Easy: Macbeth*. Hauppage: Barron's, 1984.

Durband, Alan, ed. *Shakespeare Made Easy: Romeo and Juliet*. Hauppage: Barron's, 1984.

Dusinberre, Juliet. *Shakespeare and the Nature of Women*. London: Macmillan, 1975.

Ebert, Roger. Review of "O," *Chicago Sun-Times*, August 31, 2001. <http://rogerebert.suntimes.com/apps/pbcs.dll/article?AID=/20010831/REVIEWS/108310302/1023> Accessed May 15, 2005.

———. Review of *Romeo & Juliet*, *Chicago Sun-Times*, November 1, 1996. <http://rogerebert.suntimes.com/apps/pbcs.dll/article?AID=/19961101/REVIEWS/611010304/1023> Accessed May 15, 2005.

———. Review of *10 Things I Hate about You*, *Chicago Sun-Times*, March 31, 1999. <http://rogerebert.suntimes.com/apps/pbcs.dll/article?AID=/19990331/REVIEWS/903310301/1023> Accessed May 15, 2005.

Edens, Walter, Christopher Durer, Walter Eggers, Duncan Harris and Keith Hall, eds. *Teaching Shakespeare*. Princeton: Princeton University Press, 1977.

Eisner, Will. *Comics and Sequential Art*. Tamarac: Poorhouse Press, 1985.

———. *Graphic Storytelling*. Tamarac: Poorhouse Press, 1996.

Epstein, Norrie. *The Friendly Shakespeare*. New York: Viking, 1993.

Erskine, Chris. " 'Yo, dog': Positively Shakespearean Rap," *Los Angeles Times*, November 13, 2002, E8.

Fiedler, Leslie. "The Middle Against Both Ends," in *Arguing Comics: Literary Masters on a Popular Medium*, edited by Jeet Heer and Kent Worcester. Jackson: University Press of Mississippi, 2004.

Finkelstein, Richard. "Disney cites Shakespeare: The limits of appropriation," in *Shakespeare and Appropriation*, edited by Christy Desmet and Robert Sawyer. London: Routledge, 1999.

Fischlin, Daniel and Mark Fortier. *Adaptations of Shakespeare*. London: Routledge, 2000.

Foley, F. Kathleen. "Music, murder, and maybe," *Los Angeles Times*, July 16, 2003, E3.

———. " 'Romeo' Forms a Happy Union," *Los Angeles Times*, June 7, 2001, F40.

———. "Sex, Drugs, and Shakespeare," *Los Angeles Times*, January 13, 2005, E5.

Friedlander, Paul. *Rock and Roll: A Social History*. Boulder: Westview, 1996.

Fukushima, Yoshiko. *Manga Discourse in Japanese Theatre*. London: Keegan Paul, 2003.

Gaiman, Neil. *The Sandman: The Doll's House*. New York: DC Comics, 1990.

———. *The Sandman: Dream Country*. New York: DC Comics, 1991.

———. *The Sandman: The Kindly Ones*. New York: DC Comics, 1996.

———. *The Sandman: Preludes and Nocturnes*. New York: DC Comics, 1991.

———. *The Sandman: The Wake*. New York: DC Comics, 1997.

Gans, Herbert J. *Popular Culture and High Culture*. New York: Basic Books, 1999.

Gates, Jr., Henry Louis. *The Signifying Monkey: A Theory of African-American Literary Criticism*. Oxford: Oxford University Press, 1988.

Gilroy, Paul. *There Ain't No Black in the Union Jack: The Cultural Politics of Race and Nation*. Chicago: University of Chicago Press, 1987.

Giroux, Henry A. *Channel Surfing*. New York: St. Martin's, 1997.

————. *Living Dangerously*. New York: Peter Lang, 1996.

Glassner, Barry. *The Culture of Fear*. New York: Basic Books, 1999.

Grode, Eric. "Bard or Bust: A Fanatics Vow." *American Theatre* 19, no. 7 (September 2002): 45–47.

Groom, Nick and Piero. *Introducing Shakespeare*. Cambridge: Icon Books, 2001.

Guare, John, Mel Shapiro, and Galt MacDermot. *Two Gentlemen of Verona*. NewYork: Holt, Rinehart and Winston, 1979.

Guzman, Isaac. "Boppin' with the Bard," *Newsday*, January 27, 2000, C1.

Hayasaki, Erika. "Reading, 'Riting, and Rap," *Los Angeles Times*, January 14, 2003, A1, A16.

Hebdige, Dick. *Subculture: The Meaning of Style*. London: Methuen, 1979.

Hedrick, Donald and Bryan Reynolds, eds. *Shakespeare without Class: Misappropriations of Cultural Capitol*. New York: Palgrave, 2000.

Heffley, Lynn. "Alas, poor Hamlet, he's a laughingstock," *Los Angeles Times*, August 12, 2005, E2.

Henderson, Diana E. "A Shrew for the Times," in *Shakespeare, the Movie: Popularizing the Plays on Film, TV, and Video*, edited by Lynda E. Boose and Richard Burt, 148–168. New York: Routledge, 1997.

Hill, Errol. *Shakespeare in Sable: A History of Black Shakespearean Actors*. Amherst: University of Massachusetts Press, 1984.

Hoch, Danny. "here we go, yo." *American Theatre* 21, no. 10 (December 2004): 38–40, 70–74.

Hodgson, Barbara. "*William Shakespeare's Romeo + Juliet*: Everything's Nice in America?" *Shakespeare Survey* 52 (1999): 88–98.

Holderness, Graham. "Radical Potentiality and Institutional Closure: Shakespeare in Film and Television," in *Political Shakespeare: New Essays in Cultural Materialism*, edited by Jonathan Dollimore and Alan Sinfield. Ithaca and London: Cornell University Press, 1985.

Horn, Barbara Lee. *The Age of Hair*. Westport: Greenwood, 1991.

Horn, John. " 'Chicago' Has Hollywood Saying, 'Hey, Kids, Let's Put on a Show'," *Los Angeles Times*, February 12, 2003, A1, A24.

Hutcheon, Linda. *A Theory of Parody*. New York: Urbana, 1985.

Istel, John. "Pop Goes the Musical." *American Theatre* 20, no. 3 (March 2003): 21–25.

Jameson, Fredric. *Postmodernism, or the Cultural Logic of Late Capitalism*. Durham: Duke University Press, 1991.

Jensen, Wendy. "Faces and Places," *US Magazine*, January 1996, 13–22.

Johnson, Steven. *Everything Bad is Good for You*. New York: Riverhead, 2005.

Jones, Wenzel. "Reviews: Hamlet, The Artist Formerly Known as Prince of Denmark," *Backstage West*, August 11, 2005, 17.

Jones, Jr., William B. *Classics Illustrated: A Cultural History with Illustrations*. Jefferson: McFarland and Company, 2002.

Kennedy, Dennis. "Shakespeare without His Language," in *Shakespeare, Theory and Performance*, edited by James C. Bulman. London: Routledge, 1996.

Kernan, Alvin. *The Death of Literature*. New Haven, Yale University Press, 1990.

————. *The Playwright as Magician*. New Haven: Yale University Press, 1979.

Kott, Jan. *The Bottom Translation*. Evanston: Northwestern University Press, 1987.

Krims, Adam. *Rap Music and the Poetics of Identity*. Cambridge: Cambridge University Press, 2000.

Kwitney, Alisa. *The Sandman: King of Dreams*. San Francisco: Chronicle Books, 2003.

Landsberg, Mitchell. "Hip-Hop Unlocks the Meaning of Literary Classics." *Los Angeles Times*, June 19, 2005, B2.

Lanier, Douglas. *Shakespeare and Modern Popular Culture*. Oxford: Oxford University Press, 2002.

Lefevere, Andre. "Why Waste Our Time on Rewrites? The Trouble with Interpretation and the Role of Rewriting in an Alternative Paradigm," in *The Manipulation of Literature: Studies in Literary Translation*, edited by Theo Hermans. New York: St. Martin's, 1983.

Legman, Gershon. *Love and Death: A Study in Censorship*. New York: Hacker Art, 1948.

Levine, Lawrence. *Highbrow / Lowbrow: The Emergence of Cultural Hierarchy in America*. Cambridge: Harvard University Press, 1988.

Lewis, Jon. *The Road to Romance and Ruin: Teen Films and Youth Culture*. New York: Routledge, 1992.

Lindroth, Mary. "The Prince and the Newscaster: Baz Luhrmann Updates Shakespeare for a Y2K Audience" <http://www.mtsu.edu/~english/lindroth.html> Accessed September 27, 2000.

Loehlin, James N. " 'These Violent Delights Have Violent Ends': Baz Luhrmann's Millennial Shakespeare," in *Shakespeare, Film, Fin de Siècle*, edited by Mark Thornton Burnett and Ramona Wray. New York: St. Martin's, 2000.

Luck, Otto. "*The Bomb-itty of Errors*: A Masterpiece by Any Other Name" *NYRock* (2000) <http://www.nyrock.com/reviews/2000/bomb.htm> Accessed March 28, 2002.

Lyons, Donald. "Lights, Camera, Shakespeare." *Commentary* (February 1999): 57–60.

Macdonald, Dwight, *Against the American Grain*. New York: Random House, 1962.

MacLiammoír, Micheál. From "Put Money in Thy Purse," in *Focus on Shakespearean Films*, edited by Charles W. Eckert, 79–100. Englewood Cliffs, NJ: Prentice Hall, 1972.

Manvell, Roger. *Shakespeare and the Film*. New York: Praeger, 1971.

Margolies, Dany. "Bard to the Future," *Backstage West*, August 4, 2005, 14.

Marowitz, Charles. *Prospero's Staff: Acting and Directing in the Contemporary Theatre*. Bloomington: Indiana University Press, 1986.

———. "Reconstructing Shakespeare or Harlotry in Bardolatry." *Shakespeare Survey* 40 (1988): 5–27.

Martinez, Julio. "All's Kool That Ends Kool," *Daily Variety*, May 23, 2002, 12.

McCabe, Joseph. *Hanging Out with the Dream King: Conversations with Neil Gaiman and His Collaborators*. Seattle: Fantagraphics, 2004.

McCarter, Jeremy. "Why Hip Hop Could Revitalize the Theatre—If It Wanted To" *The New Republic Online* (July 18, 2001) <http://www.tnr.com/online/mccarter 071801.html> Accessed May 29, 2002.

McCloud, Scott. *Understanding Comics*. New York: Harper Perennial, 1993.

McCloud, Scott. *Understanding Comics: The Invisible Art.* New York: Harper Perennial, 1993.

McKinley, Jesse. "On Stage and Off," *New York Times*, December 24, 1999, E12.

McMurtry, Jo. *Shakespeare Films in the Classroom: A Descriptive Guide.* Hamden: Archon Books, 1994.

Menendez, Francisco. "Redefining Originality: Pearce and Luhrmann's Conceptualization of *Romeo and Juliet.*" *Creative Screenwriting* 5, no. 2 (1998): 36–41.

Midgette, Anne. "Fall Preview/Dance," *Los Angeles Times*, September 17, 2000: Calendar 7.

Miller, Michael M. "Shake, Rattle, and Roll Speare," *Orange County Weekly*, July 14, 2000, 21.

Mills, Jeffrey H. "*Star Trek IV*: The Good, The Bad and The Unquenched Thirst," in *The Best of Trek 15*, edited by Walter Irwin and G.B. Love. New York: Roc, 1990.

Moore, Alan and David Gibbons, eds. *Watchmen.* New York: DC Comics, 1987.

Moore, Alan and David Lloyd, eds. *V for Vendetta.* New York: DC Comics, 1990.

Nyberg, Amy Kiste. *Seal of Approval: The History of the Comics Code.* Jackson: University Press of Mississippi, 1998.

" '*O*'." *Internet Movie Databasen* (2005) <http://www.imdb.com/title/tt0184791/> Accessed May 14, 2005.

"Off-off Color: Toy Story." *Time Out New York*, no. 268 (November 9–16, 2000) <http://www.tinyninjatheater.com/reviews/timeouttoytheater.shtml> Accessed July 15, 2005.

Osborne, Laurie. "Mixing Media and Animating Shakespeare's Tales," in *Shakespeare the Movie II*, edited by Richard Burt and Lynda E. Boose. New York: Routledge, 2003.

Page, Philip and Marilyn Pettit, eds. *A Midsummer Night's Dream.* Hauppauge: Barron's, 2002.

Papp, Joseph and Ted Cornell. *William Shakespeare's "Naked" Hamlet: A Production Handbook.* New York: Macmillan, 1969.

Pearce, Craig, Baz Lurhmann and William Shakespeare. *William Shakespeare's Romeo + Juliet: The Contemporary Film, The Classic Play.* New York: Bantam, 1996.

Pierce, Brook. "Reviews: Tiny Ninja Macbeth, Finally, Little Green Man." *TheatreMania.com* (August 18, 2000) <http://www.theatermania.com/content/ news.cfm/story/970> Accessed August 1, 2005.

Pipher, Mary. *Reviving Ophelia.* New York: Putnam, 1994.

Pitt, Angela. *Shakespeare's Women.* Totowa, NJ: Barnes and Noble, 1981.

Pittman, L. Monique. "Taming *10 Things I Hate About You*: Shakespeare and the Teenage Film Audience." *Literature/Film Quarterly* 32, no. 2 (2004): 144–152. <http://80-proquest.umi.com.allstate.libproxy.ivytech.edu /pqdweb?RQT=305& querySyntax=PQ&searchInterface=1&moreOptState=CLOSED&TS=112469 1219&h_pubtitle=&h_pmid=&clientId=54498&JSEnabled=1&SQ=L.+ Monique+Pittman+Taming+10+Things+I+Hate+about+You&DBId=1&da te=LL&onDate=&beforeDate=&afterDate=&fromDate=&toDate= &pubti- tle=&author=&FT=0&AT=any&revType=review&revPos=all&STYPE=all

&sortb y=REVERSE_CHRON&searchButtonImage.x=0& searchButtonImage. y=0> Accessed July 7, 2004.

Pollitt, Katha. "Sweet Swan of Avon!" *The Nation*, 262, no. 9 (March 4, 1996): 9.

Potter, Russell A. *Spectacular Vernacular: Hip-Hop and the Politics of Postmodernism*. Albany: State University of New York Press, 1995.

Pressley, Nelson. "As You Sort of Like It: Shakespeare's Mildly Hip-Hop Romp," *Washington Post*, April 6, 2000, C2.

Proschan, Frank. "The Semiotic Study of Puppets, Masks and Performing Objects." *Semiotica* 47, no. 1–4 (1983): 3–46.

Quart, Alissa. *Branded: The Buying and Selling of Teenagers*. New York: Basic Books, 2004.

Ragni, Gerome and James Rado. *Hair*. New York: Pocket Books, 1969.

Riggio, Milla Cozart, ed. *Teaching Shakespeare through Performance*. New York: Modern Language Association of America, 1999.

Roberts, Terri. "Twelfth Dog Night," *Daily Variety*, December 21, 1999, 14.

Rodman, Sarah. "Bard to the Bone," *Boston Herald*, November 29, 2000, 47, 51.

"*Romeo + Juliet*." *Internet Movie Database* (2005) <http://www.imdb.com/title/tt0117509/> Accessed May 14, 2005.

Rose, Tricia. *Black Noise*. Hanover: Wesleyan University Press, 1994.

Rozakis, Laurie. *The Complete Idiot's Guide to Shakespeare*. Indianapolis: Alpha Group, 1999.

Rozett, Martha Tuck. *Talking Back to Shakespeare*. Newark: University of Delaware Press, 1994.

Rudolph, Sarah J. "Performance Review: *The Bomb-itty of Errors*," *Theatre Journal* 54, no. 2 (2002): 307–309.

Salter, Denis. "Acting Shakespeare in Postcolonial Space," in *Shakespeare, Theory, Performance*, edited by James C. Bulman. London: Routledge, 1996.

Sammons, Eddie. *Shakespeare: A Hundred Years on Film*. Lanham, MD: Scarecrow Press, 2004.

Scholes, Robert. *The Rise and Fall of English*. New Haven: Yale University Press, 1998.

Schulenberg, Richard. "Troubadour's 'Twelfth Dog Night' at Miles Is 'The Funniest Show in Town'," *Santa Monica Mirror*, August, 18–24, 1999, n.p.

Schwartz, Delmore. "Masterpieces as Cartoons," in *Arguing Comics: Literary Masters on a Popular Medium*, edited by Jeet Heer and Kent Worcester. Jackson: University Press of Mississippi, 2004.

Scott, Michael. *Shakespeare and the Modern Dramatist*. New York: St. Martin's, 1989.

Sedgwick, Fred. *Shakespeare and the Young Writer*. London: Routledge, 1999.

Sexton, Adam. "Don't Believe the Hype: Why Isn't Hip Hop Criticism Better?" in *Rap on Rap: Straight Up Talk on Hip-Hop Culture*, edited by Adam Sexton. New York: Delta, 1999.

"Shakespeare in the Cinema: A Film Directors' Symposium." *Cineaste* 24, no. 1 (1998): 48–55.

Shakespeare, William. "Hamlet," in *Classics Illustrated 5*, adapted by Steven Grant and Tom Mandrake. New York: First Publishing, 1990.

————. *The Riverside Shakespeare*, edited by G. Blakemore Evans. Boston: Houghton Mifflin, 1974.

Shandler, Nina. *Ophelia's Mom*. New York: Crown, 2001.

Shandler, Sara. *Ophelia Speaks*. New York: Harper Collins, 1999.

Shotten, Pete and Nicholas Schaffner. *John Lennon in My Life*. New York: Stern and Day, 1983.

Simon, John. "Pearl Throwing Free Style," in *Focus on Shakespearean Films*, edited by Charles W. Eckert, 154–157. Englewood Cliffs, NJ: Prentice Hall, 1972.

Simon, Richard Keller. "Much Ado about 'Friends': What Pop Culture Offers Literature," *The Chronicle of Higher Education* 46, no. 41 (June 16, 2000): B4.

————. *Trash Culture: Popular Culture and the Great Tradition*. Berkeley: University of California Press, 1999.

Sinfield, Alan. "Give and Account of Shakespeare and Education, Showing Why You Think They Are Effective and What You Have Appreciated about Them; Support Your Comments with Precise References," in *Political Shakespeare*, edited by Jonathan Dollimore and Alan Sinfield. Manchester: Manchester University Press, 1985.

————. "Making Space: Appropriation and Confrontation in Recent British Plays," in *The Shakespeare Myth*, edited by Graham Holderness. Manchester: Manchester University Press, 1988.

Sitomer, Alan and Michael Cirelli. *Hip-Hop Poetry and the Classics*. Beverly Hills: Milk Mug Publishing, 2004.

Speaight, George. *Juvenile Drama: The History of the English Toy Theatre*. London: MacDonald and Company, 1946.

Steinberg, Shirley R. and Joe L. Kincheloe, eds. *Kinderculture: The Corporate Construction of Childhood*. Boulder: Westview, 1998.

Steranko, James. *The Steranko History of Comics Volume I*. Reading, PA: Supergraphics, 1970.

Stevenson, Robert Louis. "A Penny Plain and Twopence Coloured." *Memories and Portraits*. New York: Charles Scribner's Sons, 1900.

Storey, John. *An Introductory Guide to Cultural Theory and Popular Culture*. Athens: University of Georgia Press, 1993.

Sturak, Clara. "Shakespeare's Stayin' Alive with New Production at Miles Playhouse," *Santa Monica Mirror*, July 19–25, 2000, 12.

Taylor, Gary. *Reinventing Shakespeare*. Oxford: Oxford University Press, 1989.

"10 Things I Hate about You," *Internet Movie Database* <http://www.imdb.com/title/tt0147800/> Accessed May 14, 2005.

Toporov, Brandon and Van Howell. *Shakespeare for Beginners*. New York: Writers and Readers Publishing, 1997.

Travers, Peter. Review of "William Shakespeare's Romeo + Juliet." *Rolling Stone* (1996) <http://www.rollingstone.com/reviews/movie/_/id/5949093> Accessed May 15, 2005.

Twitchell, James B. *Branded Nation*. New York: Simon and Schuster, 2004.

Uno, Roberta. "The 5th Element" *American Theatre* 21, no. 4 (April 2004): 26–30, 85–86.

Walker, Matt. Personal Interview, November 20, 2003.

Weber, Bruce. "Rap is to Shakespeare as Bomb is to Comedy," *New York Times*, December 21, 1999, E3.

Weinart, Laura. "Fleetwood Macbeth," *Backstage West*, July 17, 2003, 11–12.

Wertham, Fredric. *Seduction of the Innocent*. New York: Rinehart and Company, 1954.

West, Greg, Jackie Boyland, et al. *Are We Reviving Ophelia?* Boston: Baker's Plays, 1998.

White, Armond. "Who wants to see ten niggers play basketball?" in *Droppin' Science: Critical Essays on Rap Music and Hip-hop Culture*, edited by William Eric Perkins. Philadelphia: Temple University Press, 1996.

Williams, Deanne. "Mick Jagger Macbeth," in *Shakespeare Survey 57: Macbeth and Its Afterlife*, edited by Peter Holland. Cambridge: Cambridge University Press, 2004. 145–158.

Wilson, A.E. *Penny Plain Two Pence Coloured*. London: George G. Harrap and Company, 1932.

Wilson, John. "Come Not to Bury Shakespeare," *Chronicle of Higher Education* 43, no. 23 (February 14, 1997): B6.

Wright, Bradford M. *Comic Book Nation*. Baltimore: Johns Hopkins University Press, 2001.

Yardley, Jonathan. "The Immortal Bard is Dying on College Campuses," *Pittsburgh Post Gazette*, January 5, 1997, E4.

Ziegler, Georgiana. *Shakespeare's Unruly Women*. Washington, DC: Folger Shakespeare Library, 1997.

Filmography

Get Over It. Prod. Michael Burns and Marc Butan. Writ. R. Lee Fleming, Jr. Dir. Tommy O'Haver. Miramax, 2000, DVD.

The Glass House. Prod. Neal H. Moritz. Writ. Wesley Strick. Dir. Daniel Sackheim. Columbia, 2001, DVD.

"O". Deluxe Edition. Prod. Eric Gitter, Anthony Rhulen, and Daniel L. Fried. Writ. Brad Kaaya. Dir. Tim Blake Nelson. Lion's Gate Films, 2001, DVD.

Othello. Prod. Julien DeRode and Orson Welles. Writ. Jean Sacha, William Shakespeare, and Orson Welles. Dir. Orson Welles. Mercury Pictures, 1952, videocassette.

Othello. Prod. John Braborn and Anthony Havelock-Allan. Writ. William Shakespeare. Dir. Stuart Burge. Warner Brothers, 1965, videocassette.

Othello. Prod. David Barron and Luke Roeg. Writ. Oliver Parker. Dir. Oliver Parker. Columbia Pictures/Castle Rock, 1995, videocassette.

Purple Rain. Prod. Robert Cavallo, Steven Fargnoli and Joseph Ruffalo. Writ. William Blinn and Albert Magnoli. Dir. Albert Magnoli. Warner Brothers, 1984, videocassette.

Renaissance Man. Prod. Sara Colleton, Elliot Abbott, and Robert Greenhut. Writ. Jim Burnstein. Dir. Penny Marshall. Touchstone, 1994, videocassette.

The Simpsons: Tales from the Public Domain. Writ. Matt Warburton, Dir. Mike B. Anderson, Episode No. DABF08, 2002.

The Taming of the Shrew. Prod. Mary Pickford. Writ. William Shakespeare (with additional dialogue by Sam Taylor). Dir. Sam Taylor. Madacy Music Group, 1929, videocassette.

The Taming of the Shrew. Prod. Richard Burton, Elizabeth Taylor, and Franco Zeffirelli. Writ. Suso Cecchi D'Amico, Paul Dehn, and Franco Zeffirelli. Dir. Franco Zeffirelli. Columbia Pictures, 1967, videocassette.

10 Things I Hate about You. Prod. Andrew Lazar. Writ. Karen McCullah Lutz and Kirsten Smith. Dir. Gil Junger, Touchstone, 1999, DVD.

Tromeo and Juliet. Prod. Lloyd Kaufman and Michael Herz, Writ. Lloyd Kaufman and James Gunn. Dir. Lloyd Kaufman, Troma Entertainment, 1997, DVD.

William Shakespeare's Romeo + Juliet. Prod. Gabriella Martinelli and Baz Luhrmann. Writ. Baz Luhrmann and Craig Pearce. Dir. Baz Luhrmann. Twentieth Century Fox, 1996, DVD and VHS.

Discography

Aerosmith. "Flesh." *Get a Grip.* Geffen 493085, 2001.

Beatles. *Magical Mystery Tour.* Apple Records CDP 7780632, 1967.

Blue Oyster Cult. "Don't Fear the Reaper." *Agents of Fortune.* Sony 85479, 1976.

Chaka Kahn. "I Feel for You." *I Feel for You.* Warner Brothers 25162, 1984.

Costello, Elvis. *The Juliet Letters.* Warner Brothers 945180–2, 1993.

Dire Straits. "Romeo and Juliet." *Making Movies.* Warner Brothers 47771, 1980.

Dylan, Bob. "Floater." *Love and Theft.* Sony 85975, 2001.

Hair: The Original Broadway Cast Recording. RCA Victor 1150–2-RC, 1968.

Hall and Oates. "Maneater." *H2O.* BMG 58616, 1982.

Indigo Girls. "Romeo and Juliet." *Rites of Passage.* Sony 61576, 1992.

———. *Swamp Ophelia.* Sony 57621, 1994.

Madonna. "Cherish." *Like a Prayer.* Sire 25844, 1989.

———. "Fever." *Erotica.* Sire 45031, 1992.

McLaren, Malcolm and the World Famous Supreme Team. *Round the Outside! Round the Outside!* Virgin 2–91599, 1990.

Merchant, Natalie. *Ophelia.* Elektra 62270, 1998.

Penn, Michael. "No Myth." *March.* RCA 68099, 1989.

Prince. *Purple Rain.* Warner Brothers 25011, 1984.

———. "1999." *1999.* Warner Brothers 23720, 1983.

Ratt. "Round and Round." *Out of the Cellar.* Atlantic 80143, 1984.

Reed, Lou. "Romeo Had Juliette." *New York.* Sire 25829, 1989.

The Reflections. "(Just Like) Romeo and Juliet." *Groups That Rocked The Sixties.* Madacy Records 1619, 1964.

Rolling Stones. "Sympathy for the Devil." *Beggar's Banquet.* Abkco 719539, 1968.

Springsteen, Bruce. "Fire." *Live 1975–1985.* Sony 65388, 1985.

———. "Incident on 57th Street." *The Wild, The Innocent and the E-Street Shuffle.* Sony 32432, 1973.

Springsteen, Bruce. "Point Blank." *The River*. Sony 36854, 1980.

Waits, Tom. "Romeo is Bleeding." *Blue Valentine*. Elektra 162, 1970.

William Shakespeare's Romeo + Juliet: Music from the Motion Picture. Capitol Records CDP8 37715 0, 1996.

William Shakespeare's Romeo + Juliet: Music from the Motion Picture: Volume 2. Capitol Records CDP72438 55567 2 2, 1997.

Index